Reprints of
Old Rituals

Scottish Rite Research Society

ב   י

Reprints of Rituals of Old Degrees

By
ARTURO DE HOYOS, 33°, Grand Cross, K.Y.C.H.
Past Master, McAllen Lodge No. 1110, AF&AM of Texas
Grand Archivist & Grand Historian

WESTPHALIA PRESS
an imprint of
Policy Studies Organization

All Rights Reserved © 2025 by Policy Studies Organization

Westphalia Press
An imprint of Policy Studies Organization
1527 New Hampshire Ave., NW
Washington, DC 20036

ISBN-13: 978-1-63723-688-8

Cover design by Jeffrey Barnes:
jbarnesbook.design

Daniel Gutierrez-Sandoval, Executive Director
PSO and Westphalia Press

All rights reserved. No part of this publication may be reproduced, stored in a retrieval system, or transmitted in any form or by any means, electronic, mechanical, photocopying, recording, or otherwise, without the prior permission of the copyright holder.

de Hoyos, Arturo, 1959–
Reprints of Rituals of Old Degrees / Arturo de Hoyos
Includes an introduction and index.

Albert Pike, 33°, 1809–1891
Sovereign Grand Commander, SJ, USA, 1859–1891
Photograph by Matthew B. Brady & Co., Washington, DC
Archives of the Supreme Council, 33°, Southern Jurisdiction, USA

Contents

INTRODUCTION IX

    The Degree of Mark Master Mason, ca.1804 x

    The Wigan Ritual of the Early Grand Encampment, ca.1801 xiv

    Grade, Mark Mason, Passed Master,
    and Royal Arch, Rite Ancien Maçonnerie d'York, 1795. xviii

        Mark Mason. 5th Degree of the Masonry of York, Ancient Rite. xx
        Past Master. Venerable of the L[odge]. 4th Degree of the Ancient Rite. xxiii
        Royal Arch — 7th Degree of the Ancient Rite. xxiii
        Excursus — The Royal Master Degree xxiv

    Knights Templar, former English Ritual, 1851 xxvi

        Masson's System of Examination of the Royal, Exalted, and
        Military Order of Masonic Knights Templar in England and Wales xxvii

    Grand Maitre Ecossais or Scottish Elder Master and Knight of St. Andrew. . . xxxvi

    Old Ceremony of Royal Arch Exaltation. xxxviii

APPENDIX (RITUALS FROM CARLILES MANUAL OF FREEMASONRY). XXXVIII

    The Mark Man and Mark Master Degree xxxviii

    A Description Of Royal Arch Masonry. 48

    Knights Templar 73

FACSIMILE (REPRINTS OF RITUALS OF OLD DEGREES) 93

    The Degree of Master Mark Mason, Being the Work of
    The Grand Council of Princes of Jerusalem of South Carolina and
    The Oldest Work Extant Anywhere. 95

    Royal Arch Exaltation 115

    The Wigan Ritual of the Early Grand Encampment, ca.1801 137

    The English Ritual for Knights Templar 157

    Grand Maitre Ecossais or Scottish Elder Master and Knight of St. Andrew. 175

    Grade, Mark Mason, Passed Master,
    and Royal Arch, Rite Ancien Maçonnerie d'York, 1795 205

    Past Master: Vemerable of the Lodge. 4th Degree of the Ancient Rite. 245

INDEX 247

Introduction

In 1879 William M. Ireland, 33°, the Assistant Grand Auditor of the Supreme Council issued a two-page list of about thirty books for sale from the Supreme Council. All of them, with the exception the *Transactions*, were "prepared by the Ven∴ Gr∴ Commander of the Supreme Council [Albert Pike, 33°], being in part complied, in part written by him."[1] Among the books listed are many which are still used today, including the *Grand Constitutions* (the fundamental law of the Scottish Rite), *Morals and Dogma* (Pike's lectures and background philosophy for the degrees), and the *Book of the Words* (his etymological dictionary on Masonic esoteric words). But under the bold heading "Reprints of Rituals of Old Degrees" appear the following lesser known titles:

> Degree of MARK MASTER MASON, being the work of the Grand Council of Princes of Jerusalem of South Carolina, and the oldest work extent anywhere.
> The WIGAN RITUAL of the EARLY GRAND ENCAMPMENT.
> GRADE, MARK MASON, PASSED MASTER, and ROYAL ARCH, RITE ANCIEN MAÇONNERIE D'YORK [Were originally translated from English into French, and used in the French West Indies in 1795.]
> KNIGHTS TEMPLAR, former English Ritual.
> GRAND MAITRE ECOSSAIS or SCOTTISH ELDER MASTER AND KNIGHT OF ST. ANDREW, being the Fourth Degree of the Degree of Ramsey.
> Old Ceremony of ROYAL ARCH EXALTATION.

Some of these rituals were from the archives of the Supreme Council, while others were given to Pike by his friend Matthew Cooke, 30°, an enthusiastic English Mason who collected rituals, and frequently researched in the British Museum. An avid collector or rituals,[2]

---

1. James D. Carter, *History of the Supreme Council, 33°* ... (1861–1891) (Washington, DC, 1967), pp. 176–77.
2. Pike's collection of rituals, in the archives of the Supreme Council, includes dozens of manuscripts, many purchased following the death of Hyacinthe Astier, an officer of the Supreme Council of France, whose library was advertised for sale in *Notice sur les livres manuscrits et imprimés sur le franc-maçonnerie, les templiers et sociétés qui en dépendent provenant du cabinet de feu M. Astier* ... (Paris: Chez D. Guillemot, 1856). Pike translated several of the texts and noted their provenance. For Pike's earliest collection of Scottish Rite Degrees, see Arturo de Hoyos, *Masonic Formulas and Rituals Transcribed by Albert Pike* (Washington, D.C.: Scottish Rite Research Society, 2010)

ix

Albert Pike would also later reprint three other important works which help us understand the evolution of the Craft Degrees: *A Mason's Examination* (1723),[3] *The Grand Mystery of Free Masons Discover'd* (1725),[4] and Samuel Prichard's *Masonry Dissected* (1730).[5]

The book you are now reading does not include a detailed analysis of the rituals reproduced herein. Rather, in the brief treatments of the degrees that follow, I hope to provide some information which will contribute to their interest. In this regard I have, for the sake of comparison, also included some earlier versions of the rituals in the Appendix. The idea occurred to me when I noticed that Matthew Cooke, in his prefatory remarks on the Royal Arch Exaltation, referred to the "old ceremony of the Royal Arch … set out in Carlisle's 'MANUAL…'" [sic]. Here, Cooke is alluding to Richard Carlile's *Manual of Freemasonry* (1836, 1845),[6] which was comprised of articles printed in Carlile's *The Republican* (1825), while he was imprisoned in Dorchester Gaol, for blasphemy and seditious libel. *The Republican* published the first exposure of English Freemasonry following the formation of the United Grand Lodge of England (1813), and allows us a glimpse of early states of many rituals.

Over the years, as I read the *Reprints of Rituals of Old Degrees* I found myself, time and again, comparing them with Carlile's earlier texts. I quickly realized that their inclusion here could only benefit the reader. Although I have a copy of *The Republican*, its rituals are marred by extraneous and unnecessary comments, which were removed when published as a stand-alone text. My included transcripts are from my earliest personal copy, *Manual of Freemasonry: in Three Parts* (1853).[7]

THE DEGREE OF MARK MASTER MASON, CA. 1804

"Mark Masonry" was originally divided into two degrees: Mark Man, and Mark Master. The two degrees are known to have been conferred as early as 1769 by Thomas Dunckerley in Portsmouth[8] (undated copies of these two degrees, printed by Carlile, follow at the end of this section). Today the Mark consists of a single degree, Mark Master Mason,

---

3. *Official Bulletin of the Supreme Council of the 33d Degree, for the Southern Jurisdiction of the United States* 10 vols. (Gr∴ Or∴ of Charleston [Washington, D.C.], June, 1890) vol. 10, No. 1: 278–82.

4. *Official Bulletin of the Supreme Council of the 33d Degree for the Southern Jurisdiction of the United States.* Vol. X (June 1890), No. 1, pp. 259–78.

5. For reasons unknown, Prichard's text was taken from a German version, translated by Hermann H. Gerdes, 32°, from *Die Zergliederte Frey-Maurer[e]y in the volume Neues Constitutionen-Buch der Alten Erwürdigen Brüderschaft der Frey-Maurer … von Jacob Anderson,* Francfurt am Mayn, 1762. *Official Bulletin of the Supreme Council of the 33d Degree, for the Southern Jurisdiction of the United States.* Vol. IX (March, 1889) No. 1, pp. 285–93.

6. Carlile's text was republished by his son in 1836 in parts; and in one volume in 1845.

7. *Manual of Freemasonry: in Three Parts. With an Explanatory Introduction to the Science, and A Free Translation of Some of the Sacred Scripture Names. By the Late Richard Carlile. Now First Collected in One Volume.* (London: Richard Carlile, Fleet Street [Printed by J.O. Clarke, 3, Raquet Court, and 121 Fleet Street], 1853).

8. Harry Carr., ed., Bernard E. Jones, *Freemasons' Book of the Royal Arch* (London: Harrap, 1957, 1969), pp. 76–77.

the administration of which differs depending upon jurisdiction. For example, in the United States the Mark Master Degree is attached to Royal Arch Chapters; in England and Wales it falls under the Grand Lodge of Mark Master Masons, while in Scotland it is considered a part of the Fellow Craft Degree, and it may be conferred in a Craft Lodge or Royal Arch Chapter.[9]

While Pike calls the ritual he printed "the oldest work extent anywhere," Albert G. Mackey noted that this copy dates from 1804, and was used by American Eagle Mark Lodge No. 1, Charleston, South Carolina. Mackey added that it "appears to have been [conferred] only on Past Master Masons of the Scottish Rite where were recognized by the possession of Scottish degrees as Past Masters," and that he "had every reason to believe that this was the ritual used at that time by the Mark lodges in America..."[10] American Eagle Mark Lodge No. 1 was under the authority of the Supreme Council, 33°, as Mackey notes in the following article.

Degree of Mark Master[11]

The degree of Mark Master, as an independent degree, is of comparatively modern date, and is confined principally to the United States. But few European Royal Arch Masons are in possession of it. In England, Mark Masonry is at this time practiced in some of the Chapters and Lodges, but it is, says Dr. Oliver, "by the tolerance and not by the sanction of the Grand Lodge." When we speak of the modern character of the degree, we, of course, allude to it as a distinct and independent grade There can be no doubt of the antiquity and truthfulness of the traditions and legends connected with it; but it is most probable that they were formerly connected with the degree of Fellow Craft, of which Mark Masonry is illustrative, just as Royal Arch Masonry is illustrative of the third degree. Since the organization of Royal Arch Chapters in this country, those bodies have taken the Mark degree under their superintendence, and it is now conferred, as is well known, as the first of the capitular degrees. But the control of the degree was probably assumed by the Chapters, rather because it was found floating about, without any definite superintending power, than because of any connection that had existed between it and the Royal Arch before the latter was taken from the Lodges and made a distinct jurisdiction, as it was in 1797. In the English Chapters no provision is made for its being conferred, nor, as we have already said, is it usual to find English Royal Arch Masons in possession of it. When they arrive in

---

9. The interested reader may also refer to Revd. Neville Barker Cryer, *Tell Me More About the Mark Degree* (London: Lewis Masonic, 2007).

10. Albert G. Mackey, et al., "The Mark Degree" in *The History of Freemasonry. Its Legends and Traditions. Its Chronological History.* (New York and London: Masonic History Company, 1898, 1906), vol. 3, pp. 817, 827.

11. Albert G. Mackey, *"Degree of Mark Master,"* in C[harles] Moore, ed., *The Masonic Review* vol. 7 (October Cincinnati, Ohio: J. Ernst, 1851), No. 1, pp. 17–19.

this country, it is generally, necessary to "heal" them, by bestowing the degree, before they can be admitted into our Chapters. With these facts in view, it becomes interesting, as an historical inquiry, to discover how the Mark degree was controlled before its direction was assumed by the Grand Chapters. As some assistance to the elucidation of this question, we append the following copy of a Warrant of Constitution, granted in 1803, in Charleston, for holding a Mark Lodge, and which was a revival of a previous warrant issued by the same body in 1802. By this document, the original of which is in the archives of the Supreme Council of the thirty-third degree for the Southern Jurisdiction of the United States, it will be seen that Mark Masonry was at that time, in South Carolina at least, considered as being attached to the Scotch rite, and warrants were issued by Councils of Princes of Jerusalem, the sixteenth degree in that rite. Whether similar Councils, at that time in existence in some of the Northern States, were also in the habit of exercising the same powers, we are at present unable to say. But the following document, which we have closely copied from the original, for whose authority we vouch, we offer as an interesting contribution to the history of the degree in this country. The warrant is as follows:

By the Glory of the Grand Architect of the Universe.
Lux E Tenebris.

From the East of the Grand of the Most Sublime Council of Princes of Jerusalem, under the Celestial Canopy of the Zenith which answers to the 32° 45' North Latitude.

Whereas, on the twenty-first day of January, 5806, and of the Christian Era 1802, a Warrant was granted by the Grand Council of Princes of Jerusalem, to sundry brethren, Master Mark Masons, for the purpose of establishing a Lodge of Mark Masonry, in this city, to be known and distinguished by the name of the American Eagle Mark Lodge, No. 1, said Warrant having been returned to the Grand Council and deposited among the Archives, and an application for a new Warrant to bear the same name and number; And whereas the Grand Council from the conviction that the establishment of a Lodge of Mark Masonry would facilitate and advance the progress of the Royal Art in the Sublime degrees:

Do deem it expedient to grant this our Warrant, authorizing and empowering our beloved and worshipful brother, Emanuel De La Motta, *Grand Overseer* or *Master*, and our beloved and worshipful brother, Frederick Dalcho, as *Senior Warden*, and our beloved and worshipful brother, Solomon Harby, as *Junior Warden*, to congregate and establish a Lodge of Mark Masonry, who, as well as their successors in office, shall diligently and faithfully discharge and execute the duties and functions appertaining to such lodge, (which duties and functions shall be considered as comprising the passing the Symbolic Chair previous to their initiation in the mysteries of said lodge) agreeably to ancient form and usages, as heretofore

INTRODUCTION

established in such lodges. And also to frame bye-laws for their local government. Provided, nevertheless, that such forms, usages, and bye-laws, are not repugnant to the constitutional laws of this Grand Council.

In witness whereof, we, the undersigned, Officers of the Grand Council of Princes of Jerusalem, in open Council, at Charleston, South Carolina, have hereunto set our hands and affixed the Grand Seals of the Illustrious Order, in the place where the Greatest treasures are deposited, the beholding of which fills us with joy, comfort and acknowledgment of all that is great and good. Near the B.B. and under the C.C. this fifth day of the month called Shebat, 5563, which answers to the twenty-seventh day of February, Anno Lucis 5807, of Mark Masonry 2215, and of the Christian Era 1803.

JN. MITCHELL,
Pres, and Most Enlightened.
FRED'K. DALCHO,
Senior Most Enlightened.
ISAAC AULD,
Junior Most Enlightened
JOSEPH BEE, *Secretary.*

We derive three historical facts from this document, which are worthy of notice.

In the first place, in 1802, five years after the organization of Grand Chapters in Pennsylvania and New England, Mark Lodges were established in South Carolina by the Princes of Jerusalem under the Scotch rite. The first Chapter established in that State was at Beaufort, in 1805, and from that period, the Mark degree seems to have been placed exclusively under the Royal Arch Jurisdiction.

Secondly—From the same document we learn that the presiding officer of a Mark Lodge was called the "Grand Overseer," and not as now, "Right Worshipful Master." There is an allusion to this title in the charge of the degree, first published by Webb, and adopted in all succeeding Monitors, in which the candidate is directed so to act that his conduct "may stand the test of the Grand Overseer's square."

Thirdly—We learn from this document that at that time (in the Scotch rite, at least,) none but Past Masters could receive the Mark degree, and hence the lodge was authorized as a preparatory step, to pass its candidates through the Chair. We are unable to say whether this was or was not always and everywhere the case, but some light is thrown upon the subject by the fact that the Chisel and Mallet, the working tools of the Mark Master, were originally considered as belonging, with their symbolic explanation, to the Past Master's degree, and are so set down in Hutchinson's "Spirit of Masonry," published in 1788. Webb was the first writer who appropriated them to the Mark degree.

It is in this way that the old documents, scattered throughout the country, must, by the isolated facts that they contain and the deductions that may be drawn from them, be made subservient to the history of Masonry in America.

Mackey's points are well taken. The ritual does indeed appear archaic in several regards. It is notably more "Masonic" as it is devoid of scriptural readings and other religious connotations, including those regarding the keystone. Its charge (pp. 12–13) is more primitive than the earliest printed monitorial version in Webb's *The Free-Mason's Monitor* (Albany, 1797).

The close connection between this ritual, and the Supreme Council at Charleston, is evinced by a lecture beginning on pages 8–10 ("My dear Bro∴, in receiving …") which is nearly a verbatim copy of the early charge used prior to conferring the Ineffable Degrees of the Lodge of Perfection,[12] while it also shares some language with the *Circular throughout the Two Hemispheres* (1802), which was the first document issued by the Supreme Council, 33° at Charleston. It may also be noted that pages 9–10 borrow from William Hutchinson's *The Spirit of Masonry* (1775).[13] As a side-note it can be further mentioned that the lecture was later used in the lecture of the Discreet Master Degree in the Ancient and Primitive Rite of Memphis.[14]

THE WIGAN RITUAL OF THE EARLY GRAND ENCAMPMENT, CA. 1801

As explained in Bro. Matthew Cooke's brief preface this is a copy of a manuscript preserved in Wigan, Lancashire, dated 1801. The copy was made for him by Brother John Yarker, who added the following in his *Notes on the orders of the Temple and St. John and the Jerusalem Encampment, Manchester* (1869).[15]

> … Sir Thomas Dunckerley died, and was succeeded in the Grand Mastership of the Order by the Right Honorable Thomas Lord Rancliffe, of Portman Square, London. We have seen that under the authority of York, the Encampments granted their own certificates, copies of which of later date will appear, but from 1791 regular returns were required and certificates issued by the Grand Conclave of London, the charge for registration and certificate being 5s. These certificates are headed with a small geometrical engraving, a modified form of which is yet found on the Irish certificate, and contains the Maltese Cross, Double-headed Eagle, Interlaced Triangles, Three Crossed Swords, Six Banners, the Secret Cypher of the Order, &c. They are as follows:–

---

12. See the copy transcribed by Perez Snell ca.1830, in Arturo de Hoyos, *The Scottish Rite Ritual Monitor and Guide* 3d ed. (Washington, DC: The Supreme Council, 33°, 2011). pp. 1031–33.

13. Compare with William Hutchinson, *The Spirit of Masonry in Moral and Elucidatory Lectures* (London: J. Wilkie & W. Goldsmith, 1775), pp. 185–86.

14. Calvin C. Burt, *Egyptian and Masonic History of the Original and Unabridged Ancient and Ninety-six (96°) Degree Rite of Memphis* (Utica, New York: White and Floyd, 1879) pp. 145–47. See also Calvin C. Burt, *Ritual of the Degrees, Lectures and Standard Work, Rules, Regulations, Constitutions and Laws, for the Instruction and Guidance of the Craft of the Egyptian Masonic Rite of Memphis, from the Fourth to the Ninety-fifth Degrees, for the Continent of America*. In 4 vols. (Chicago: Sovereign Sanctuary (95°) of the Valley of Chicago, 1867), pp. 13–17.

15. John Yarker, *Notes on the Orders of the Temple and St. John and the Jerusalem Encampment, Manchester* (Manchester: Guardian Steam Press, 1869), pp. 24–25.

INTRODUCTION

"In the name of the Holy
and undivided Trinity
(the engraving)
T.P.K. Initium Sapient[ia]e
Amor Domini.

THOMAS DUNCKERLEY, of Hampton Court Palace, in the county of Middlesex, Most Eminent and Supreme GRAND MASTER of the Royal and Exalted, Religious and Military Orders of H.R.D.M. Grand Elected Masonic Knights Templars K.O.D.S.H. of St. John of Jerusalem, Palestine, &c., &c., &c., under the patronage of his ROYAL HIGHNESS PRINCE EDWARD.

These are to certify that Sir —, of the Conclave and Chapter of —, held in their field of Encampment at , is registered in the Grand and Royal Conclave of England.

Given at London the 24th day of June, A.L. 5798, A.D. 1794, A.O. 676. By command of the Most Eminent and Supreme Grand Master.

The Seal attached to the Dunckerley certificates is the same as that on the Jerusalem warrant, but one of 1796 issued by Thomas Lord Rancliffe, has the impression of a fine seal engraved in silver of the Rose Croix, which is yet in possession of the Grand Vice-Chancellor. The former bears a column surmounted with rays of light, and square, level, and plumb rule; behind are two swords crossed; below, "A.L., 5795; " (or 1791) "LXXXI." At the sides of the column are—Mitre, Maltese Cross; Patriarchal Cross, Jerusalem Cross; Six Stars; Two Letters;[16] and round the seal the inscription, "R.O., H.R.D.M., K.O.D.H. K.T.P., H.P.R.; IN HOC SIGNO VINCES." The whole is surmounted by the emblem of the Red Cross of Constantine, a Double-headed Eagle. The last-mentioned Seal has a ladder of Seven Steps; behind are Cross Swords, Circle, and Thirty-three Stars; at the foot of the Ladder is the letter M, and at the top a Glory, the letter N, Triangle, and Cubic Stone; various letters are scattered about; the dates 1118, 1314; the ages 3, 5, 7, 9, 27, 81; the letters P.K., H.M., &c.

"Trinity Sunday, May 22nd, 1796. Sir Baptist Ronchetti, G.C.—April 23rd, 1797. Sir David Torr chosen R.G.C.—April 8th, 1798. The officers chosen were Sir William Young, R.G.C.—November, 1798. There were only three members present, and their patience was tired, some of the brethren having been absent six months."

---

16. The Seal of the Priors of the Order of St. John found in the Temple Church, London, in 1830, has:— "On one side the Holy Sepulchre of Jerusalem, with the Saviour in his tomb, at his head an elevated cross, above a tabernacle or chapel, from the roof depends two incense pots, surrounding this:— Fr. Berengarii Custos pauperum Hospitalis Jherusalem. Reverse: —A holy man in the attitude of prayer before a patriarchal cross, on either side of which are the letters Alpha and Omega, and under the first letter a star." [—Yarker's note]

There now occurs an interval of four years, in which no meeting seems to have been held. We have had an opportunity of seeing many changes, and although it would be a difficult matter to say what either the York or the Dunckerley working (if different) was at the period, yet a copy of the Temple lectures as used after the death of Baron Rancliffe, in 1801, has been placed in my hands by Sir Knt. Thomas Lonsdale Bold, and though they may be derived from the latter, yet the officers do not seem quite to correspond with either, and may possibly be the lectures of an older system than either of these two revisions. The Preface is as follows:-

"The Order of High Knight Templars consists of 21 members assembled in Grand Chapter and Royal Encampment. The Grand Master or Captain General is the head, with Captains commanding, Standard Bearers, &c. At all processions are carried a sword and scabbard, with a blue silk cushion fringed with black. Each Knight a broad ribbon across the breast, hanging down to the left side, tied with blue ribbon, in a bow knot, with the Star of the Order on the left breast. At the bottom of the ribbon or scarf hangs a short sword or dagger, also the image or picture of St. John hangs pendent to a blue silk ribbon at the middle of the breast. The habit or ensign of the Order are a marble girdle, cap star and garter, or cross. The Cross or Star of the Order is made of blue silk twist with gold, irradiated with beams of blue. The Knights of this Order are esteemed clearly the greatest Military Order in the world.

The manner of electing a Knight of this order is—when the Grand Master or Captain General, with the consent of the whole, desire to install a candidate, he draws a letter on which is the Cross of the Order, which is sent to the candidate as follows:—"Conclave of — A.D. 1801. We, the Captain General, &c., &c., of the Grand Encampment of the Most Noble, Holy, Invincible, and Magnanimous Order of High Knights Templars, at our Castle, Conclave, or Encampment, in— Commanding:—To A. B. send greeting:—For the zeal and fidelity you have shown in defending our rights in Masonry we have elected you to become one of this Order, therefore we command and require you to repair to us at our Castle, Conclave, or Encampment aforesaid, on — day the day of A.D. 1801, at o'clock, to be installed and receive the ensigns of the order. Given at &c., &c. (Signed) A. B., Captain General.'"

Emblems: Eye, with triangle; St. John; Skull and Cross bones, with I.H.S. W.; Sword and Sceptre; Star; Ladder, five steps; Hour Glass and Scythe, Urn; Twelve Lights; Lamb; Porch, with cock; Cross, five steps.

INTRODUCTION

Grade, Mark Mason, Passed Master, and Royal Arch, Rite Ancien Maçonnerie d'York were originally translated from English into French, and used in the French West Indies in 1795.

As Pike explained in his introduction to these degrees the manuscript,[17] from which they were translated, was originally discovered in the archives of the Grand Lodge of Louisiana. Although they are in French, they are based on undiscovered originals in English, which were translated for use in the French Caribbean in the late eighteenth century. The French manuscript is in the handwriting of Achille Huet de Lachelle, an enthusiastic and prominent Mason, who was among other things, the Provincial Grand Master of the Rose Croix de Kilwinning (Royal Order of Scotland) for the Isle of Saint Domingue (now Haiti). De Lachelle's manuscript is comprised of three sections: (1) *Rose Croix D'héredom de Kilwining. 18me Grade de la maçonnerie ou Le 4me de la 5me∴ classe*, (2) *Rite Ancien Maconnerie D'York. Grade, Mark Macon & Grade Royale Arch*, (3) *Instituts Généraux Maçonniques*, and only the second part is included herein. For reasons unknown, the degrees of the second section are not presented sequentially:

Mark Maçon — 5me∴ Grade de la maconnerie D'York. Rit antien
Royale Arche — 7me∴ Grade du rite ancien
Passe master. Vénérable de L☐ 4me∴ Grade du rit ancien

Missing from the collection are the degrees of Super-excellent Mason, and the Royal Master, both of which are mentioned in the Royal Arch Degree. The rituals of de Lachelle's collection correspond quite well with the content, but not necessarily the order, of "The 7 Seven Degrees of the Ancient or English Rite" (Les 7 Grades Du Rite Ancien ou Anglais) in a manuscript[18] belonging to Pierre Joseph Duhulquod,[19] Senior Warden of the Lodge *Réunion des Coeur*, in the Orient of Jeremie, Island and Coast of Saint Domingue. Duhulquod's manuscript was as accurate certified on April 16, 1803, by Antoine Bideaud, 33°.[20] It will readily be seen that these early "York Rite" rituals differed somewhat from the

---

17. This bound manuscript is now in the Archives of the Supreme Council, 33°, S.J., Washington, D.C.
18. *Royal Arche et du Rit Ancient. Appti∴ Compon∴ Mtre∴ Ex. Mtre∴ Marque Maçon: Royal Master Royal Arch.* The thirty-three page ms. actually includes ritual information on the 13°, Knight of the Royal Arch, followed by the seven classes of Masonry: (1) Apprentice, (2) Fellow, (3) Master, (4) Past Master (*Passe Mtre∴ ou Ex Mtre∴*), (5) Mark Mason, (6) Super Excellent Mason, and (7) Royal Master. Then follows the Royal Arch, called the "22d Degree of the new Rite, and the last of the Ancient." (Archives of the Supreme Council, 33°, S.J., Washington, D.C.)
19. A veteran of the battle of New Orleans, he was also known as "Pierre Joseph Dulcot." See Jane Lucas De Grummond and Ronald R. Morazan, *The Baratarians and the Battle of New Orleans* (Baton Rouge: Louisiana State University Press,), pp. 72, 258.
20. Bideaud, who signed himself as "Sovereign Grand Inspector General of the Thirty-third Degree, and Sovereign Grand Commander for Life for the French Windward and Leeward Islands" (les îles francaise du Vent et Sous le Vent), certified that the rituals conform to those in his archives.

xvii

forms commonly used today throughout most of the United States. Today's York Rite owes itself primarily to the ritual revisions of Thomas Smith Webb, who received his Royal Arch Degree in Philadelphia in 1796.

Pierre Joseph Duhulquod's Mark Master jewel is similar to that described in de Lachelle's rituals. The letters HTWSJTKS signify "Hiram Tyre will send Jabulum to King Solomon."

INTRODUCTION

Mark Mason, 5th Degree of the Masonry of York, Ancient Rite

The Mark Master Degree, as commonly used in the United States today, includes the use of a symbolic keystone upon which appears the letters H∴T∴W∴S∴S∴T∴K∴S∴ within a circle. The letters are variously interpreted, depending upon jurisdiction. The circular device and letters are also found on a "Chapter Penny" or "Shekel," presented to members, and in the center of the circle the member inscribes his personal "mark"—a unique design which identified him. Before the practice of using a coin, however, American Mark Master Masons often wore a "jewel" or medallion around their necks, which resembled the one drawn here. They were often oval, or shield-shaped, and might be adorned with filigree work, or various symbols, or with the mallet and chisel (the working tools of a Mark Master). Alternatively, the jewel could be a simple circular medallion.[21]

American Style Mark Master Jewel

Mark Master Jewel of Frederick Phile

In de Lachelle's and Duhulquod's early French rituals, however, we find something else. Differing by a single letter we they read H∴T∴W∴S∴J∴T∴K∴S∴, signifying "Hiram Tyre will send *Jabulum* to King Solomon."[22] Before explaining the significance of the name Jabulum, it is interesting to note that this variant appears to have also been used in at least one part of the United States. The Mark Master Mason jewel of Frederick Phile (ca.1740–93), seen here, uses the same letters as these French rituals.[23] Its significance was

---

21. The letters in a circle can be found, for example, on the flap of the apron allegedly given by the Marquis de Lafayette to George Washington in 1784.
22. In what a manuscript which is very similar to Duhulquod's, but apparently written not long afterwards, the letters HTWWSTKS appear, meaning "Hiram of Tyre will send back the son of the widow to Solomon." See *Document 167-o-f. Collection de rituels du Rite Ancien d'York* (Latomia, 2009), p. 24.
23. The jewel is owned by the National Heritage Museum of the Supreme Council, 33°, N.M.J., Lexington, Massachusetts. Its photograph and Phile's brief biographical information appear on their web page < http://nationalheritagemuseum.typepad.com/library_and_archives/mark-medals/ >. Posted August 27, 2013.

xix

likely overlooked because the engraving is in cursive. Phile, who was from Philadelphia, must have commissioned the jewel after receiving the degree in New York City's Holland Mark Lodge (founded 1788), and before his death in 1793.

In early forms of the Royal Arch Degree conferred in the United States the name "Jabulum" appears as "Jabulon"[24] and "Jahbuhlun"[25] although its meaning was not explained (the earliest ritual usage of the name I have seen is in the "Perfect Scot Elect or Holy Arch, called the Square"[26] Degree, allegedly received by Stephen Morin in England in 1744).

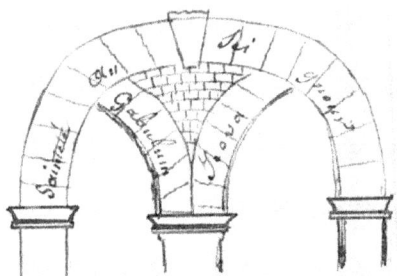

In old rituals these are variants of the name of an explorer who, with two others, made a significant discovery beneath an arch. The names of the explorers differ slightly in different manuscripts and rites. Some early French rituals call them Jabulon, Johaben, and Stolkin,[27] while the Order of the Royal Secret often used Gibulum, Joabert, and Stolkin.[28] In celebration of having made the valuable discovery, the name of the most intrepid explorer was repeated. Duhulquod's manuscript includes the accompanying drawing of an arch with the words "Holiness to the Lord" and "Gabulum, Jeova," hinting at the legend. For reasons likely attributable to pronunciation,

---

24. See "Knight of the Royal Arch" in Arturo de Hoyos, *Freemasonry's Royal Secret* (Washington, DC: Scottish Rite Research Society, 2014), pp. 265–84. An unattributed ritual collection in the Archives of the Supreme Council, 33°, S.J. includes both the "Royal Arch Chapter" (with Jabulon), and the "Royal Arch" (with Jobert, Stokin, and Gibulum [sic]).

25. Ex-Mason David Bernard explained, "There is a great difference in the manner of giving the Royal Arch word in the different chapters. Sometimes it is given in the opening ... sometimes they commence with the word GOD, each one pronouncing a letter of it in succession, until they have each pronounced every letter of the word, then the word JEHOVAH, a syllable at a time, and then the word JAHBUHLUN, as described. There are also chapters where the latter word is not known, and there are others in which the word is not given at all at opening." de Hoyos, *Light on Masonry* (2008), p. 346.

26. The degree of *Parfait Elu Ecossais ou la Voute Sacre appellee le quarré* uses the form "Gabalon," signifying "favorite friend or zealous Mason." It was the name which Solomon gave to the Perfect Elus, which are called "Gabalons." In the ritual the candidate pronounces the word "God" and then "Ga-ba-lon" in syllables. As a "Scottish" (*Ecossais*) degree, it may support the theory that the early Scots Master Degree included material later found in the Royal Arch. Indeed, the first page includes material which is very much "Royal Arch" in character, including the use of a triangle, hieroglyphs, and the phrase *In principio erat Verbum et Verbum erat apud Deum* (In the beginning was the Word, and the Word was with God). The ritual has been modified however, evident by its mention of later degrees, including Perfect Master, Elu of the Nine, Knight Elect, and Grand Architect (ms. p. 28). Notes in the text assert that Morin received the degree in 1744. The author appreciates his fellow Texas Mason, Bro. Josef Wages, for sharing the *Parfait Elu Ecossais* manuscript with him.

27. See Paul Naudon, *Histoire rituels et tuileur des haut Grades Maçonniques* (Paris: Dervy, 1993), p. 317.

28. de Hoyos, *Freemasonry's Royal Secret* (2014), p. 84. The 1783 *Franken MS.* calls the latter Guibelum.

INTRODUCTION

the J-form of the name was preserved in the York Rite, while the G-form is found in the Order of the Royal Secret, and the Scottish Rite. Interestingly, the latter preserves a more complete form of the degree and legend than the York Rite. It should be noted that there are many variations of this name, and that they are sometimes confused in the manuscripts. In some, Gibulum is the name of the explorer, and Jabulum (or even Zabulon) is a significant word, while in others, they may be reversed.

It is noteworthy that in several places de Lachelle's manuscript actually shows a transition from Jabulum to Gibulum. The *J* and *a* of the former name are written over with *G* and *i*, and on one page de Lachelle neglects to correct the name one time. In all instances of his translation, however, Pike adopts the *G*-form of the name.

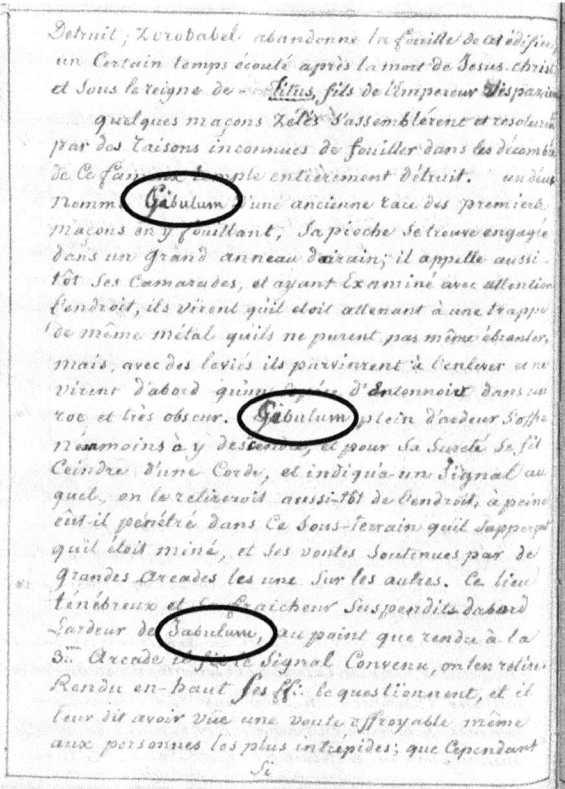

Achille Huet de Lachelle's manuscript shows the transition from Jabulum to Gibulum.

xxi

Past Master, Venerable of the L[odge], 4th Degree of the Ancient Rite

Not much need be said about this brief degree. It consists primarily of an obligation, and the sign and word of a Past Master, which are different from those traditionally encountered. The manner in which the words appear is anagrammatic. M∴A∴h∴O∴B∴M∴O∴ is *Mohabon*, and G∴I∴U∴M∴B∴V∴L∴ is *Gibulum* (in Duhulquod's manuscript G∴I∴B∴U∴L∴U∴M∴ means "Excellent Master"). De Lachelle's manuscript also includes the following two illustrations for this degree, neither of which is captioned.

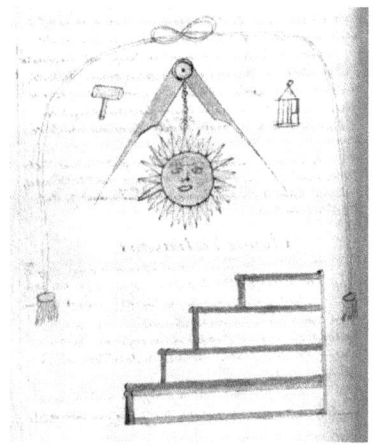   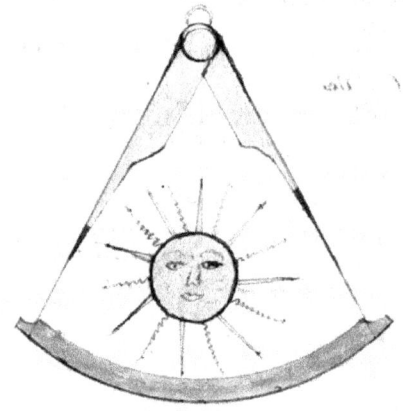

Past Master Tracing Board   Past Master's Jewel

Royal Arch, 7th Degree of the Ancient Rite

This ritual is rather full and complete and, although part of the "York Rite," it yet includes material commonly found in the Order of the Royal Secret and later, in the Scottish Rite. Interestingly, there are two membership jewels described (the "Grand Cordon and Jewel," p. 23/34), the first of which is almost identical to the Jewel used by the Scottish Rite. Unfortunately, these are not sketched in the manuscript.

There are several unusual features which will be noted by the reader. One is an early formula used in opening, "We three, by friendship and confidence united ..." (p. 24/35), another is the fact that the candidate is admitted on the basis that he is a Super-excellent Mason and Royal Master, who has governed a lodge (i.e., is a Past Master).

INTRODUCTION

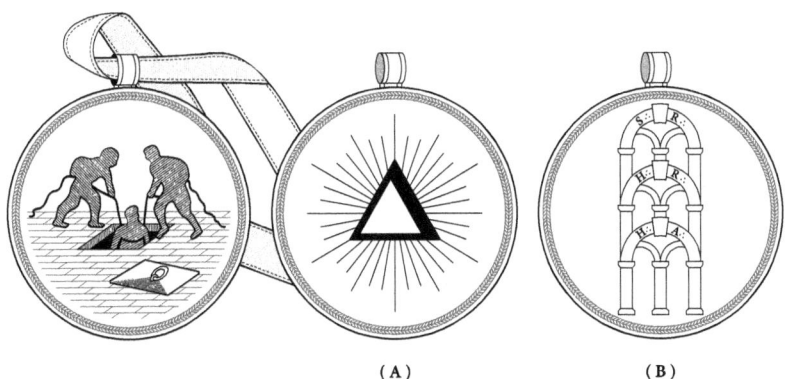

(A)   (B)
Royal Arch Grand Cordon and Jewel

Excursus, The Royal Master Degree

Although the Royal Master Degree is mentioned in de Lachelle's Royal Arch Degree, there is no hint concerning the ritual's content. The early history and origins of the Royal Master Degree are unknown. It is believed that Thomas Lowndes first conferred the degree around 1805, in New York,[29] and the earliest known records are those of his Columbian Council No. 1, New York, which date from 1810.[30]

Does de Lachelle's manuscript, dating to ca.1795, provide evidence that the Royal Master Degree existed before 1805? Perhaps Duhulquod's manuscript, dated 1803, may help answer the question. The similarity between de Lachelle's and Duhulquod's rituals is strong, and the fact that they were used in same area of the world may suggest that Duhulquod's Royal Master ritual may be the one mentioned in de Lachelle's Royal Arch Degree. I have translated Duhulquod's brief Royal Master Degree below to show that it may indeed have provided rudimentary content to Thomas Lowndes. Further, this primitive degree seems also be related to the degree now known as "Ark and Dove" or "Royal Ark Mariner."

---

29. *Proceedings of the Grand Council, Royal and Select Masters of the State of Vermont at the 45th Annual Assembly In the City of Burlington, Tuesday, June 9th, A.D. 1903, A∴Dep∴ 2903.* Vol. 5 (Windsor, Verm..: Journal Company, Book and Job Printers, 1903) No. 8, Appendix: "Report on the Committee on Correspondence 1903," p. 15.

30. *The Hudson River Trestle Board* vol. 5 (Newburgh, New York, April 15, 1906), No. 68, p. 577. See also Eugene E. Hinman, Ray V. Denslow, and Charles C. Hunt, *A History of the Cryptic Rite*, 2 vols. (Tacoma, Wash.: General Grand Council R. & S.M., U.S.A., 1931), vol. 1, pp. 606–7.

REPRINTS OF RITUALS OF OLD DEGREES

ROYAL MASTER
7TH DEGREE
THE PAINTING OF THE [LODGE] IS IN BLUE.
TOKEN
CROSS THE HANDS TOGETHER, IN THE MANNER
OF FORMING A DOUBLE ✥ [CROSS]

PASS WORD
N∴O∴É∴ [NOAH]
SACRED WORD
A∴L∴P∴H∴A∴ E∴T∴ O∴M∴E∴G∴A∴
The Sign
With the index finger of the right hand, the other fingers closed, pointing at an object at in air, saying Voià qu'il vient (in English) Lo, he com[eth,] which is the sense of Noah in the ark.

INTRODUCTION

Knights Templar, former English Ritual, 1851

The ritual is rather full and complete, and not much need be said, other than that is it not the ritual currently used. An even earlier version of the English Knight Templar ritual printed by Richard Carlile in *The Republican* (1825),[31] appears in the Appendix. The ritual provided by Bro. Cooke is nearly identical to one printed by *The Perfect Ceremonies of the Masonic Knights Templar, Knight of Malta, Mediterranean Pass, and Rose Croix de Heredom Degrees* (1876),[32] although the latter also included the ceremony of consecrating an Encampment of Knight Templar. It also included a catechism for the Degree, which follows here for the sake of completion.

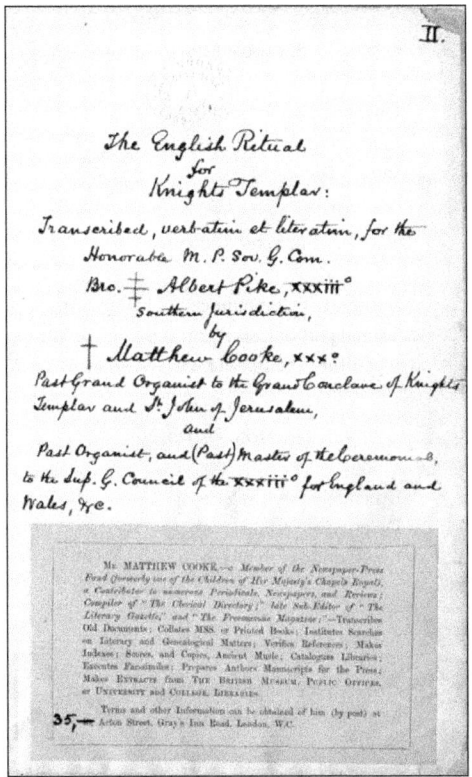

---

31. Richard Carlile, *The Republican* vol. 12 (London, Friday, Oct. 7, 1825), No. 12, pp. 420–33.

32. *The Perfect Ceremonies of the Masonic Knights Templar, Knight of Malta, Mediterranean Pass, and Rose Croix de Heredom Degrees* (London: Privately Printed for A. Lewis, 1876), pp. 9–84.

REPRINTS OF RITUALS OF OLD DEGREES

Masson's System of Examination of the Royal, Exalted, and Military Order of Masonic Knights Templar in England and Wales

Preface.

In order to harmonise with the general working of Encampments, the System is divided into Sections and Clauses, for greater clearness, and to admit of being given as time may admit.

Section First.

Clause I.   Qualification of Candidates.
        II. Preparation and Admission.
        III. Introduction.

Section Second.

Clause I.   First part of Communication before Introduction.
        II. Second part of Communication before Introduction.
        III. Investiture and Installation.

Section Third.

Clause I.   Explanation of Mysteries.
        II. Description of Encampment.
        III. Explanation of Symbols.

Q. From the South-west Angle?
A. By the North-west Angle.

INTRODUCTION

First Section.
First Clause.

Q. What are the necessary qualifications for the admission of a Candidate for the Order?
A. There are three.
Q. Name them?
A. 1st, That he should have been received by Holy Baptism an Inheritor of the Kingdom of Heaven. 2d, That his life and actions, during his state of manhood, should have evinced a strict adherence to the precepts of the Captain of our Salvation. 3d, That he should have been regularly initiated into the three probationary degrees of Masonry, and exalted to the sublime degree of R. A. M.

Second Clause.

Q. How many preparations are necessary before he can be admitted?
A. Three.
Q. Name them?
A. 1st, That he should be prepared in mind; 2d, That he should be prepared in spirit; 3d, That he should be prepared in humility.
Q. Why in mind?
A. That he may properly consider, that as genuine merit is the pass to preferment, whether he feels himself justified in his claim.
Q. Why in spirit?
A. Because, as our Order is both religious and military, he should not neglect to consider whether he can fairly present himself as a Disciple of Christ, and brave enough in the hour of danger to resist the unprovoked attacks of the Children of Darkness.
Q. Why in humility?
A. To commemorate the first garments adopted by our glorious predecessors before the Crusades, who, in humble attire of Pilgrims, travelled through dangers and difficulties to Jerusalem, there to offer up their prayers at the Shrine of their Saviour; and in this appearance alone ought a Candidate to be received into an Encampment of Knights Templar.

Third Clause.

Q. The Candidate being thus prepared, whither is he conducted?

A. By the Outposts he is conducted to the entrance of the Encampment.

Q. How does he gain admittance?

A. By four sounds of the trumpet; or, in time of peace, by four knocks at the outward gate of the Encampment.

Q. To what does this allude?

A. To the number of degrees he has obtained in Masonry.

Q. Who came to his assistance?

A. The representative of the 2d Captain, attended by a Herald.

Q. What did he demand?

A. Who comes here?

Q. The reply?

A. A poor pilgrim on his travels, who, hearing that a Knights Templar Encampment is established here, craves admission.

Q. What further inquiry was made?

A. From whence he came, and for what purpose? to which he answers: —From the West, going to Jerusalem, there to pray for the forgiveness of his own sins and those of his fellow creatures.

Q. Upon what ground did he prefer his request?

A. By his possessing the Secrets of the H. R. A.

Q. What was next done?

A. The Aide-de-camp of the 2d Captain, having ascertained his possession of the Secrets, desired him to wait the commands of his Chief.

Q. What was the result?

A. With the approbation of the Knights assembled, the E. C. directed the Candidate to be admitted with caution and in ancient form.

INTRODUCTION

Second Section.
First Clause.

Q. The Candidate being admitted within the entrance of the Encampment, what caution is observed?

A. The Second and First Captains satisfy themselves of the claim of the Candidate, and then introduce him.

Q. What follows?

A. The Can., not being in possession of any test by which he can claim free admission, is rejected, and being refreshed with bread and water, is ordered to undergo the probation.

Q. Why is he refreshed with bread and water?

A. These were and are considered by those who enter on their pilgrimage on earth as the staff of life.

Q. How many years is a Novice to serve before he can be admitted a Member of the Order?

A. Fifteen years.

Q. Describe the servitude?

A. Seven years as a pilgrim to try his piety; seven years as a soldier to try his faith; and one year of penance and mortification to try his fidelity.

Q. Is no shorter period allowed?

A. Only in cases of individual merit, and then only by the power of the E. C., emanating from the G. C.

Q. Is the Candidate subject to any obligation?

A. I, A. B., in the name of the Holy Trinity, and in the presence of the Knights here assembled, do hereby and hereon most solemnly promise and swear never to reveal the secrets of a Knight Templar to any one beneath that degree, unless it be to a Candidate for the same, in a lawful Encampment of Knights Templar, and then only whilst acting as a regularly installed Commander. I furthermore solemnly promise, that I will faithfully defend and maintain the holy Christian faith against all unprovoked attacks of its enemies; that I will not shed the blood of a Knight Templar in wrath, unless it be in the just wars of Sovereign Princes or States; but, on the contrary, will defend him, even at the risk of my life, where or whensoever his life or his honour may be in danger. That I will, to the utmost of my power, protect the near and dear relatives and connexions of K. T., and if possible prevent all harm, danger, or violence to which they may be exposed. Lastly, I do most sincerely promise to be obedient to the supreme authorities of the country in which I do or may reside, and strictly to observe and maintain the ancient laws and regulations of the Order, the Statutes of the Grand Conclave of England and Wales, and to answer and obey, so far as lies in my power, all summonses which I may receive, the same being duly marked. To all these points I swear fidelity, without evasion, equivocation, or mental reservation of any kind, under no less penalty than the loss of life, by having my head struck off and placed upon a pinnacle or spire, my skull sawn asunder, and my brains exposed to the scorching rays of the sun, as a warning to all infidels and traitors. So help me Christ, and keep me steadfast in this my solemn obligation.

Second Clause.

Q. What are the names of a Soldier of Christ?

A. Strengthened by FAITH, having the Breastplate of RIGHTEOUSNESS, and his feet shod with the preparation of the Gospel of Peace. He is armed with the Shield of Faith, the Helmet of Salvation, and the Sword of the Spirit.

Q. Being thus armed, what is entrusted to his particular care?

A. The S. and P. W. of a Crusader.

Q. Give me the Sign?

A. (*Done*.)

Q. To what does it allude?

A. * * * *

Q. Give me the P. W.?

A. (*Done*.)

Q. To what does it allude?

A. * * * *

Q. The Candidate having proved his valour as a Christian warrior, what is entrusted to him then?

A. The knowledge and import of the Sacred Word.

Q. What was next entrusted to him?

A. The emblems of Life and Death are particularly recommended to his contemplation.

Q. Why such awful emblems?

A. That his thoughts should never wander from the serious consideration of the uncertainty of human existence, and the awful situation in which he has placed himself in reference to his obligation.

Q. The Candidate having fully served the 15 years, what follows?

A. He is declared a Novice of the Order, entrusted with G. S. and G. P. W., and allowed to retire for meditation and repose.

INTRODUCTION

Third Clause.

Q. The Novice being now entitled to greater honours, how did he obtain them?

A. By virtue and perseverance.

Q. Describe the manner?

A. Having announced himself in due form to the Representative of the 2d Captain, he is re-admitted, examined by the 2d and 1st Captains, and afterwards by the E. C.

Q. What is a Casual Sign, as alluded to?

A. A certain motion of the hand, which can only be understood and answered by those who have been regularly installed.

Q. Give me the Casual Sign?

A. (Done.)

Q. To what does it allude?

A. * * * *

Q. Give me the Gd. P. W.?

A. (Done.)

Q. To what does it refer?

A. The prophecy against Syria and Israel, as recorded in Holy Writ.

Q. The Novice being thus received, what follows?

A. After the Grand Prelate has impressed on his mind the duty he is ever to observe towards God, his neighbour, and himself, he is refreshed with the cup of memory.

Q. Thus refreshed, what was next presented to him?

A. The test of his sincerity; which with his blood is in token also of his faith, and which possesses a new name no man knoweth but he who has received it.

Q. Being now in possession of this great and mysterious memorial, what was next ordered?

A. The Novice was ordered to advance to the East, and under the holy banner of our Order, to receive the honour of Knighthood in ancient form.

Q. Describe that form?

A. Being handed by the 2d Captain to the foot of the throne, he kneels on his left knee, while the Knights appear in full armour. The E. C. places his sword on his shoulder; creates him a Knight; and in that character he raises him as Knight Companion of the Royal, Exalted, Religious, and Military Order of the Holy Temple and Sepulchre of Christ, and orders him to be solemnly invested with the insignia of the Institution.

Q. What concludes the Installation?

A. Having been entrusted with the G. S., W., and G., by the Emt. Cr., he is most respectfully conducted to his stall; and by the Heralds in the S. W. and the N. W. he is regularly proclaimed, and which the assembly acknowledges by a regular salute of arms.

Third Section.
First Clause.

Q. What mysterious knowledge is entrusted to the members of our Order?

A. The G. S., the G. W., and the G. G.

Q. What next?

A. The description of our Encampment, and the hidden import of those emblems and symbols which are indispensable in a Chapter of the Order.

Q. Please give me the Gd. S.?

A. (*Done.*)

Q. To what does it allude?

A. * * * *

Q. Give me the G. W.?

A. (*Done.*)

Q. What does it express?

A. * * * *

Q. Give to the Kt. next you the G. G.?

A. (*Done.*)

Q. What does it imply?

A. That we are to support each other through dangers and difficulties, and to stand or fall together in defence of the Christian Faith, against all unprovoked attacks of its enemies.

INTRODUCTION

S%%%%%%econd Clause.

Q. How is an Encampment of K. Templars situated?
A. Due E. and W.
Q. What is its form?
A. A close square.
Q. On what ground do we place our sacred banner?
A. On sacred ground.
Q. What makes the ground sacred?
A. The Holy Cross raised in the centre of a triangle.
Q. Why is the Holy Cross placed in the centre?
A. That situation being equally distant from the exterior lines, it enables every individual in the Encampment to behold the emblem he bears, and to which he has sworn fidelity.
Q. Is there any other reason?
A. Yes. That in this sign we hope to conquer; from which reason the Crusaders adopted the motto—"In hoc signo vinces."
Q. How is the Triangle in the Encampment represented?
A. By the situation of the Em. Com. and the two leading Captains, who from their situation figuratively represent the extremities of each angle, those intersecting the Close Square from the S. W. and N. W. to the point, thereby forming a triangle between two parallel lines.
Q. What does the T. represent?
A. The Triune Essence of Deity.
Q. For what reason do we consider the Western side the basis of the triangle?
A. For the reason, the nations to the N., S., and West, from their geographical situation, could not at once co-operate together, but being actuated by one and the same laudable motive, they united in the East, and thus formed by their union a triangle of Wisdom, Strength, and Beauty.

Third Clause.

Q. What is considered a Chapter of the Order?

A. A Congregation of Knights in H. Conclave, during any cessation of Hostility or War.

Q. For what purpose do they congregate?

A. To maintain the Stability and Honour of the Order, and to receive such Novices as are deserving to be admitted among them.

Q. What do we principally behold in a Chapter of Knights Templar?

A. A Representation of the Holy Sepulchre.

Q. Why so?

A. Because the recovery of the Holy Sepulchre was the ground plan of the Crusades.

Q. What further objects attract your attention?

A. The emblem of our Faith, the guide of our Life, and the hope of our Salvation.

Q. How are they represented?

A. By the Cross, the Sacred Volume, and Holy Gospel.

Q. Do we not assign another reason for the Cross, than being only an emblem of our Faith?

A. Yes. We consider also that it represents the tree of Death and the tree of Life. For as by the first Adam Sin and Death were brought into the world, so by the second Adam we hope for life everlasting.

Q. What do we next discover?

A. The emblem of Mortality, and the severe punishment of Infidelity.

Q. How are they represented?

A. By a human Skull and Saw.

Q. For what purpose are they placed before us?

A. To remind us of our obligation, and to avoid the punishment incurred by Simon of Syracuse.

Q. Do we acknowledge any other symbols in our Chapter?

A. Yes. Twelve Lights, composed of Three Large and Nine Lesser Lights.

Q. How are they situated?

A. They are so placed as to form a triangle to the emblems already described, the Greater Lights placed at the extremity of each angle, and these intersected by the Lesser Lights.

Q. What do these Lights represent?

A. The Twelve Apostles. The three larger represent the three favoured Apostles of Christ—Peter, James, and John; and the nine lesser, the less favourite Apostles, including Judas Iscariot, who betrayed his Lord and Master.

End of Masson's System of Examination.

INTRODUCTION

Grand Maitre Ecossais or Scottish Elder Master and Knight of St. Andrew, being the Fourth Degree of the Degree of Ramsay

The significance of this degree has largely been overlooked by historians of the Scottish Rite. A copy of the ritual, called "Grand Master Ecosé, or Scot[t]ish Elder Master and Knight of St. Andrew" is in Frederick Dalcho's collection (dated 1801–02) of Supreme Council rituals. It was mentioned in the *Circular throughout the Two Hemispheres* (December 4, 1802) as one of the degrees communicated "free of expence, to those Brethren, who are high enough to understand them."[33] More importantly, it one of degrees mentioned in Dalcho's Thirty-third Degree patent, occupying a position between Prince of Lebanus and Chief of the Tabernacle. It's a matter of curiosity that it the Grand Master Ecosé is the only degree named on his patent which is not currently a part of the Scottish Rite. This begs the question if it perhaps was once conferred as such?

Dalcho's Patent (May 25, 1801)	Circular (December 4, 1802)
[18] Sovereign Prince of Rose Croix de Heroden	[18] Sovereign Prince of Rose Croix de Heroden
[19] Grand Pontif	[19] Grand Pontif
[20] Master ad Vitam – Grand Master of all Symbolic Lodges	[20] Grand Master of all Symbolic Lodges
[21] Patriarch Noachite Chevalier Prussian	[21] Patriarch Noachite or Chevalier Prussian
[22] Prince of Lebanus	[22] Prince of Lebanus
[23] Grand Master Ecosé – Knight of St.Andrew, &c &c &c	[23] Chief of the Tabernacle
[24] Chief of the Tabernacle	[24] Prince of the Tabernacle
[25] Prince of Mercy	[25] Prince of Mercy
[26] Knight of the Brazen Serpent	[26] Knight of the Brazen Serpent
[27] Commander of the Temple	[27] Commander of the Temple
[28] Sovereign Knight of the Sun, Prince Adept	[28] Knight of the Sun
[29] K∴H∴ Knight of the White and Black Eagle	[29] K—H
[30] Prince of the Royal Secret	[30] Prince of the Royal Secret
[31] Prince of the Royal Secret	[31] Prince of the Royal Secret
[32] Prince of the Royal Secret	[32] Prince of the Royal Secret
[33] Sovereign Grand Inspector General	[33] Sovereign Grand Inspector General

More importantly, the Grand Master Ecosé is one of the sources used by Frederick Dalcho in creating the first ritual of the Thirty-third Degree.

---

33. The degree is one of three appended to the "Jamaican Francken Manuscript." See de Hoyos, *Freemasonry's Royal Secret* (2014), pp. 285–301.

Dalcho's Grand Master Ecosé, or Scot[t]ish Elder Master and Knight of St Andrew (c.1801)	Dalcho's Sovereign Grand Inspector General (c.1802)
"How adorable and astonishing are the rays of that Glorious Light, which sends forth its bright and brilliant beams from the Holy Ark of Alliance and Covenant …	"How adorable & astonishing are the rays of the glorious light, which sends forth its orient and brilliant beams from the Highest Heavens –
We adore the Great & Mighty Jehovah, who exists from Eternity, glorified by his great and mighty name for ever and ever …" (p. 15)	We adore the Great & Mighty Jehovah who exists from Eternity, Glory be to his Great and Almighty name for ever and ever – " (p.10)
"Let us with the deepest veneration and duty adore the fountain of the glorious spirit who is the Most Merciful & benificent Ruler of the Universe and all the creatures it contains.…" (p. 15)	"Let us with the deepest veneration and duty <piety>, humbly adore the fountain of that Glorious spirit, who is the Most Merciful and Benificent Ruler of the Universe, and all the creatures it contains.…" (p. 10)

The Grand Master Ecosé itself is alchemical and symbolic, and is discussed by Pike in *Morals and Dogma*,[34] but the "Rite of Ramsay" never existed. The degrees of the "Rite" (listed by Pike on page 24)[35] reveal that it was, as Arthur Edward Waite, wrote "an imaginary antedated version of the Rite of Strict Observance…."[36] As for its name, the title "Scots Master" is the oldest and among the most common in the various rites, orders, and systems of the fraternity. The ritual printed by Pike is actually a modification of a degree called "Scottish Master and Knight of St. Andrew of the Thistle."[37]

---

34. Arturo de Hoyos, *Albert Pike's Morals and Dogma: Annotated Edition* (Washington, D.C.: Supreme Council, 33°, 2011, 2013), 28:909–28.
35. Jean-Marie Ragon, *Orthodoxie maçonnique: suivie de la Maçonnerie occulte, et de l'initiation hermétique* (Paris: Dentu, 1853), pp. 116–17.
36. Arthur Edward Waite, *The Secret Tradition in Freemasonry* (New York: E. P. Dutton & Co., Inc., 1937), p. 201.
37. "Schottischer Meister und Ritter des Heiligen Andreas zur Distel," in Friedrich Ludwig Schröder, *Ritualsammlung*. 26 vols. (Rudolstadt: Geheimdruck; Wesselhöft in Jena, 1805–16), vol. 1, pp. 1–32.

INTRODUCTION

Old Ceremony of Royal Arch Exaltation

In 1813, when the "Moderns" and "Antients" Grand Lodges merged to form the United Grand Lodge of England, their compact declared that "pure Antient Masonry consists of three degrees and no more, viz. those of the Entered Apprentice, the Fellow Craft, and the Master Mason including the Supreme Order of the Holy Royal Arch." That statement notwithstanding, it was not until 1834 that work began to harmonize the ritual of the Royal Arch.

Although Ill. Ireland's circular advertises this as the "old ceremony" it was actually the ritual in use during Pike's and Cooke's lifetimes, as the latter explained in his brief preface. Bro. Cooke noted that the "old ceremony" was actually that printed by Richard Carlile in *The Republican* (1825), which was not updated when the *Manual of Freemasonry* was printed in 1835.

Older Degrees from Carlile's *Manual of Freemasonry*, Corresponding to those Printed by Pike

Richard Carlile was the first person to publish an exposure of the English Freemasonry following the formation of the United Grand Lodge of England, in 1813. Carlile, a free thinker, was a great champion of freedom of the press. He published the works of Thomas Paine, and was jailed for blasphemy and seditious libel. While in prison he published *The Republican*, which included his exposure of Freemasonry. His exposé included virtually all of the degrees practiced in England at the time, and even included that variants printed by William Finch. Shorn of its anti-Masonic remarks, the text was improved and later published in parts by his son as the *Manual of Freemasonry* (1836); a one-volume edition appeared in 1845. The following texts were transcribed from my oldest personal copy, dated 1853.

A Description of the Masonic Degree of Mark Man.[38]

The ceremony of opening the lodge, as far as it goes, is precisely the same as in the Fellow Crafts degree, and would be superfluously printed. The Catechism will be all that is necessary to explain the distinctions of the degree. The Masons call it a LECTURE; but a lecture, in fact, is a discourse read, and not a catechism.

Catechism.

WORSHIPFUL MASTER. Brother Senior Warden, in what manner do we prepare our candidates in this degree?

SENIOR WARDEN. As a Fellow Craft, with the additional characteristic of this degree on his apron.

W. M. What is that characteristic?

S. W. The ten mathematical characters, to correspond with the nine figures and cypher in arithmetic; the signature of Hiram Abiff, and the mark of this degree.

W. M. Why is he thus prepared?

---

38. Richard Carlile, *The Republican* vol. 12 (London, Friday, August 19, 1825), No. 7.

S. W. To denote the official duties of this class of Masons at the building of King Solomon's temple, and the discovery made by the brethren, when they were repairing the temple.

W. M. Being thus prepared, in what manner did you enter?

S. W. By three reports (knocks), varying in sound from those of a Fellow Craft.

W. M. Having gained your admission, how were you dealt with?

S. W. I was conducted round to repair the temple in a manner peculiar to this degree, and having made a valuable discovery, I afterwards received the solemn obligation to keep sacred the secrets of this Order. After I had taken the obligation and sealed it in the usual manner, I was raised in the ancient form of a Master Mason.

W. M. Having thus bound yourself to keep sacred the secrets of this Order, what were the mysteries with which you were then entrusted?

S. W. The sign, token, and word of a Mark Man.

W. M. What does the sign denote?

S. W. The penalty of the obligation.

W. M. Why was it introduced into this Order of Masonry?

S. W. To commemorate the signal used by our ancient brethren of this degree, when the first temple was erected in the city of Jerusalem.

W. M. What was that signal?

S. W. The trumpet.

W. M. Why was it used?

S. W. To denote the approach of danger.

W. M. What does the grip or token denote?

S. W. One of the penal laws of ancient Tyre united with the famous link of a Mark Man.

W. M. What does the word denote?

S. W. Everything past, present, or to come.

W. M. Why was this grand, majestic word introduced?

S. W. To hold in commemoration a very remarkable circumstance that occurred on the morning that the foundation stone of the temple was laid. Whilst King Solomon was in the act of congratulating our Grand Superintendent, Hiram Abiff, on the occasion of his having discovered the celebrated problem in masonry and geometry, one of the precious stones fell from the royal crown to the ground, which, being perceived by the senior master of the Order of Mark Men, who, with the chief officers, were in attendance on this grand and solemn assembly, he picked it up and returned it to the king. This stone was of the carbuncle kind, and represented the tribe of Judah and our Saviour. It was formed into that great and glorious name, which King Solomon permitted to be used in the test word of this degree, in commemoration of its having been found by one of the chief brethren of this Order.

W. M. What was the original number of Mark Men at the building of King Solomon's temple?

S. W. Two thousand.

W. M. Who were they?

APPENDIX

S. W. The Senior and Junior Wardens of the Fellow Crafts Lodges.

W. M. How many lodges of Mark Men were there in the city of Jerusalem?

S. W. Twenty.

W. M. Why limited to twenty?

S. W. In allusion to the height, length, and breadth of the sanctum sanctorum, or holy of holies.

W. M. How many Masons in each lodge?

S. W. One hundred.

W. M. What was the employ of these mark men?

S. W. To mark the materials, as they came out of the hands of the workmen, to enable them to put them together with greater facility and precision, when brought from the quarries of Tyre, the Forests of Lebanon and the clay ground of the Jordan, between the Succoth and Zarthan, to the holy city of Jerusalem.

W. M. What were the peculiar marks on that occasion?

S. W. Certain. mathematical figures, consisting of squares, levels, and perpendiculars, that King Solomon commanded to be used on that occasion, which have ever since been denominated the *Freemasons' Secret Alphabet* or *Mystic Characters*.

W. M. Can you describe those characters?

S. W. With that circumspection peculiar to Masons, I will meet you on the line parallel, by giving you one part, leaving you to your own free will in giving the remainder.

W. M. I will thank you to proceed.

The S. W. rises, salutes the W. M. with the sign, advances to him, and lays his two penal fingers[39] (first and second) on those of the W. M., and thus forms the index to the secret alphabet, by joining the horizontal parallel to two perpendicular parallels.

W. M. What is the mark of this degree?

S. W. The H T or Tau in ancient characters.

W. M. What is the chief signature of this degree?

S. W. The first is H. A. B., and the word is STODAN.

W. M. In what manner are they depicted in a Mark Man's lodge?

S. W. On the under surface of the key-stone of King Solomon's Arch, which they discovered to be a little loosened, at the time that they were inspecting the subterraneous passages, and making preparations for the repairs of the temple.

W. M. What else was there discovered?

S. W. Round the circle surrounding the letters H. A. B., and between the other letters forming the remainder of the signature of this degree, we found conspicuous in Hebrew characters the word *Amasaphus*, or, as some say, *Amethyst*.

---

39. "A square, its portions, and the different positions, into which those portions may be placed, with the aid of the dot, will form an alphabet of twenty-four letters, without the use of a quarter or single side, such as the Roman I. This is the secret alphabet of Masonry. It is very probable, that the circle, triangle, and square, their divisions, and the varied divisions of those divisions, first gave the idea of letters and an alphabet. The Egyptian letters are plainly of this character. One of the Greek letters is a triangle. The circle is common in almost all alphabets; the square in many, the united divisions of both in all." –*Carlile's note.*

W. M. How many Mark Men were there employed in the quarries of Tyre?
S. W. Fourteen hundred.
W. M. How many lodges were there in those quarries?
S. W. Fourteen.
W. M. How many Mark Men in each lodge?
S. W. One hundred.
W. M. What was the pay of each Mason in this degree per day?
S. W. Nine shekels, equal to £1. 2s. 6d. of our money.
W. M. What was the sum total paid on this class of workmen, at the finishing of the temple of Jerusalem?
S. W. Six million, two hundred and twenty-five thousand, seven hundred and fifty pounds.
W. M. What was delineated on this ancient coin?
S. W. On one side, the pot of manna, and the words, *Shekel of Israel*; on the other, *the rod of Aaron budding*, with the word, *Jerusalem the Holy*.
W. M. Give me the historical account of this degree?
S. W. At the building of King Solomon's temple, the valuable and curious key-stone, containing many valuable coins and the ten letters in precious stone work which Hiram Abiff took so much pains to complete, was lost, supposed to have been taken away by some of the workmen, and a reward was offered by King Solomon for the speedy finding or making of another to fit the place. An ingenious Entered Apprentice made one and fixed it in the vacancy in the arch, which, being known to some of the Fellow Crafts, they conceived it a disgrace to their Order to let an inferior degree bear the palm of honour. They therefore, in the heat of jealousy, took it and threw it into the Brook Kedron, adjacent to the temple. A reward was also offered for the finding of this second stone, which excited the brother who had made it, to go, with two other Entered Apprentices, in pursuit of it; and when they had found it, they received equally among them the last reward, and with it the degree of a Fellow Craft. The Brother who made it received the first reward to his own share for his ingenuity, and had the honour with his two Companions to fix it the second time in the arch, previous to which, the brother who made it cut on the under-side the word Amasaphus; and in addition to his former rewards, he was honoured with the degree of Mark Man, which is done by going round the Lodge of a Mark Man putting in his hands as a fellow craft to receive his wages. He is desired to state on what ground he claims those honours, and having informed them of his discovery and what he had made, they then acknowledge his claim to be just; and he being desired to fetch the said key-stone, he finds it in his way to the arch, by kicking against the ring of it concealed under ground, the original key-stone that Hiram Abiff had made, with the proper characters and signatures to it. He is then taught to put in his hands in due form for the payment of his wages, after which he receives the secrets of this degree.
W. M. Brethren, I now crave your assistance in closing this lodge of mark men.
(*The Brethren stand round the Lodge in due form.*)

APPENDIX

W. M. Brother Senior Warden, what is the internal signal for closing this Order?
S. W. Three reports varying in Sound.
W. M. By whom are they given?
S. W. By the Worshipful Master and Wardens.
W. M. When are they to be given?
S. W. Immediately after all the brethren of this degree have given the proper sign.
W. M. Brethren, be pleased to give me the sign. (*The reports are then given.*)
W. M. Why are those reports given?
S. W. As a perpetual memorial of the labour of our ancient brethren in the three famous places where the materials of the temple were prepared:—the Quarries of Tyre, the Forests of Lebanon, and the Clay Ground of the Jordan between Succoth and Zarthan.
W. M. To what do the reports further allude?
S. W. To the class of workmen that compose this degree.
W. M. Then, Brethren, as the master of that class, I declare this lodge duly closed, till our Fellow Craft brethren have furnished us with fresh materials to be MARKED and PASSED to the spot on which we intend to erect a building to the service of the Grand Architect of heaven and earth.

Description of the Degree of Mark Master.

The opening of the lodge in this degree exhibits nothing different from that of the others, but in the distinctive sign, word, token, and knocking.

Lecture or Catechism.

W. M. Brother Senior Warden, you will describe the form of preparation that the candidate has to undergo in this degree?
S. W. He is first prepared in the character of a Master Mason, with this additional characteristic on his apron—the H T is reversed, and in the *ancient Masonic form*.
W. M. For what reason is he so prepared?
S. W. To point out the chief duties that this class of workmen had to perform when the materials were brought to them to be marked and passed in due form.
W. M. In what manner did you enter the lodge after your preparation?
S. W. With five reports, and all of them distinct and loud.
W. M. Why did you give this signal of your approach?
S. W. To denote the No. of this degree as the fifth.
W. M. There is a second reason for this branch of the ceremony?
S. W. In allusion to the peculiar number and class of workmen employed in and about that magnificent building in the holy city of Jerusalem.

W. M. Having gained your admission, how were you dealt with in this degree of a Mark Master?

S. W. I was conducted round the lodge five times.

W. M. For what reason?

S. W. To point out to me that, without the full enjoyment of the five external senses, I could not have received the privileges of this degree.

W. M. In what manner were you proved as to the possession of those senses?

S. W. After traversing from west to east, I was commanded to kneel to hear and receive the benefit of the prayer; and having been taught to repeat it from the delivery of the proper officer, my possession of this faculty was fully acknowledged.

In the second round, the Holy Bible was presented to me, from which I was desired to read that passage where the word of a Master Mason is to be found. This ceremony proved the faculty of *seeing*.

In the third round, the compasses were opened at an angle of ninety degrees, and applied from the guttural to the pectoral part of my body, till my countenance, on some particular emotion, denoted that I retained the noble faculty of *feeling*.

In the fourth round, the pot of manna was presented to me, and having partaken of its contents, and declared the same good, the proper officer acknowledged my possession of the faculty of *tasting*.

I was then delivered over to the Senior Warden, who kindly conducted me round, for the last probation, to the Right Worshipful Master in the east, where, standing in due form behind the sacred altar, I was taught to kneel before the pot of incense: being commanded to pronounce its contents, I was acknowledged by the master to be in possession of all the five external senses, and was accordingly passed in due form to receive the further ceremony of this degree.

W. M. What was the chief thing that entitled you to the sacred Mysteries of this Order?

S. W. My free acceptance of the great and solemn obligation.

[*He then seals the sacred obligation by pressing the Holy Bible to his lips five times, and is raised from the foot of the altar, in due ancient form, both hands on the Holy Bible, &c.*]

W. M. Having now by the most solemn ties of honour, fidelity, and brotherly love, bound yourself to the religious performance of your sacred test, what was your reward for that voluntary sacrifice?

S. W. The communications of its sacred mysteries.

W. M. Name the three first.

S. W. The sign, token, and word of a Mark Master.

W. M. What does the sign denote?

S. W. The penalty of the obligation.

W. M. Why was it introduced in this degree?

S. W. In commemoration of the signal used by the ancient brethren of this Order, at the erection of that famous temple in the holy city of Jerusalem, by our most excellent Grand Master, Solomon, King of Israel.

W. M. What was that *signal*?

APPENDIX

S. W. The celebrated Light House on the highest part of Mount Lebanon.
W. M. For what purpose was it there set up?
S. W. To guide and direct the ancient mariners employed in fetching gold, ivory, and precious stones, from Ophir, for the ornamental parts of the temple.
W. M. What does the token denote?
S. W. Another of the penal laws of ancient Tyre united with the link of a Mark Master.
W. M. What does the word denote?
S. W. Omnipotent, omnipresent, omniscient.
W. M. To what does it further allude?
S. W. To one of the names of the Almighty Creator of heaven and earth; which name, with all its glorious attributes, King Solomon caused to be entirely displayed in the centre of his audience-chamber. It was this grand ineffable name, with all its glorious attributes subjoined, and aided by the admirable eloquence and wisdom of Solomon, that wrought the conversion of his noble friend and ally the great and learned King of Tyre; and which he, in conjunction with Solomon and our grand superintendent, Hiram Abiff, conferred on the brethren of this degree as one of their distinguishing *characteristics*.
W. M. What was the original number of Mark Masters at the building of the first, glorious temple of Jerusalem?
S. W. One thousand.
W. M. Who were they?
S. W. The right worshipful Masters of the Fellow Crafts Lodges.
W. M. How many lodges were there in this degree during the building of King Solomon's temple?
S. W. Twenty.
W. M. Why confined to twenty?
S. W. In allusion to the breadth of the holy place.
W. M. How many masons in each lodge?
S. W. Fifty.
W. M. What was the employ of these masons?
S. W. To re-examine the materials, after they were brought to Jerusalem, that every part might duly correspond, and prevent confusion and mistake, when they were employed in fitting the respective parts to their proper places; and by their additional marks, in the form of an equilateral triangle, they proved and fully passed the work previously examined by the Mark Men.
W. M. What were the marks or characters used by the brethren of this degree?
[Here the brother, instead of answering in the usual manner, gives the division of the Tau, in the ancient and masonic character, formed by his hands thus; and the right worshipful Master answers him with his Hiram in a similar manner.]
W. M. How many Mark Masters were there employed in the quarries of Tyre?
S. W. Seven hundred.
W. M. How many lodges were there in the quarries of Tyre?

S. W. Fourteen.

W. M. How many Mark Masters in each lodge?

S. W. Fifty.

W. M. What was the pay of each Mark Master per day?

S. W. Twenty-five shekels, equal to 3l. 2s. 6d. of our money.

W. M. What was the sum total paid to this class of workmen at the building of the first temple at Jerusalem?

S. W. Thirty-one millions, one hundred and twenty-eight thousand, seven hundred and fifty pounds.

W. M. What was delineated on that ancient coin?

S. W. The same as on that of the Mark Man, with the addition of the proper signature.

W. M. Brethren, I now crave your assistance to close this lodge. (*They rise and stand in due order as Mark Masters.*)

Brother Senior Warden, what is the internal signal for closing this degree?

S. W. Five reports.

W. M. By whom are they given?

S. W. By the right worshipful Master and his wardens.

W. M. When are they given?

S. W. Immediately after the brethren have all given the signs of this degree.

W. M. Let that sign be given. (*It is given and the reports or knocks follow.*) Why are these reports given?

S. W. In allusion to the five points of fellowship.

W. M. What is the second allusion?

S. W. The five noble offerings for the glorious temple of Jerusalem. First, the grand offering of Araunah the Jebusite on the holy mount Moriah. Second, the noble offering of King David. Third, the princely offering of King Solomon.

Fourth, the mariners' and voluntary offering of the princes and mighty men of Jerusalem. And, lastly, the magnificent offering of the celebrated Queen of Sheba.

W. M. What is the third allusion of these reports at the close of the lodge?

S. W. To the class of workmen that composed this Order.

W. M. Then, brethren, as master of that class, I declare this lodge duly closed, until our brethren have furnished us with fresh materials for labour in our mystical science of free and accepted masonry.

APPENDIX

A Description
of
Royal Arch Masonry

The Masons of this degree are called *Companions*, and when assembled a *Chapter*. They are so arranged as to form the figure of an arch. There are nine officers. Zerubbabel, as Prince; Haggai, as Prophet; Jeshua, as High Priest; the three principal officers, or High Chiefs, form the key-stones of the arch. Principal, Senior, and Junior Sojourners form the basis. Ezra and Nehemiah, Senior, and Junior Scribes, one on each side; Janitor or Tyler without the door. The Companions assembled make up the sides of the arch, representing Jachin and Boaz, the pillars of Solomon's Temple. In the front of the Principals stands an altar, on which are the initials of the names of Solomon, King of Israel; Hiram, King of Tyre, and Hiram Abiff. When convenient, an organ should be in the Chapter Rooms. A Chapter is considered a type of the Sanhedrim of the Jews.

To Open a Chapter.

The principal officers having robed, and taken their sceptres, all take their stations in the Arch.

Zerubbabel, as Prince, thus addresses them:—

Companions, assist me to open the chapter. Companion Junior Sojourner, what is the chief and constant care of every Royal Arch Mason?

J. S. To prove the chapter properly tiled.

Z. See that duty done.

(*The Junior Sojourner gives one knock on the door, which is answered from without by the Janitor, and then says*)—Most Excellent, the chapter is properly tiled.

Z. Companion Junior Sojourner, your duty in the Chapter?

J. S. To guard the First Veil, and to allow none to enter but those who are in possession of all pass-words, signs, and tokens thereunto belonging; and not then without first acquainting the Senior Sojourner.

Z. Companion Senior Sojourner, your duty in the chapter?

S. S. To guard the Second Veil, and to allow none to enter but those who are in possession of all pass-words, signs, and tokens thereunto belonging; and not then without first acquainting the Principal Sojourner.

Z. Companion Principal Sojourner, your duty in the chapter?

P. S. To guard the Third Veil, and to allow none to enter but those who are in possession of all pass-words, signs, and tokens thereunto belonging; and not then without first acquainting the Principals.

Z. Companion Ezra, your duty in the chapter?

E. To register all records, acts, laws, and transactions, for the general good of the chapter.

Z. Companion Nehemiah, your duty in the chapter?

N. To aid and assist Companion Ezra in his duty, and to introduce all candidates for exaltation.

Z. Companion Jeshua, your duty in the chapter?

J. To aid and assist in carrying on the Lord s works.

Z. Companion Haggai, your duty in the chapter?

H. To aid and assist in completing the Lord's works.

Z. Companions, let us pray:

O God, thou Great and Grand Architect of the Universe, Grand Prince, causer of all existence, at thy word the pillars of the sky were raised, and its beauteous arches formed. Thy breath kindled the stars, adorned the moon with silver rays, and gave the sun its resplendent lustre. We are assembled in thy Great name to acknowledge thy power, thy wisdom, and thy goodness, and to implore thy blessing. We pray thee, O Gracious God, to bless us in our undertaking through life for this great end. Endue us with a competence of thy most holy spirit, that we may be enabled to trace thee out in all thy wonderful works, as far as it is agreeable to thy divine will, that thy praises may resound with the fervent love of thy creatures from pole to pole; and rebound from the vaulted canopy of the heavens, through universal nature. Grant this, O God, Amen.

Z. In the beginning was the *word*.

H. And the *word* was with God.

J. And the *word* was God.

Z. Companions, Principals, what are the great attributes of these mysterious words?

H. Omniscience.

J. Omnipotence

N. Omnipresence. To the all-wise, all powerful, and all present Being, around whose throne may we hereafter engage.

Z. Most excellent Haggai, from whence came you?

H. From Babylon.

Z. Most excellent Jeshua, where are you going?

J. To Jerusalem.

Z. Most excellent chiefs, why leave you Babylon to go to Jerusalem?

H. To assist in rebuilding the second temple, and to endeavor to obtain the sacred word.

Z. Let us celebrate this grand design (which is done as follows):

The three principals and each three companions form the triangles, and each of the three takes his left-hand companion by the right-hand wrist, and his right-hand companion by the left-hand wrist, forming two distinct triangles with the hands, and a triangle with their right feet, amounting to a triple triangle, and then pronounce the following words, each taking a line in turn:—

APPENDIX

As we three did agree,
In peace, love, and unity,
The sacred word to keep;
So we three do agree,
In peace, love, and unity,
The *sacred word* to search;
Until we three,
Or three such as we, shall agree,
This Royal Arch Chapter to close.

The right hands, still joined as a triangle, are raised as high as possible, and the word JAO-BUL-ON, given at low breath, in syllables in the following order, so that each companion has to pronounce the whole word:—

1st.	2nd.	3rd.
Jao	Bul	On
—	Jao	Bul
On	—	Jao
Bul	On	—

Z. Companions, is the *word* correct?

On each set replying in the affirmative, Z. gives five knocks, and declares the chapter duly opened. The J. S. gives the five knocks on the door, and is answered from without by the five knocks from the Janitor. The companions then take their seats.

Z. Companion Ezra, you will read the minutes of the last chapter.

(*This being done, Z. inquires if any companion, has anything to propose.*) If there be no candidate for exaltation, the following charge, or lecture, or both, are delivered:—

The Charge.

Companions, the masonic system exhibits a stupendous and beautiful fabric, founded on universal wisdom, unfolding its gates to receive, without prejudice or discrimination, the worthy professors of every description of genuine religion or knowledge; concentrating as it were into one body their just tenets, unencumbered with the disputable peculiarities of any sect or persuasion. This system originated in the earliest of ages, and among the wisest of men. But it is to be lamented, that to the desponding suggestions of some of the weaker minds among our own fraternity, the prejudices of the world against our invaluable institution are in a great measure imputable. Unable to comprehend the beautiful allegories of ancient wisdom, they ignorantly assert that the rites of masonry are futile; its doctrines inefficient. To this assertion, indeed, they give, by their own misconduct, a semblance of truth, as we fail to discern that they are made wiser or better men by their admission to our mysteries.

Companions, I need not tell you, that nature alone can provide us with the ground of wisdom; but masonry will teach and enable us to cultivate the soil, and to foster and strengthen the plant in its growth. Therefore, to dispel the clouds of ignorance, so inauspicious to the noble purpose of our order and to hold forth a moral whereby we may see the power and greatness of the all-wise Disposer of events, the Royal Arch Degree gives us an ample field for discussion, by which we are shown, in the sad experience of the once-favourite people of God, a lesson how to conduct ourselves in every situation of our existence; and that when fortune, affluence, sickness, or adversity attend us, we ought never to lose sight of the source from whence it came, always remembering that the power which gave is also a power to take away. Having in itself this grand moral which ought to be cultivated by every man among us—"to do unto others as we would wish to be done by:" and it is the ultimatum of all terrestrial happiness, imitating in itself every virtue man can possess. May we, as companions, so study virtue, as to hand down to posterity a name unspotted by vice, and worthy of imitation.

APPENDIX

To Close a Chapter

Z. (*Knocks to order, and says*): Companion Junior Sojourner, the constant care of a Royal Arch Mason?
J. S. To prove the chapter tiled.
Z. Let that duty be done.
(*The J. S. gives the five knocks, which are answered from without by five from the Janitor.*)
J. S. (*With the penal sign.*) Most Excellent, the chapter is close tiled.
Z. (*Gives the five knocks, and says.*):
Companions, assist me co close this Royal Arch Chapter.

The chiefs, sojourners, and companions form into threes, join hands and feet, give the word, as at opening, and pronounce as follows:—

As we three did agree,
In peace, love, and unity,
The *sacred word* to keep;
So we three do agree,
In peace, love, and unity,
The *sacred word* to keep;
Until we three,
Or three such as we, shall agree,
This Royal Arch Chapter to open.

Zerubbabel, Junior Sojourner, and Janitor, give the five knocks, and the Prince declares the chapter closed.

Some chapters close in this short way:—The companions, scribes, and sojourners stand round the floor-cloth, exhibiting the penal sign. The three principals form a triangle, each holding to the Bible. They salute the book, and pass it round for each person present to do the same. Then they form the grand triangle, and say:—We three do agree, this Royal Arch Chapter to close, and, in love and unity, the sacred word of a Royal Arch Mason to keep, and not to reveal it to anyone in the world unless it be when three, such as we, do meet and agree, a Royal Arch Chapter to open.

The Exaltation.

The candidate for exaltation having been ballotted for and approved, is conducted by the Junior Scribe to the door. Four knocks are given by the Janitor.

The Junior Sojourner, within, says: Most Excellent Zerubbabel, a report (*making the penal sign.*)

Z. See who wants admission. .

J. S. (*Opening the door.*) Who comes there?

Brother N——, who has duly and truly served his time as an Entered Apprentice, passed the degree of a Fellow-Craft, and has been, in due time, raised to the sublime degree of a Master Mason, upon the five points of fellowship, with the respective signs, words, and pass-words thereunto belonging; and lastly, having been duly elected master of a lodge of Master Masons, installed in the chair and entrusted with the grip and word, the sign and salutation of a Past Master, now presents himself, properly prepared, for admission into this chapter, and for exaltation into the sublime degree of Royal Arch Masonry.

J. S. Halt, while I make due report.—(*He repeats the application to Zerubbabel.*)

Z. Companions, is it your wish that Brother N—— be admitted?

C. It is, most excellent.

Z. Companion Junior Sojourner, is he in possession of requisite particulars, and properly prepared?

J. S. To the best of my knowledge, most excellent.

Z. Let the candidate be admitted in due form. (*The form is to pass the candidate under an arch made by the companions holding their rods so as to resemble a Gothic arch. He is placed in the west.*) Brother N——, we understand that you seek preferment in our order; but, before you can be admitted, we must first ascertain whether you voluntarily offer yourself for the mysteries of this exalted degree?

Br. N. I do.

Z. We must also further ascertain, whether you are properly qualified to receive the mysteries of this exalted degree.

The High Priest Jeshua advances, orders him to kneel, and thus prays:—

Almighty God, who art the sole Architect of the Universe, at whose command the world burst forth from chaos, and all created matter had its birth, look down, we pray thee, at this time in a more peculiar manner, on this thy servant, and henceforth crown him with every blessing from thine inexhaustible store. But, above all, give him grace to consider well his present undertaking, that he may neither proceed therein lightly, nor recede from it dishonourably; but pursue it steadily, ever remembering the intention, which is the acquisition of true wisdom and understanding, by searching out thy great and glorious works, for promoting thy honour and glory, for the benefit of the whole creation and his own eternal welfare. So mote it be.

APPENDIX

Brother N—— is then led to the altar, where the Prophet Haggai receives him, exhorts him on the solemn nature of his situation, and appraises him that he now stands before a representation of the Grand Sanhedrim, or famous court of Judicature among the ancient Jews.

The High Priest here reads the second chapter of the book of Proverbs:—

"My son, if thou wilt receive my words, and hide my commandments with thee; so that thou incline thine ear unto wisdom, *and* apply thine heart to understanding; yea, if thou criest after knowledge, and liftest up thy voice for understanding; if thou seekest her as silver, and searchest *for* her as for hid treasures; then shalt thou understand the fear of the Lord and find the knowledge of God. For the Lord giveth wisdom, out of his mouth cometh knowledge and understanding. He layeth up sound wisdom for the righteous: he is a buckler to them that walk uprightly. He keepeth the paths of judgment, and preserveth the way of his saints. Then shalt thou understand righteousness, and judgment, and equity; yea, every good path. When wisdom entereth into thine heart, and knowledge is pleasant unto thy soul, discretion shall preserve thee, understanding shall keep thee; to deliver thee from the way of the evil man, from the man that speaketh froward things; who leave the path of uprightness, to walk in the ways of darkness; who rejoice to do evil, and delight in the forwardness of the wicked; whose ways are crooked, and they froward in their paths: to deliver thee from the strange woman, even from the stranger which flattereth with her words; which forsaketh the guide of her youth, and forgetteth the covenant of her God. For her house inclineth unto death, and her paths unto the dead. None that go unto her return again, neither take they hold of the paths of life. That thou mayest walk in the way of good men, and keep the paths of the righteous. For the upright shall dwell in the land and the perfect shall remain in it. But the wicked shall be cut off from the earth, and the transgressors shall be rooted out of it."

Obligation.

Zerubbabel then administers the obligation.

"I, A. B., of my own free will and accord, in the presence of the Grand Architect of the Universe, and this Chapter of Royal Arch Masons, do hereby and hereon most solemnly and sincerely promise and swear, in addition to my former obligations, that I will not reveal the secrets of this degree to any of an inferior degree, or to anyone except he be a true and lawful Companion Royal Arch Mason, or within the body of a just and legally constituted chapter, under the penalty of having the crown of my skull struck off, in addition to all my former penalties. So help me God, and keep me firm in this my obligation of a Royal Arch Companion." (*Kisses the Bible five times.*)

Z. In whom do you put your trust?
Br. N. In Jehovah.
Zerubbabel makes the following exhortation:—

In the name of that Omnipotent Being, arise, and may the remembrance of the sprig of cassia, which was found on the grave of him, who was truly the *most excellent* of Masons, and who parted with his life, because he would not part with his honour, ever stimulate his successors to imitate his glorious example; that the essence of virtue may enshrine our moral laws, and like the beautiful rose of Sharon, in conjunction with the lily of the valley, exalt our intellectual part. When death, the grand leveler of all human greatness, hath drawn his sable curtain round us, and when the last arrow of our mortal enemy hath been dispatched, and the bow of this mighty conqueror broken by the iron arm of time, when the angel of the Lord declares that time shall be no more, and when, by this victory, God hath subdued all things to himself, then shall we receive the reward of our virtue, by acquiring the possession of an immortal inheritance in those heavenly mansions veiled from mortal eye, where every secret of masonry will be opened, never to be closed. Then shall the great Jehovah, the Grand Master of the whole Universe, bid us enter into his celestial lodge, where peace, order, and harmony shall eternally reign. (*The candidate is directed to retire.*)

Ceremony of Passing the Veils.

The following ceremony, called "Passing the Veils," is dispensed with in some chapters; but as it is an original part, it is introduced to make this work complete.

The candidate is prepared with a blindfold, his knees are bared, and his feet slipshod, with a cable-tow round his waist. The three sojourners act as the guardians of the three veils. The Junior scribe is the conductor of the candidate, and gives four knocks at the door of the First Veil, which is opened, and the candidate admitted by giving the Past Master's word, *Giblum*, and the sign. He is conducted round that part of the room, while the High Priest reads the third chapter of Exodus, verses 1 to 6:—

"Now Moses kept the flock of Jethro, his father-in-law, the priest of Midian; and he led the flock to the backside of the desert, and came to the mountain of God, even to Horeb. And the angel of the Lord appeared unto him in a flame of fire, out of the midst of the bush; and he looked, and, behold the bush burned with fire, and the bush was not consumed.

(*The bandage is taken from the candidate's eyes, and he sees a bush on fire.*) And Moses said, I will now turn aside, and see this great sight, why the bush is not burnt. And when the Lord saw that he turned aside to see, God called unto him out of the midst of the bush, and said,—Moses, Moses. And he said, Here am I. And he said, Draw not nigh hither; put off thy shoes from off thy feet (*the candidate here has his shoes slipped off*), for the place whereon thou standest is holy ground. Moreover he said, I am the God of thy father, the God of Abraham, the God of Isaac, and the God of Jacob. And Moses hid his face; for he was afraid to look upon God."

The High Priest Jeshua then reads the 13th and 14th verses of the same chapter:—

APPENDIX

"And Moses said unto God, Behold, when I come unto the children of Israel, and shall say unto them, The God of your fathers hath sent me unto you; and they shall say to me, What is his name? what shall I say unto them? And God said unto Moses, I AM THAT I AM. And he said, Thus shalt thou say unto the children of Israel, I AM hath sent me unto you."

The candidate is here informed that I AM THAT I AM is one of the words of the Royal Arch Degree, or the Pass-word from the First to the Second Veil.

This constitutes the passing of the First Veil. The candidate is then led to the Second Veil, and challenged by the Guard, who demands the *Pass-Word*, which is given by the candidate:—I AM THAT I AM. He enters the Second Veil, wherein is placed the figure of a Serpent and Aaron's Rod. Jeshua reads the first five verses of the fourth chapter of the Book of Exodus:—

"And Moses answered and said, But, behold, they will not believe me, nor hearken unto my voice; for they will say, The Lord hath not appeared unto thee. And the Lord said unto him, What is that in thine hand? And he said, A rod. And he said, Caste it on the ground. And he cast it on the ground and it became a serpent; and Moses fled from before it. And the Lord said unto Moses, Put forth thine hand, and take it by the tail. And he put forth his hand and caught it, and it became a rod in his hand: that they may believe that the Lord God of their fathers, the God of Abraham, the God of Isaac, and the God of Jacob, appeared unto thee."

The candidate is told to pick up the rod cast down before him; that the act is the sign of the Second Veil, and that the Pass-words are *Moses*, *Aaron*, and *Eleazer*. With these words he passes the Guard of the Third Veil. Jeshua reads from the 6th to the 9th verses of the fourth chapter of Exodus:—

"And the Lord said furthermore unto him, Put now thine hand into thy bosom. And he put his hand into his bosom; and when he took it out, behold, his hand was leprous as snow. And he said, Put thine hand into thy bosom again. And he put his hand into his bosom again; and plucked it out of his bosom, and behold, it was turned again as his other flesh. And it shall come to pass, if they will not believe thee, neither hearken to the voice of the first sign, that they will believe the voice of the latter sign. And it shall come to pass, if they will not believe also these two signs, neither hearken unto thy voice, that thou shalt take of the water of the river, and pour it upon the dry land; and the water which thou takest out of the river shall become blood upon the dry land."

The candidate is told that the signs of the leprous hand and the pouring out of the water are the signs of the Third Veil, and that HOLINESS TO THE LORD are the pass-words to the Sanctum Sanctorum. He is shown the ark of the covenant, containing the tables of stone, the pot of manna, also the table of shew-bread, the burning incense, and the candlestick with seven branches. After which, he is withdrawn to enter as a Sojourner.

REPRINTS OF RITUALS OF OLD DEGREES

Re-Entry of the Candidate.

(*The five knocks are given at the door.*)

J. S. Who comes there?

N. Three Sojourners from Babylon, who wish to offer their services to the Sanhedrim sitting in council, to assist in the rebuilding of the Temple.

J. S. Wait, while I report to the Most Excellent Principals. Most Excellent,—Three Sojourners crave admission to offer their services for the rebuilding of the Temple.

Z. Let them be admitted. (*They are accordingly admitted.*) Sojourners, what is your request?

S. First, we beg leave, Most Excellent, to sojourn among you; and having heard that you are about to rebuild the Temple of the Lord, we beg your acceptance of our best service in promoting that glorious work.

Z. We greatly commend your conduct, and should be glad to know who you are.

S. We are of your own kindred and people, sprung from your tribes and branches, and from the same original stock, equally with you, descendants of our forefathers Abraham, Isaac, and Jacob. But we have been under the displeasure of Almighty God, through the offences committed by our ancestors, who deviated from the true Masonic principles and laws, and not only committed numberless errors, but ran into every kind of wickedness; so that the Almighty, being displeased, gave his judgment against them, by the mouth of Jeremiah and other prophets, by whom he declared, that the fruitfulness of the Lord should be spoiled—their city become desolate and an abomination, and that they should feel the weight of his wrath for seventy years. This actually began to be fulfilled in the fourth year of the reign of Jehoiakin—A. L. 3398.

Z. Our knowledge of the facts, and the candour with which you have related them, leave no doubt of your sincerity; but we beg to be informed who were your immediate ancestors.

S. We are not of the lineage of that race of traitors, who fell away during the siege and went over to the enemy, when liberty and kindred had most need of their assistance: nor of the lower class of the people left behind by Nebuzaradan, the chief of Nebuchadnezzar's officers, to cultivate the vineyards and for other servile purposes; but the offspring of those princes and nobles carried into captivity with Zedekiah. The seventy years of captivity being expired, and the anger of the Lord appeased, he hath stirred up the heart of Cyrus King of Persia and Babylon, who hath issued his proclamation, saying—"Who is there of the Lord's people, his God be with him, and let him go up to Jerusalem which is in Judea, and build him a house to the Lord God of Israel; for he is the only true and living God." We, therefore, have taken the advantage of this proclamation, and have returned for that purpose.

Z. Sojourners, how have you been employed during your captivity in Babylon?

S. In Masonry, Most Excellent.

Z. What do you mean by Masonry?

APPENDIX

S. That grand and universal science which includes all others; but more especially that which teaches the knowledge of ourselves, and the duties incumbent on us as men and Masons.

Z. In what labour do you wish to engage?

S. We deem the lowest situation in the Lord's house an honour; therefore, we only beg employ.

Z. Your humility bespeaks your merit, and we doubt not but you are qualified for some superior office. Those being full, you will be furnished with tools for the purpose, and we, for the present, shall appoint you to go and prepare for the foundation of the Second Temple. But let me lay this injunction upon you—that should you meet with anything belonging to the First Temple, you will communicate no part thereof to anyone, until you have faithfully made your report to the Sanhedrim here sitting in chapter. Go, and may the God of Abraham, Isaac, and Jacob, be with you and prosper you.

The sojourners retire, and are furnished with a pickaxe, shovel, and crow-bar, of the ordinary size, generally made of wood, and kept for that purpose. After a short time, they return, give the knocks, and enter as before. During their absence, they are supposed to have been at work, and to have made a discovery, of which they come to make a report.

After being duly reported and admitted, they are thus addressed:—

Z. Sojourners, we are informed that you have made a discovery.

S. We have, Most Excellent; for being at our work early this morning, our companion broke up the ground with his pickaxe; and we judging from the sound thereof that it was hollow, called upon our companion with his shovel to clear away the loose earth, and discovered the perfect crown of an arch. With my crow-bar I removed the key-stone. Our curiosity was excited to know what it contained; but being afraid of danger, we cast lots who should first go down, which lot, Most Excellent, fell upon me. We also agreed upon proper security against danger. I was then let down with a cable tied round my waist, and another at each hand. Having arrived at the bottom without impediment, I gave the signal for my freedom, and in searching the arch, found this scroll. From the want of light, I could not discern its contents; for the sun had but just come to the portico of the eastern door, and darting its beams parallel to the plane of the horizon, I could not discover what it contained. I, therefore, gave the agreed signal, and was drawn up. We have, as in duty bound, thus come to make our report.

Z. The discovery you have made is of the greatest importance. It is no less than the long-lost book of the holy law. You now see that the world is indebted to Masonry for the preservation of this sacred volume. Had it not been for the Masonic wisdom and precaution of our Grand Master, this the only remaining copy of the law, would have been lost at the destruction of the Temple. We cannot too much praise you for your fidelity and promptness in this discovery and report; and you will now return and make further search, observing, as before, the same precaution.

(*The Sojourners retire; after a while return, and are admitted as before, to report further discoveries, as follows:—*)

Z. Sojourners, we are informed that you have made another discovery.

S. We have, Most Excellent; for, on recommencing our labour, we found a second crown of an arch, and with difficulty removed the key-stone. On descending the arch, nothing of consequence was found; but judging from the sound thereof that it was hollow beneath, our curiosity was excited for a further search. We discovered a key-stone of a third arch; on removing it, the sun, having now gained its meridian height, darted its rays to the centre. It shone resplendent on a white marble pedestal, whereon was a plate of gold. On this plate was engraved a triple triangle, and within the triangles some characters which are beyond our comprehension; therefore, we have, as in duty bound, brought it, and made our second report.

Z. Pray, Sojourners, give us that which you have found, and explain the characters.

S. That, Most Excellent, we should be glad to do; but must confess our ignorance, like wise men. We should deem it too great a presumption in us to attempt it.

Z. Sojourners,—These three mysterious words, in a triangular form, is the long-lost sacred word of the Master Mason, and is too incomprehensible for individual expression; but in reward for your industry and zeal, you will now be put in possession of a full explanation of this the Grand Omnific Royal Arch Word. (*This is communicated to the candidate in due form* […].)

Z. In drawing forth the third key-stone, you have obtained the Grand Omnific word, the prayer being the first, and the obligation the emblem of the second keystone, as moral similitudes of material things. I have now to make you acquainted with the following five original Royal Arch Signs:—

The first is the penal Sign, which is given by circling the forehead with the thumb and forefinger of the right hand, alluding to the penalty of the obligation; and also in allusion to the Sojourner's guarding his eyes from the intensity of the sun's rays, when the perpendicular reflection shone so brilliantly on the gold plate, which was found on the pedestal at the withdrawing of the third key-stone of the secret arch, and which contained the Grand Omnific word; and further, in allusion to the fall of man.

The second is the Reverential Sign, or Sign of Sorrow, which is given by laying the right hand on the forehead for support, and the left at the heart in a bowing humble attitude. It represents the attitude in which our first parents met Jehovah in the garden of Eden after their transgression.

The third is the Penitential, or Supplicatory Sign, which is given with the hands raised in the attitude of prayer, and the knees slightly bent, in allusion to the expulsion of our first parents from the garden of Eden.

The fourth is the Monitorial Sign, or Sign of Suffering, which is given by placing the right hand on the heart, and supporting an inclination of the head with the left, in allusion to the pain that arose from toil in having to till the land.

The fifth is the Fiducial Sign, or the sign of Faith and Hope, which is given by raising the hands above the head, in allusion to the prospect of redemption from the fall.

APPENDIX

I have now to invest you with the badges of a Royal Arch Mason, the apron, sash, and jewel. They are badges of honour and of our order. The apron and sash are of mixed colours, purple radiated with crimson. The purple implies awe and reverence, and the crimson in rays signifies justice tempered with mercy.

The character on the apron is designated the Triple Tau, one of the most ancient of emblems; and as Masonry is the science of sciences, so this emblem may be styled the emblem of all emblems, for it is the grand emblem of Royal Arch Masonry; and its depth of meaning reaches to the creation of the world, and all that is therein.

The jewel is a double triangle within a circle of gold. The intersecting triangles denote the elements of fire and water.

The sun in the centre with its diverging rays is an emblem of the Deity. The encircling ring is an emblem of eternity and infinity, whose centre is everywhere and circumference nowhere, denoting omnipresence and perfection.

I have now to congratulate you on your exaltation. You will now take your station in the chapter, and when a lecture is delivered, the mysteries into which you have been initiated will be further explained.

Lecture.
First Section.

Q. Are you a Royal Arch Mason?
A. I am.
Q. How shall I know you to be such?
A. By the Royal Arch Sign.
Q. Can you give me that sign?
A. I can. (*He gives it.*)
Q. Where did you learn that sign?
A. In a Royal Arch Chapter.
Q. Who were present 1.
A. The three principals, Zerubbabel the Prince of the people, Haggai the Prophet, and Jeshua the High Priest, with the rest of the companions, men chosen for virtue and moral rectitude; the better to enable them to superintend the carrying on of the works of the Second temple.
Q. How did you gain admittance?
A. By having been initiated into the first degree of Masonry, as an entered Apprentice, passed to the Degree of a Craft, raised to the sublime Degree of a Master Mason, by being in possession of a Past Master's word and signs.
Q. Do you recollect the Past Master's word?
A. I do.
Q. Will you give it to me?
A. Giblum, or in some chapters Chibbelum.

Q. What does that word denote?
A. An excellent Mason.
Q. When admitted, how were you placed?
A. On both knees to receive the benefit of a prayer.
Q. How were you then disposed of?
A. I was led to the altar, where the prophet Haggai received me, and gave me an exhortation.
Q. Can you give me the substance of it?
A. I can:—That as I was about to undertake a solemn and glorious work in entering into an obligation before the grand Sanhedrim, it was essential that sincerity and truth should accompany all the future undertakings of my life.
Q. Did you enter into that obligation?
A. I did, after the High Priest had read a portion of Scripture. (Prov. C. ii.)
Q. Can you repeat the obligation?
A. I can. (See the exaltation.)
Q. What was then required of you?
A. In whom did I put my trust.
Q. Your answer?
A. In Jehovah.
Q. Why were you obligated?
A. To teach me to avoid the offences committed by our ancestors, who, deviating from true Masonic principles and laws, brought on themselves and their posterity that heavy burthen, and on their city and temple that ruin and desolation, whereby the holy word was so long lost, and afterwards so miraculously discovered.
Q. What was next said to you?
A. I was ordered to arise in the name of that omnipotent Being, and the Principal, Zerubbabel, delivered the following exordium.[40]
Q. How were you next disposed of?
A. I was desired to retire, to be further prepared.

Second Section.

Q. How were you prepared to pass the veils?
A. I was blindfolded, both knees bare, both feet slip-shod, and a cable-tow round my waist.
Q. How did you gain admission to the first veil?
A. By four knocks, the Past Master's word and sign.
Q. Why were your feet slip-shod?

---

40. Carlile's text points to his page 112, where the "Charge" was printed.

APPENDIX

A. In allusion to the condition of Moses, before the burning bush in the wilderness, who was told to put his shoes from off his feet, for the place whereon he stood was holy ground.

Q. Why were your knees bare?

A. That I might offer up my prayers to the Great Jehovah, in the most humble manner, to thank him for mercies received, crave pardon for past offences, and implore his aid and protection in my future conduct.

Q. Why was the cable-tow used?

A. In commemoration of a singular benefit derived from it by the sojourners, in preparing the foundation of the second Temple.

Q. After entering the first veil, what happened to you?

A. I was led round, and desired to be attentive to a portion of Scripture (Exodus, chapter 2, verses 1 to 6), and when I halted, the bandage was removed from my eyes.

Q. What was then presented to your notice?

A. THE BURNING BUSH. I was also entrusted with the passwords.

Q. Have you remembered those pass-words?

A. I have.

Q. Will you give them to me?

A. I AM THAT I AM.

Q. How did you pass the guard of the second veil?

A. By the benefits of the pass-words I have just given.

Q. On entering the second veil, what was presented to your notice, and how were you disposed of?

A. The figure of a serpent and Aaron's rod were pointed out to me, and I was desired to be attentive to a portion of scripture (Exodus, chap. 4, verses 1 to 5), and was taught the sign and pass-words.

Q. What is a sign?

A. Picking up Aaron's rod, in allusion to the serpent.

Q. Have you got the pass-words?

A. I have.

Q. Will you give them to me?

A. MOSES, AARON, ELEAZER.

Q. What gained your admission to the third veil?

A. The sign and pass-words with which I was entrusted in the second veil.

Q. On passing the third veil, what was said to you?

A. I was again desired to be attentive to a portion of scripture which was read to me (Exodus, chap. 4, verses 6 to 9), and taught the signs and pass-words to the sanctum sanctorum.

Q. Can you give me those signs and pass-words?

A. I can. (*He gives the sign as at page* 119, *and the passwords*), HOLINESS TO THE LORD.

Q. To what else was your attention directed in the third veil?

A. I was shown the ark of the covenant, containing the tables of stone and golden pot of manna: also the table of shew bread, the burning incense, and the candlestick with seven branches.

Q. Did those signs and pass-words gain you admission to the sanctum sanctorum?

A. They did.

Q. How were you disposed of?

A. I was desired to withdraw, to prepare for further instruction.

Third Section.

Q. On your next application how were you accosted?

A. The junior sojourner demanded who I was.

Q. Your answer?

A. A sojourner from Babylon, who begs to offer his services in rebuilding the temple.

Q. What was the reply?

A. I was desired to wait until reported to the principals sitting in Sanhedrim.

Q. Were you then admitted?

A. I was, and my request was demanded by the most excellent Zerubbabel.

Q. What was the nature of your request?

A. To sojourn and assist in rebuilding the temple.

Q. What attention was paid to your application?

A. I was complimented on my offer of service, and had to explain of what kindred and lineage I was.

Q. Your explanation?

A. That I was descended from their own kindred and people, sprung from their own tribes and branches, from the same original stock, equally with the descendants of your forefathers, Abraham, Isaac, and Jacob. But that we had been under the displeasure of Almighty God, through the offences committed by our ancestors, who deviated from true Masonic principles and laws, and not only committed numberless errors, but ran into every kind of wickedness; so that the Almighty, displeased, gave judgment against them, by the mouth of Jeremiah and other prophets, by whom he declared that the fruitfulness of the Lord should be spoiled, their city become desolate, and an abomination, and that they should feel his wrath for seventy years.

Q. What was next said to you?

A. I was complimented on my candour and sincerity, and asked who were my immediate ancestors. To which I replied that I was not of the lineage of that race of traitors, who fell away during the siege of that city, and went over to the enemy, when liberty and kindred had most need of their assistance, nor of the lower class of people left behind by Neburzaradan, the chief of Nebuchadnezzar's officers, to cultivate the vineyards, and for other servile purposes: but the offspring of those princes and nobles carried into captivity with Zedekiah.

APPENDIX

Q. Were you questioned on the occasion of your return?

A. I was; and explained, that the seventy years of captivity having expired, and the anger of the Lord appeased, he hath stirred up Cyrus, King of Persia and Babylon, to issue his proclamation that those of the Lord's people who were inclined, might go up to Jerusalem and rebuild the temple, for that he, Cyrus, had discovered the God of Israel to be the only true and living God..

Q. What further enquiry was made you?

A. I was asked how I had been employed in Babylon. I answered in Masonry: and to a question as to what it meant, that it was the grand and universal science, that included all other sciences, but more especially the moral one, which formed the knowledge of ourselves and the duties incumbent on us as men and Masons.

Q. Were you asked in what labour you wished to engage?

A. I was, and stated that I deemed the lowest situation in the Lord's house an honour, and therefore I only sought employ.

Q. How were you then disposed of?

A. I was accepted with the injunction, that as all the superior offices were filled, I should be furnished with tools to prepare the foundation of the second temple; but that if I found anything belonging to the first temple, I was not to discover it to anyone, until I had faithfully made a report to the Sanhedrim in chapter.

Q. Did you make any discovery?

A. I did. Being at work with my companions early in the morning, breaking up the ground with my pick-axe, and judging from the sound thereof that it was hollow, I called upon one of them to remove the soil with his shovel, when I discovered the perfect crown of an arch. Finding that it had no entrance, with my crow-bar I removed the key-stone. Our curiosity was excited to know what it contained; but afraid of danger, we drew lots which should descend. The lot fell upon me. I was let down with a cable-tow round my waist, which was held by my two companions, and to which I held with my hands. Having reached the bottom, I found a scroll; but from the want of light I could not discern its contents, for the sun had but just come to the portico of the eastern door, and darted its beams parallel to the plane of the horizon. Remembering the injunction of the Sanhedrim, I was drawn up by signal, and proceeded to make the report.

Q. What did it prove to be?

A. The long-lost book of the law, for the preservation of which, Zerubbabel observed, we had been indebted to Masonry; for, if our Grand Masters had not used their Masonic wisdom and precaution in the construction of this arch, this the only remaining copy of the law, would have been lost at the destruction of the temple.

Q. Was anything further said to you on that occasion?

A. I was praised for my fidelity and promptness in the discovery and report, and ordered to return and make further search, observing the same precaution.

Q. Was there any further discovery?

A. There was. On recommencing the search, we found a second arch, beneath the first. The key-stone was removed with great difficulty. Descending that arch, nothing was found in it; but judging from the sound that it was hollow beneath, we made further search, and found the key-stone of a third arch. In removing it, the sun having gained its meridian height, darted its rays to the centre. It shone resplendent on a white marble pedestal, whereon was a plate of gold. On this plate was engraved a triple triangle, and within the triangles some characters, of which we immediately proceeded to make report. When we made the report, we were asked if we understood the characters on the gold plate, to which we replied in the negative.

Q. Were you instructed as to what they meant?

A. We were. Zerubbabel informed us, that the mysterious characters, within the double triangle, were the long-lost word of the Master Mason, and too incomprehensible for individual expression; but that, in reward for our industry and zeal, we should be put in possession of a full explanation of this, the *Grand Omnific* Word of a Royal Arch Mason. We were further told, that as the drawing of the third key-stone had obtained us the grand omnific word, it had been so obtained by the prayer, which was an emblem of drawing the first, and the *obligation*, which was an emblem of drawing the second keystone, as similitudes of material things.

Q. Were you then invested?

A. I was invested with the sash and apron of a Royal Arch Mason: and also entrusted with the various branches of their laws and mysteries.

Fourth Section.

Q. What are you?

A. A citizen of the world, a brother to every worthy Mason, and a companion for those of our Royal Arch Degree.

Q. Pray, sojourner, who are you?

A. Of your own kindred and people, sprung from the noble and illustrious race of ancestors whose honours we hope to merit, by a steady pursuit of wisdom, truth, and justice.

Q. From whence came you?

A. From the Grand Royal Arch Chapter of Jerusalem.

Q. Who were present?

A. Zerubbabel the Prince of the people, Haggai the prophet, and Jeshua the High Priest.

Q. What do the Principals of the Royal Arch Chapter represent.

A. Zerubbabel, Haggai, and Jeshua, represent the three keystones, by which we learn, that in drawing them forth, the discovery is complete; and by the passing of the sojourner through each of these offices, the mystical knowledge of our Royal Arch Chapter is to be obtained.

Q. What do the two scribes represent?

APPENDIX

A. The two scribes, Ezra and Nehemiah, represent the two columns or pillars, that supported the entrance of the Arch; and thereby, also, is signified, their duty of registering and entering on our records every act, law, or transaction, for the general good of the chapter.

Q. What do the three sojourners represent?

A. The three sojourners represent the three stones, whereon the three Grand Masters kneel to offer up their prayers for the success of their work. And hereby we have a lesson, that in every thing we undertake, we ought to offer up our prayers to the Almighty for success.

Q. Why do we, as Royal Arch Masons, sit in this form?

A. To represent the Holy Royal Arch and hereby, we have a lesson to pursue unity and concord; for as one stone drawn from an arch endangers the whole, so may the improper conduct of one member endanger the whole chapter.

Q. Why was the ceremony of drawing the three key-stones observed?

A. To teach us not to rely on our own reasoning and abilities for our conduct through life; but to draw forth our rules or government from the law and the prophets, and also to commemorate the discovery of the Royal Arch.

Q. What was this part of their discovery?

A. The pedestal of perfect white marble, worked in the form of a double cube. On the top a plate of gold containing the figure of a triple triangle. Within the figure are the mysterious characters, which the Grand and Royal Chapter informed us were the grand omnific word itself.

Q. Were you entrusted with the grand word?

A. I was. They gave me the grand movement, taught me the sign, and entrusted me with the sacred word, which is too incomprehensible for an individual to express.

Q. Was that word ever lost?

A. It was.

Q. In what manner?

A. By the untimely death of our Grand Master, Hiram Abiff, who was slain by a conspiracy of the craft, in order to extort it from him; therefore, as the word was incomprehensible without three Grand Masters being present, another word was substituted in its room, until the Grand Architect of the universe caused it to be discovered.

Q. How was that discovery made?

A. By the three sojourners preparing for the foundation of the second temple, who made the report thereof to the Royal Arch Chapter. As the labourers were clearing away the rubbish, they Perceived the crown of an arch. At the time of the destruction of the temple, the roof and walls fell in, and remained full seventy years a heap of rubbish. The arch, being unknown to any but the three Grand Masters, was their secret and royal council room. It was made and remained proof against the destroying flames and fury of the enemy, until the discovery was made and its contents known.

Q. At what time did that discovery happen?

A. The discovery was made in the first year of the reign of Cyrus, King of Persia and Babylon, on the return of the Jews from the Babylonish captivity. The three sojourners discovered the pedestal perfect and entire, having withstood the fury of the flames and rage of war, being defended by HIM who hath declared that he would place his word there, never to pass away. Hence we may learn the vanity of all human pursuits against the arm of Omnipotence.

Fifth Section.

Q. Can you describe the grand pedestal?

A. It was on a chequered pavement, to represent the uncertainty of life and the instability of things terrestrial. It was of perfect white marble, cut into the form of the altar of incense, being the only true double cube, and thereby, both in figure and colour, the most perfect emblem of innocence and purity.

On the base of the pedestal is the letter G, which signifies Giblum, a common name for all Masons who are masters of their business. Hereby, we have a lesson of humility and brotherly love: for there is no doubt, it was most highly finished, as the work of the great Hiram Abiff himself; he would not assume the honour, but affix the common name, that every companion might be a sharer. On the front were inscribed the names of the three most excellent grand masters. On the top was a plate of gold, in which was engraved a triple triangle, and within the figure the grand omnific word.

Q. Can you explain the jewel?

A. On the bottom of the scroll is inscribed the motto: Nil nisi clavis deest,—*nothing but the key is wanting*; which may be taken in its literal sense. Then, the circle is an emblem of eternity, with the motto: Talia si jungere possis, sit tibi scire satis,—*if thou canst comprehend these things, thou knowest enough.*

The two intersecting triangles denote the elements of fire and water, with a motto, declaring that the wearer is desirous of doing his duty, and filling up, with justice, that link in the chain of creation, wherein his great Creator had thought proper to place him. Within is another triangle, with the sun in its centre, its rays issuing forth at every point, an emblem of the Deity, represented by a circle, whose centre is everywhere and circumference no where, denoting his omnipresence and perfection.

It is also an emblem of geometry. And here we find the most perfect emblem of the science of agriculture: not a partial one, like the Basilidean, calculated for one particular climate or country: but universal, pointed out by a pair of compasses issuing from the centre of the sun, and suspending a globe denoting the earth, and thereby representing the influence of that glorious luminary over both the animal and vegetable creation: admonishing us to be careful to perform every operation in its proper season, that we lose not the fruits of our labour. Under these, is the compound character, or the Royal Arch Mason's badge.

Q. What explanation have you to give of this deeply mystical character?

APPENDIX

A. It signifies, in its figurative appearance as T. H., Templum Hierosolyma, the Temple of Jerusalem, and is always used as the Royal Arch Mason's badge, by which the wearer acknowledges himself a servant of the true God, who had thereby established his worship, and to whose service that glorious temple was erected. It also signifies Clavis ad Thesaurum, a key to a treasure; and Theca ubi res pretiosa deponitur, a place where a precious thing is concealed; or Res ipsa pretiosa, the precious thing itself. Hence we have the greatest reason to believe, that what was there concealed was the sacred name itself. But these are all symbolical definitions of the symbol, which is to be simply solved into an *emblem of science of the human mind*, and is the most ancient symbol of that kind, the prototype of the cross, and the first object in every religion or human system of worship. This is the grand secret of Masonry, which passes by symbols, from superstition to science; as ignorance dealing with ancient mysteries and symbols passed from science to superstition.

Q. Explain the five grand original signs.

A. The first parents of mankind, formed by the Grand Architect of the Universe, in the utmost perfection, both of body and mind seated in a paradise of pleasure, bounteously supplied with means for the gratification of every appetite, and at full liberty for enjoyment, to the end of time itself, with only one prohibition by way of contract, whereon should depend their immortality, soon became disobedient, and thereby obnoxious to sin, misery, and death. To preserve us from which, and as a memento to guard us from the like error, we adopted the *penal sign*.

Scarcely had our first parents transgressed, conscious of their crime, and filled with shame and horror, they endeavoured to hide themselves from the presence of that Being, in whom before had been their chief delight; but hearing the summons of his awful voice, and unable to bear the splendour of his appearance, in a humble bending posture, they approached with awe and palpitation of heart, their right hand at their forehead for support, and their left at their heart, as a shield against the radiant glory; and hence arose the *reverential sign*, or *sign of salute*.

It was now they heard pronounced the dreadful sentence, that the ground, for their sakes accursed, should no longer pour forth in such abundance; but themselves be driven from that happy region, to some less friendly climate, there to cultivate the hungry soil, and so earn their daily food by sweat and labour. Now banished from the presence of their God, and impelled by the wants and calls of nature to constant toil and care, they became more fully sensible of their crime, and with true contrition of heart, they, with clasped hands, implored forgiveness; and hence arose the *penitential or supplicatory sign*, or *sign of sorrow*.

Now fervent prayer, the grand restorer of true peace of mind, and only balm to heal a wounded conscience, first raised a gleam of hope, and encouraged them to pursue their daily task with greater cheerfulness: but seized with weariness and pain, the sure effects of constant toil and labour, they were forced to lay their right hands to the region of the heart, and their left as a support to the side of their heads; and thus arose the *monitorial sign*, or *sign of admonition*.

Now their minds being more calm, their toil seemed less severe, and cheered by bright-eyed hope, with uplifted hands and hearts, they clearly saw redemption drawing on; and hence arose the last sign, called the *fiducial sign*, or *sign of faith, and hope*.

Q. Why do we use rods in the Chapter?

A. In Anno Lucis 2513, our most excellent grand master Moses, tending the flock of Jethro, his father-in-law, at the foot of Mount Sinai, was called by the Almighty, and commanded to go down into Egypt, and deliver his brethren from their cruel bondage. Moses, then in banishment, greatly hesitated, saying, Who am I, that I should go? The Lord, to encourage him, promised to be with him. Moses, still doubting, begs of him a sign, to convince him of his power, and to confirm his promise. The Lord asked, what is in thine hand.

Moses answered, A rod. The Lord said unto him, Cast it on the ground. This done, it immediately became a serpent: and Moses fled from it. The Lord said unto Moses, Put forth thine hand, and take it by the tail; and it became a rod.

With this rod he smote the two rocks in the wilderness, from whence the waters gushed out. With this rod he divided the waters of the Red Sea, and made them to stand as two great heaps. With this rod he wrought his wonders in the land of Egypt; and, therefore, to commemorate these singular events, and as emblems, we make that use of them in our Royal Arch Chapter.

Q. What definition have you of the banner of the Chapter?

A. The banners of the twelve tribes of Israel, which we have for many purposes, especially to commemorate the great wonders which he wrought for the children of Israel during their travels in the wilderness, where they were first setup around their encampments, and about which each tribe was to pitch its respective standards. The devices thereon were emblematical of their posterity and after ages.

APPENDIX

Knights Templar.[41]

The Ceremony of Installation in the Masonic Cross Degree of Knights Templar of Jerusalem, Knights Hospitallers of St. John of Jerusalem, Palestine, Rhodes, and of Malta.

Historical Prelude.

Profane History gives us no account of these Knights anterior to the time of the Crusades; but the Revelation of Sacred History and Ancient Mystery, supposes them to have been orders in the degrees of the Temple, as they now assume to be in Masonry. The title of Hospitaller is traceable only to a provision for pilgrims journeying to Jerusalem in Palestine; while the distinction of Knights of Rhodes and of Malta was acquired in the crusade wars, by their Knights getting and defending the possession of those islands. They had two residences in London: that which is now called St. John's-square, and the Temple by the river.

Modern Varieties.

In the Masonic Degree of Knights Templar, the names of the officers vary in different Encampments. The following are found amongst them:—Grand Master, Grand Prior, Grand Sub-Prior, Grand Captains first and second, Grand Orator, Grand Prelate, Grand Chancellor, Grand Chaplain, Grand Recorder, Grand Drapers, Grand Preceptor, Grand Herald, Grand Equerries, Grand Almoner, Grand Councillor, Grand Admiral, Grand Treasurer, Grand Hospitaller, Grand Marshal or Grand Vice-Admiral, Grand Bailiff, Grand Commander, Grand Master of the Ceremonies, Equerries of the Outposts, and a Janitor or Tyler.

Some encampments make the Order of Malta to be distinct from that of the Templar; while others create a Knight at once as a Knight Hospitaller of St. John of Jerusalem, of Palestine, of Rhodes, of Malta, and Knight Templar of Jerusalem.

The Signs of the Order.

The Penal Signs are the Chin or Beard Sign, which is a right hand thumb and finger stroking the chin or beard; and the Saw Sign drawing the thumb or finger across the forehead, as indicative of the penalty of having the skull sawn asunder.

---

41. Richard Carlile, *The Republican* vol. 12 (London, Friday, Oct. 7, 1825), No. 12, pp. 420–33.

The Grand Sign is emblematic of the death of Jesus Christ on the Cross, with arms extended, head dropping on the right shoulder, and the right over the left foot.

THE WORD is *Emanuel*. The Grand Word of all is *Adonai*. The Word *Necum*, which signifies *revenge*, is also used by the Knights Templar on the Continent, and sometimes in this country.

THE GRIP is to grasp each other's arms across, above the elbow, to represent a double triangle.

There is no exact regularity or fixed form in these Degrees of Chivalry, as they are not recognised by the Grand Lodge of England.

THE PASS-WORDS vary in encampments to the following extent: *I am that I am*, *Jao-bul-on*, *Jerusalem*, *Calvary*, *Golgotha*, *Arimathea*, *Emanuel*, *Ehihu* or *Elihu*.

In the Maltese Order, *Eli, Eli, Lama Sabacthani*, are the grand words: and *Gethsemane*, *Capharsoleum*, or *Caiphas* and *Melita*, are with some the pass-words.

The Mediterranean Pass.

There is a pass-word and grip called the Mediterranean Pass. These knights were in the habit of traversing the Mediterranean Sea. Such as had served a year against the Mahometans were entitled to the pass-word and grip, which enabled them to return free from molestation by their brother knights. The word is *A-montra*, a corruption of the French verb *Montrer*, to shew, to shew a sign. The knights on one side hail, by a trumpet, those of the other with A-montra. It is answered by the token, which is to seize a man by the thigh, as if in the act to throw him. The real pass-word is *Maher-shalal-hash-baz*, also spoken through a trumpet.

The banners of the encampment are two: the first, black, with a white maltese cross of eight points, which is called the number of the Knights Hospitallers of St. John; the second, white, with a red cross, which is that of the Templar. The Grand Commander has his own family banner.

A candidate for installation is habited as a pilgrim, with sandals, mantle, staff, and cross, scrip and wallet, a belt or cord round his waist, with bread and water, and, in some encampments, a burthen on the back, which is made to fall off at a view of the cross. The whole ceremony is purely Christian, according to the vulgar notions and the literal sense of Christianity.

In the following ceremony the officers are a Grand Commander, First and Second Captain, Past Grand Commander, Grand Prelate, Grand Herald, Master of the Ceremonies, Grand Registrar, and Grand Orator, Equerries of Outposts, and Janitor.

APPENDIX

Ceremony or Form of Opening an Encampment.

G. C. Does it meet with your approbation, sir knights, to open this grand Christian encampment?

Answer (all). It does.

G. C. Sir knights, assist me to resume the duties of this grand Christian encampment. To order, as Knights Templar.

(All draw their swords, and rest the points on the left hand.) Sir Knight First Captain, what is the first duty of Knights Templar met together in arms?

F. C. To see the grand Christian encampment well guarded both within and without, and the sentinels well posted.

G. C. Sir Knight First Captain, are the guards and sentinels well posted on their respective duties, and this grand Christian encampment secure?

F. C. I will issue your commands to that effect. (First to the Second Captain)—See that the guards and sentinels be well posted on their respective duties, and that this grand Christian encampment be secure.

S. C. Trumpeter, sound the alarm. (*This being done and answered by the sentinels, the Second Captain reports to the First*)—The guards and sentinels are properly posted on their respective duties, and all is well.

F. C. Grand Commander, the guards and sentinels are properly posted on their respective duties, and all is secure.

G. C. What is it?

F. C. Faith in Jesus Christ, peace and good-will towards men.

G. C. Where is the Second Captain's place in this grand Christian encampment?

F. C. In the north-west.

G. C. (*To the Second Captain.*) Your Christian duty when there placed?

S. C. As Christ arose at high meridian and ascended into heaven to bring glad tidings to the believing world; so it is my duty to preside in the north-west, to call the sir knights from the field to refreshment, that the Grand Commander may have the pleasure, and the sir knights the profit consequent.

G. C. You have a second duty.

S. C. To receive, obey, and disperse all general orders from the Grand Commander and the First Captain, and to see them duly executed. Also, to guard the entrance of the grand Christian encampment, that none pass therein, but those who are duly qualified.

G. C. Where is the situation of the First Captain in this grand Christian encampment?

S. C. In the south-west.

G. C. (*To the First Captain.*) Your Christian duty when there placed?

F. C. Joseph of Arimathea, being a just and devout man, went to Pilate to beg the body of our Lord and Saviour Jesus Christ, which being granted he wrapped it up in clean linen and laid it in a new sepulchre wherein never man was laid, and closed the entrance thereof, which closed the first day of man's

salvation. And the First Captain guards this sepulchre.

G. C. You have a second duty.

F. C. To receive and dispatch all general orders from the Grand Commander to the Second Captain, and to see them punctually obeyed.

G. C. (*To the Past Grand Commander.*) The Grand Commander's place in this grand Christian encampment?

P. G. C. In the east.

G. C. His Christian duty when there presiding?

P. G. C. Very early on the first day of the week, came Mary Magdalene and the other Mary to the sepulchre.

And lo ! there had been a great earthquake, and an angel of the Lord descended from heaven; rolled back the stone which covered the entrance to the sepulchre, and sat thereon. Which opened to us life from death: for as by the first man Adam, came death: so by the second Adam, came life everlasting. So it is the Grand Commander's place to preside in the east to superintend, govern, and regulate the grand Christian encampment, by projecting schemes and plans for its general welfare, and to see that all orders and distinctions are preserved and duly executed with every becoming warlike enterprise. To order the sound of the alarm—to call the sir knights from refreshment to the field—to fight the battles of our Lord and Saviour Jesus Christ, and, after the grand prelate has offered up his prayer, to open the grand Christian encampment.

The Grand Prelate prays thus:—O thou great Emmanuel and God of infinite goodness, look down upon this conclave with an eye of tender compassion, and incline our hearts to thy holy will, in all our actions, through Jesus Christ our Lord. Amen. (*He then, reads the first six verses of the last chapter of the Gospel according to St. Mark.*)

"And when the sabbath was past Mary Magdalene, and Mary the *mother* of James, and Salome, had brought sweet spices, that they might come and anoint him. And very early in the morning the first day of the week, they came unto the sepulcher at the rising of the sun. And they said among themselves who shall roll us away the stone from the door of the sepulchre? And when they looked, they saw that the stone was rolled away: for it was very great. And entering into the sepulchre, they saw a young man sitting on the right side, clothed in a long white garment; and they were affrighted. And he saith unto them, be not affrighted: Ye seek Jesus of Nazareth, which was crucified: he is risen; he is not here: behold the place where they laid him."

G. C. (*The knights in the posture of the grand sign.*) As our blessed Saviour's resurrection from the dead opened life and salvation unto men; and as all those who sincerely believe on him may rest assured of eternal life through his name; the life of grace with all its comforts here—the life of glory with all its unutterable blessedness hereafter, both being effectually obtained by the death and resurrection of Jesus Christ who

APPENDIX

hath opened the kingdom of heaven to all believers. So, in his names of Christ our prophet, Christ our priest, Christ our king, I now open this grand Christian encampment, for the dispatch of such business as may come regularly and duly before us.

P. G. C. So mote it be.

(*The swords of the G. C. and the two captains are then placed in the form of a triangle, on the floor, opposite to the G. C. All the other Knights sheath their swords.*)

N. B. In some encampments, the G. C. merely pronounces that it is his will and pleasure, that this grand Christian encampment be open for the dispatch of business. This is repeated by the two captains and the Master of the Ceremonies. After which, the G. C. pronounces it open in the name of Christ our prophet, Christ our priest, and Christ our King.

Ceremony or Form of Closing an Encampment.

G. C. Sir knights, assist me in the duties of closing this grand Christian encampment. To order, as Knights Templar. (*All draw their swords and rest their points on their left hands.*) Sir Knight First Captain, what is the constant duty of Knights Templar when under arms?

F. C. To see the grand Christian encampment well guarded, both within and without, and the sentinels well posted.

G. C. Sir Knight First Captain, are the guards and sentinels well posted on their respective duties, and this grand Christian encampment secure?

F. C. I will issue your commands to that effect.

(*First to the Second Captain.*) See that the guards and sentinels be well posted on their respective duties, and that this grand Christian encampment be secure.

S. C. Trumpeter, sound the alarm. (*This being done and answered by the sentinels, the Second Captain reports to the First.*)—The guards and sentinels are properly posted on their respective duties; and all is well.

F. C. Grand Commander, the Guards and sentinels are properly posted on their respective duties; and all is secure.

G. C. With what is it secured?

F. C. Faith in Jesus Christ, peace and good will to all men.

G. P. (*Praying.*) May the blessing of our Heavenly Captain descend upon us, and remain with us now and ever more, Amen. (*Reads the last six verses of the fifteenth chapter of the Gospel according to St. Mark.*)

"And now when the even was come, because it was the preparation, that is, the day before the sabbath, Joseph of Aramathæa, an honourable councillor, which also waited for the kingdom of God, came, and went in boldly unto Pilate, and craved the body of Jesus. And Pilate marvelled if he were already dead: and calling unto him the centurion, he asked him whether he had been any while dead. And when he knew it of the centurion, he gave the body to Joseph. And he brought fine linen, and took him down, and wrapped him in the linen, and laid him in a sepulchre which was hewn out of a rock, and rolled a stone unto the door of the sepulchre. And Mary Magdalene and Mary *the mother* of Jesus beheld where he was laid."

P. G. C. So mote it be. (*The Knights in their grand sign, posture.*)

G. C. When our Saviour's agony was at the summit, and he knew that all things were accomplished, having received the vinegar, he said, *it is finished*. He then bowed his head, gave up the ghost, surrendered that life, which otherwise could not have been taken from him, as a ransom for many, and freely resigned his soul into his father's hands. The work of redemption completed—the full atonement made—all the types and prophecies fulfilled—the laws magnified by a perfect obedience unto death—the justice of God satisfied, and salvation to sinners secured. Thus was our great surety laid under the arrest of death, and consigned to the silent mansions of the grave, that he might make the clods of the valley sweet to us; prepare our bed of dust, perfumed with his own glorious body, and comfort us in the reviving hope of following him through the grave, the gate of death, into a joyful immortality. After our blessed Saviour's example, may we, by faith, when time shall be no more, cheerfully commend our departing souls to our heavenly Father's keeping, until the happy resurrection morn, when fashioned like unto Christ's glorious body, our sleeping ashes shall be reanimated that we may then be taken to dwell with him in his eternal kingdom, where all terrestrial things will close. So, in his names of Christ our prophet, Christ our priest, and Christ our king, I now close this grand Christian encampment, until that time you are next summoned to attend by my orders from the Grand Registrar.

P. G. C. So mote it be.

Ceremony of the Installation.
Preparation of the Candidate.

Habited as a Pilgrim, with sandals, mantle, a belt or cord round the waist, a staff with a cross, scrip and wallet, with bread and a bottle of water, having been elected by ballot, or otherwise, according to the custom of the encampment, the candidate is conducted by the Master of the Ceremonies to the entrance of the encampment. On the approach, an alarm is sounded with a trumpet, and a report is made within by the Second Captain.

2nd C. Grand Commander, an alarm at the outpost.

G. C. Ascertain the cause, and accordingly report.

2nd C. (*To the equerry without.*) See who approaches our encampment.

E. Who comes here?

C. A pilgrim, on his travels, hearing of a Knights Templar's Encampment, has come with a hope of being admitted.

E. From whence came you?

APPENDIX

C. From the wilderness of Judea, which I have traversed, exposed to great danger, until I met with this worthy knight, who promised me protection and safe conduct to the Holy City.

E. Do you come of your own free will?

C. I do.

E. What are you desirous to do?

C. To devote my life to the services of the poor and the sick for the sake of Jesus Christ, and to pray for my own sins with those of the people.

E. What recommendation have you?

C. The Sign and Word of a Royal Arch Mason.

E. Have you worked at the second temple?

C. I have.

E. Have you received Christian Baptism?

C. I have.

E. Do you believe in God the Father, God the Son, and God the Holy Ghost?

C. I do.

E. Do you believe that God the Son was made man to save us?

C. I do.

E. Do you believe in the inspiration of the Holy Ghost?

C. I do.

E. Are you willing to protect the Christian Faith, at the expense of your life?

C. I am.

E. Wait while I make a report to the grand Christian encampment.

(*Report.—To the Second Captain.*)

A weary pilgrim from the wilderness who claims attention, and craves admission to join the encampment.

2nd C. Is he worthy of admission?

E. I have put to him the usual probationary questions, and have received satisfactory answers and proofs.

2nd C. Grand Commander, a poor weary pilgrim from the wilderness craves admission.

G. C. Is he worthy to be admitted?

2nd C. He has given satisfactory answers.

G. C. Let him be admitted under the proper form. (*The candidate is admitted: a saw is applied to his forehead at his entrance by the 2nd Captain. All the sir knights appear under arms.*)

2nd C. (*To the candidate on his entrance: with the saw to his forehead.*) Who are you that dare approach thus into our encampment?

C. A poor weary pilgrim from the wilderness of Judea.

2nd C. Have you come of your own free will?

C. I have.

2nd C. What are you desirous to do?

C. To devote my life to the service of the poor and sick for the sake of Jesus Christ, and to pray for my own sins with those of the people.

2nd C. What recommendation have you?

C. The Sign and Word of a Royal Arch Mason.

2nd C. Give me that sign and word. (*He gives them*). Have you worked at the second temple?

C. I have.

2nd C. Have you received Christian Baptism?

C. I have.

2nd C. Do you believe in God the Father, God the Son, and God the Holy Ghost?

C. I do.

2nd C. Do you believe that God the Son became man to save us?

C. I do.

2nd C. Are you willing to protect the Christian Faith at the expense of your life?

C. I am.

(*This examination is repeated by the F. C. and G. C.*) The candidate is ordered to kneel on both knees for the benefit of a prayer, and the Grand Prelate prays thus:—O Emmanuel, our great heavenly captain, look down, we beseech thee, on this encampment of thy devoted servants, and impart thy holy Spirit to the candidate now before us, that he may become a good and faithful soldier in thy service, and be worthy of thy acceptance and salvation.

P. G. M. So mote it be.

G. C. As we must have a further trial of your faith, you must perambulate the encampment seven times, in order to prepare yourself, by meditation, to take a solemn obligation. (*This is done.*)

G. C. You must now kneel on both knees, take the Gospels in your hand, and receive the obligation from our Grand Prelate.

G. P. Pilgrim, you are kneeling at the altar for the purpose of taking a solemn obligation, appertaining to the degree of a Knight Templar. If you are willing to proceed, repeat your Christian and surname, and say after me:—

Obligation.

I, A. B., in the name of the Blessed Trinity, and in commemoration of St. John of Jerusalem, that first faithful soldier and martyr of Jesus Christ, do most solemnly promise and swear that I will never illegally reveal the secrets of a Knight Templar to a Royal Arch Mason, nor to any person beneath the dignity of this noble order, nor aid in the Installation of a Knight Templar, unless five are present, under the penalty of all my former obligations.

APPENDIX

(*The pilgrim's staff and cross are taken away, and a sword placed in his hand by the Grand Commander, who says*)—In the name of the Father, Son, and Holy Ghost, I arm you with this sword, which you will employ in the defence of the Gospel of our Lord and Saviour Jesus Christ, against all opposers.

I do furthermore swear, that with this, the sword of my faith, I will guard and defend the sepulchre of our Lord Jesus Christ, against all Jews, Turks, infidels, heathens, or other opposers of the Gospel.

I do furthermore swear, that I will never knowingly draw the blood of a brother Knight Templar, nor cause it to be drawn in wrath; but will espouse his cause, knowing it to be just, though I should endanger my own life. Even when princes are engaged in war, I will not forget the duty which I owe to him as a brother. If ever I willfully violate this my solemn compact, as a brother Knight Templar, may my skull be sawn asunder with a rough saw, my brains taken out and put in a charger to be consumed by the scorching sun, and my skull in another charger, in commemoration of St. John of Jerusalem, that first faithful soldier and martyr of our Lord and Saviour. If ever I willfully deviate from this my solemn obligation, may my light be put out from among men, as that of Judas Iscariot was for betraying his Lord and Master.

(*Here the sword is taken from the candidate, and a skull placed in his hand.*)

Furthermore, may the soul that once inhabited this skull, as the representative of John the Baptist, appear against me in the day of judgment, so help me God, our Lord Jesus Christ, and keep me steadfast in this my solemn obligation of a Knight Templar, and of St. John of Jerusalem.

(*The Grand Prelate then directs the candidate to kiss the Gospels seven times, to rise, to deposit the skull on the triangular table, resume the staff, and thus addresses him:—*).

Pilgrim, thou hast craved admission to pass through our solemn ceremonies, and enter the asylum of our encampment; by the sandals, staff, and scrip I judge thee to be a child of humility: charity and hospitality are the grand characteristics of this most Christian order. In the character of Knights Templar, we are bound to give alms to the poor and weary pilgrims travelling from afar, to succour the needy, feed the hungry, clothe the naked, and bind up the wounds of the afflicted.

As you are desirous of enlisting in this noble and glorious warfare, lay aside the staff and take up the sword, fighting manfully thy way, and with valour running thy course: and may the Almighty, who is a strong tower and defence to all those who put their trust in him, be thy support and thy salvation.

I now place in your hand a lighted taper, and admonish you to perambulate the encampment five times in solemn meditation; and if you have any prejudice or enmity with any Christian man, as a qualification for further honours, it is necessary you should forgive, otherwise fly to the desert; and rather than appear unworthily among us, shun the knights of this order.

(*At the end of this perambulation, the candidate stops before a cross, when his wallet or burthen is made to fall from his back. He is then divested of the pilgrim's dress, conducted to the Grand Commander, and required to kneel. The Grand Commander lays his sword on the candidate's right and left shoulder and on the head, and says*—I hereby install you a Masonic Knight Hospitaller of St. John of Jerusalem, Palestine, Rhodes, and Malta, and also a Knight Templar. *The Grand Commander then takes the candidate by the hand, and says*—Rise, Sir Knight A. B.; receive a hearty welcome into the Christian Order, which will be ever ready to defend and protect you.)

G. C. I now invest you with the paraphernalia of the order. First, I clothe you with a mantle. Receive it as the Lord's yoke; for it is easy and light, and will bring rest to your soul. As a habit, it is of little worth, and we promise you nothing but bread and water.

Secondly, I invest you with apron, sash, and jewel. The emblems within the triangle, the star on the sash and the Maltese cross jewel, you will have explained in the lecture.

Lastly, I present you with a shield and sword, which, in the hand of a valiant and Christian Knight, is endowed with three most excellent qualities. Its hilt with *justice*; its *blade* with *fortitude*; its point with *mercy*; which gives this important lesson, that having faith in the justice of our cause we must press forward with undaunted fortitude, ever remembering to extend the point of mercy to a fallen foe.

I shall now make you acquainted with the signs, words, and tokens, and our Grand Herald will then proclaim your installation.

First, the Mediterranean pass-word and sign. The hailing word is *A-montra*. The pass-word is *Mahershalalhashbaz*. The sign is to seize a man by the thigh, as if in the act of throwing him overboard.

The Knights Templar signs and words are, first the penal sign, which is to draw the fore-finger or the thumb across the forehead, indicative of the penalty of having the skull sawn asunder. The grand sign is to represent Jesus Christ on the cross, arms extended, head drooping on the right shoulder, right foot laid over the left. The word is *Emanuel*. The grand word of all is *Adonai*. *Necum* is also used by some Knights Templar, particularly on the continent.

The token or grip, is to grasp each other's arms across above the elbow, to represent the double triangle.

The motto of a Knight Templar is, *In hoc signo vinces.*

Our worthy companion, the Grand Herald, will now proclaim your installation.

G. H. In the name of the Holy Trinity, and by order of the Grand Commander: hear ye, Sir Knights, that I proclaim Sir Knight A. B. to be duly installed Knight Hospitaller of St. John of Jerusalem, Palestine, Rhodes, and Malta, and a Knight Templar. (*To be thrice proclaimed.*)

In some encampments, the following is a concluding part of the ceremony:—

One of the equerries, dressed as a cook, with a white night cap and apron, and a large kitchen knife in his hand, suddenly makes his entrance, and kneeling on one knee before the new Sir Knight, says: Sir Knight, I admonish you to be just, honourable, and faithful to the Order, and not to disgrace yourself, or I, the cook, will hack your spurs from off your heels with my kitchen knife. He then retires.

At the conclusion of the ceremony of installation, it is usual for bread or biscuit to be handed round to the Sir Knight. A cup of wine is presented to the Grand

APPENDIX

Commander, called the cup of brotherly love. He drinks, and desires the Sir Knights to pledge him in that cup of brotherly love, in commemoration of the laſt supper of out grand heavenly Captain, with his twelve Disciples, whom He commanded thus to remember Him. (*The cup is passed round.*)

The Grand Orator usually delivers the following charge:—

Charge.

G. O. Sir Knight Companion, as you have passed the firſt degrees of Masonry, and have been balloted for, admitted and dubbed a Knight Companion of our moſt Chriſtian and sublime Order, you are to mark and learn all those parts of our rules and myſteries which you will find to be ingeniously calculated to form and qualify you to engage in services of great moment. We have been informed that you earneſtly desired and sought to be admitted, initiated, and united to our Chriſtian order; and that from free and disintereſted motives, abſtracted from pecuniary or secular views; so we kindly entreat you to receive the inſtructions which we do now or may hereafter inculcate and enjoin. However ſtrange and difficult our ceremonies may at firſt appear, we truſt that you will persevere with unremitting zeal, and expect that you will be modeſtly inquisitive and uniformly attentive, in order to acquire such pleasing inſtructions as will be moſt expedient to forward the great purposes of rational and social converse.

From what has been suggeſted, it appears that the order of Knights Templar is universally acknowledged to be the moſt sublime and refined, the moſt Catholic and efficiently useful department of Freemasonry. Its votaries are formed into a select body, self-exiſting and self-dependent only, being under no subordination whatever, the great and immutable scheme of Chriſtian morality excepted.

As we are orderly assembled for the moſt valuable of all purposes, so we are likewise enlightened in a peculiar manner and ſtrongly connected in the bonds of brotherly love, governed by certain and allowed rules, supported by decency, guarded by secrecy, skilled in myſtery, both delightful and inſtructive, possessing the affection of each other, and seriously devoting ourselves thereto at ſtated times and seasons, apart from all temporal concerns; conversing together without dissimulation or reserve, and abounding in mirth, affability and good humour.

We conceive you to be well informed in the three great qualifications which are essential to form the character of a grand Mason—morality, secrecy, and brotherly love, and shall not therefore rehearse them here.

We expect that you will join with us in all things, in labour and refreshment, in silence and mirth, always rejoicing with us in proſperity, and sympathizing with us in adversity, and to be, like the reſt of your brethren, obedient to the Grand Commander, or his Deputy, reſpectfully attentive to all the presiding officers, decent and diligent while in the encampment, and always ready either to give or receive inſtruction. You are on no account to disobey the summons of your Encampment; but, if your time will possibly allow, be punctual to the hour appointed. To all these promises, we expect that you will cheerfully comply, and we sincerely wish you much success in the issue of your labours.

As an earnest of your desire to fulfil the respective duties which you have just heard proposed, you will be pleased to attend to the Grand Commander, who will question you on the great subject of Christian charity, that great scheme of brotherly love, which has been framed by the all-wise Providence, to procure for mankind, and more especially for Masons, the highest happiness. In the course of your answer, you shall have requisite assistance.

G. C. Wherein doth Christian charity, or the love of which you have just now heard, consist?

Sir Knight. In doing all the good offices for, and shewing unfeigned kindness towards a brother. If he be virtuous, it will make us esteem him. If he be honest, but weak in judgment, it will raise our compassion to commiserate and aid him. If he be wicked, it will incline us to give him pious admonition and timely exhortation, in order to reclaim him: and if he reform, it will augment our happiness. But if through perverseness and self-will, he continues in an idle course and evil habit, it will excite our pity to pray for him, and if possible to administer to his necessities. It will at all times throw a veil over the reproach he may deservedly incur; but if his character shall at any time suffer violence without a just cause, I will then exert my best abilities to wipe off every unjust aspersion by openly vindicating his character in a fair and honourable way. If from birth, honour, state, or wealth, he is my superior, it will teach me to be attentive, tractable, obliging, and modestly submissive. If he be my inferior, it will make me affable, courteous and kind. If he be my equal, it will teach me to preserve equity and candour towards him, in a social way. Lastly, if I receive good from him, it will make me thankful and desirous to requite it. If I receive evil at his hands, it will make me slow to anger, easy to be entreated, and of long forbearance, when impelled to exact restitution. In this last act of infliction, mercy shall always triumph over judgment, to my brother's edification and enlargement.

G. C. I thank you, Sir Knight Companion, for the ready earnest which you have so cheerfully given of your intention to serve your brethren, with respect to your abilities and their several necessities and conditions in life. The Grand Registrar will now read the rules of our Grand Christian Encampment, in order that the Knights Companions may be more fully informed of their whole duty, and become better prepared to acquit themselves agreeably to the honourable and friendly confession, which our worthy companion and the rest of the Knights have already made.

G. R. Sir Knight Companion, the Grand Commander has signified his pleasure to me, that the rules be now read, which have been subscribed by all the Sir Knights Companions of this Grand Christian Encampment. Hear ye, hear ye, each and all, Sir Knights Companions present, the whole of the rules of your Grand Christian Encampment, as they have been written for your own good peace, order, and pleasure, and afterwards distinctly heard, assented to, and freely subscribed, not by another, but by and for yourselves.

APPENDIX

All answer, We will hear.

G. R. And, whereas, the Sir Knights Companions of this most Christian Order and Encampment of High Knights Templar have drawn up, approved, and agreed to the following rules, the better to prevent feuds, controversies, animosities, or debate, with a single eye to the glory of God, the honour of his Majesty, the welfare and prosperity of the kingdom, and the well-being and happiness of each other, all of which they profess most religiously to observe; they are now to be declared and known.

Lecture.

Q. Where were you prepared to be made a Knight Templar?

A. Adjoining a Grand Christian Encampment.

Q. How were you habited?

A. As a pilgrim, with sandals on my feet, a mantle on my shoulders, a staff with a cross in my hand, a belt round my waist, a scrip and wallet, with bread and a bottle of water.

Q. How were you introduced?

A. In that condition I was led towards the entrance of the Grand Christian Encampment, by the Master of the Ceremonies, and a trumpet was sounded.

Q. What followed?

A. I was challenged by an Equerry.

Q. What was that challenge?

A. Who came there.

Q. Your answer?

A. A pilgrim, on his travels to the holy city, hearing of a Knights Templar Encampment, has come with a hope of being admitted.

Q. What other questions were put to you?

A. I was asked from whence, and if came of my own free will, and what I was desirous of doing.

Q. Your answer to these questions?

A. That I came of my own free will from the wilderness of Judæa, which I had traversed, exposed to great danger until I was met by the worthy Knight who accompanied me, and who promised me protection and safe conduct to the holy city; and that I was desirous to devote my life to the service of the poor and the sick, for the sake of Jesus Christ, and to pray for my own sins with those of the people.

Q. Were you further examined?

A. I was asked what recommendation I brought with me.

Q. Your answer?

A. The sign and the word of a Royal Arch Mason.

Q. Were they called for?

A. They were.

Q. How were you further tried?

A. In being asked if I had worked at the Second Temple; if I had received Christian Baptism; if I believed in God the Father, God the Son, and God the Holy Ghost; if I believed that God the Son was made man to save us; if I believed in the inspiring power of the Holy Ghost; and if I was willing to protect the Christian faith at the expense of my life. To all which I answered in the affirmative.

Q. What occurred next?

A. I was ordered to wait until a report had been made to the Grand Commander and the Sir Knights of the Encampment.

Q. How were you admitted?

A. A saw was placed to my forehead by the Second Captain, after examining me over again on the same subjects presented by the Equerry. I thus entered the Encampment, and found the Sir Knights under arms. I was subjected to the same examination by the First Captain and by the Grand Commander; after which, I was ordered to kneel on both knees, and receive the benefit of a prayer from the Grand Prelate.

Q. What was further said to you?

A. The Grand Commander said, we must have a further trial of your faith. You must perambulate the Encampment for meditation and further preparation.

Q. What was done with you then?

A. I was conducted to the west, desired to kneel on both knees, with my face to the east, my hand on the gospels; in which position I received the first part of my obligation.

Q. Be pleased to repeat it.

A. I, A. B., in the presence of the Holy Trinity, and in memory of St. John of Jerusalem, that first faithful soldier and Martyr in Christ Jesus, do most solemnly promise and swear, that I will never illegally reveal the secrets of a Knight Templar to a Royal Arch Mason, nor to any person beneath the dignity of this noble order; nor aid in the installation of a Knight Templar unless five are present, myself included, under the penalty of all my former obligations.

Q. After you had received the first part of your obligation, what was then done with you?

A. My staff was taken from me, and I was presented with a sword as a substitute, with my hand still on the Holy Gospels, and in this prostrate form I was taught to repeat the second part of my obligation.

Q. Be pleased to deliver it.

A. I do furthermore swear, that, with this the sword of my faith, I will guard and defend the tomb and sepulchre of our Lord and Saviour Jesus Christ, against all Jews, Turks, Infidels, and Heathens, and other opposers of the gospel.

Q. After you had taken the second part of your obligation, what did the Grand Commander do with you? Did he not address you on the presentation of the sword?

APPENDIX

A. He said, in the name of the Father, Son, and Holy Ghost, I arm you with this sword, as a distinguishing mark of our approbation; and I am persuaded that you will only employ it in the defence of the gospel of our Lord and Saviour Jesus Christ, against all those who may oppose the same.

Q. Be pleased to conclude the obligation.

A. I do furthermore swear, that I will never knowingly draw the blood of a Brother Knight Templar, nor cause it to be drawn in wrath; but will espouse his cause, knowing it to be just, though I should endanger my own life. Even when princes are engaged in war, I will not forget the duty which I owe him as a brother. If ever I willfully violate this my solemn compact, as a Brother Knight Templar, may my skull be sawn asunder with a rough saw, my brains taken out and put in a charger to be consumed by the scorching sun, and my skull in another charger, in memory of St. John of Jerusalem, that faithful soldier of our Lord and Saviour. If ever I willfully deviate from this my solemn obligation, may my light be put out from among men, as that of Judas Iscariot was for betraying his Lord and Master; furthermore, may the soul that once inhabited this skull, as the representative of St. John the Baptist, appear against me in the day of judgment: so help me God, and keep me steadfast in this my solemn obligation of a Knight Templar.

Q. Was anything added?

A. I was ordered to kiss the gospels seven times, and received the charge of the Grand Prelate, who exhorted me to fight manfully and run my course with valour, trusting in our Lord and Saviour Jesus Christ.

Q. What were you then desired to do?

A. I was then ordered to take a lighted taper in my hand, and to perambulate the encampment five times, in solemn meditation, with the admonition, that if I had either prejudice or enmity towards any man, I was to dismiss it as a necessary qualification for further honours; and that, if I would not forgive my enemies, I had better fly to the desert, to shun the sight of the Knights of this order, than to appear so unworthily among them. This I promised to do.

Q. How were you then disposed of?

A. The veil was taken from the cross, at the sight of which my burthen fell from my back.

Q. And then?

A. I was divested of my pilgrim's dress, desired to kneel, and to receive the order of Knighthood.

Q. How was that done?

A. The Grand Commander laid his sword on both my shoulders and my head, and bade me rise a Masonic Knight Hospitaller of St. John of Jerusalem, Palestine, Rhodes, and Malta, and also a Knight Templar: giving me a hearty welcome into the Christian Order, that would be ever ready to defend and protect me.

Q. What followed?

A. I was entrusted with the signs, words and tokens, clothed with the mantle of the Order, at which I was told to receive the Lord's yoke, for it was easy and light, and would bring rest to my soul, and that I was promised nothing but bread and water, with that habit of little worth.

Q. What next?

A. I was invested with the apron, sash and jewel.

Q. What was then explained to you?

A. The Encampment and its furniture. First, the three Equilateral Triangles representing the Trinity in unity, in the centre of which was placed the omnipotent and all seeing eye. Second, the figure of St. John of Jerusalem holding out the Cup of Salvation to all true believers. Third, the Cock which was a memento to Peter. Fourth, the Lamb. Fifth, the Cross on Mount Calvary. Sixth, the Five Lights on the New Testament, as emblematical of the birth, life, death, resurrection, and ascension of our blessed Redeemer. Seventh, the Sword and Sceptre. Eighth, the Star which appeared at the birth of Jesus. Ninth, the Ladder with the Five steps. Tenth, the Saw. Eleventh, the Sepulchre and Gospels. And Twelfth, the Cup.

Q. What was then explained?

A. The seven agonies of our Saviour. First, that which he experienced in the Garden of Gethsemane. Second, being seized as a thief or assassin. Third, his being scourged by the order of Pontius Pilate. Fourth, the placing on his head a crown of thorns. Fifth, the mockery and derision of the Jews by putting on him a scarlet robe, and a reed in his hand as a sceptre. Sixth, nailing him to a cross; and Seventh, the piercing of his side.

Q. What was finally done?

A. My installation was thrice proclaimed by the Grand Herald, and I partook of bread and wine, in commemoration of the Lord's Supper, with the whole of the Sir Knights in the Encampment drinking from the cup of brotherly love.

The Facsimile

Reprints of Rituals of Old Degrees

THE DEGREE

OF

MASTER MARK MASON,

BEING THE WORK OF

THE GRAND COUNCIL OF PRINCES OF JERUSALEM,

OF

SOUTH CAROLINA,

AND

THE OLDEST WORK EXTANT ANYWHERE.

FROM

A Mss. in the Archives of the Supreme Council at Charleston.

MASTER MARK MASON.

FORM OF THE LODGE.

The *Chief Officer*, who is placed in the East, represents H∴ A∴, and is styled *Respectable Overseer*. He wears a bright yellow triangular collar around his neck, to which is suspended the Past Master's Jewel, gilt, with the representation of a twenty-four-inch guage, hung horizontally thereto. In his hand is a twenty-four-inch guage.

The *Senior Warden*, in the West, is styled *Worshipful Senior*. He wears the same kind of collar, with the same Jewel; but instead of the guage, a square is suspended. On the pedestal before him is a wooden square.

The *Junior Warden*, in the south, is styled *Worshipful Junior*. He wears the same kind of collar and Jewel; but suspended to the latter is a sun-dial, with the gnomon pointing to high twelve. In his hand is a *Hiram*.

To the left of the R∴ O∴ stands the *Senior Minor*, with a white wand, six feet long. Round his neck the same kind of collar and Jewel, but suspended to it the representation of a cubic stone.

To the right of the Senior Warden stands the *Junior Minor*, decorated as the Senior Minor.

In the North sits the *Treasurer*, decorated with the same kind of collar and Jewel, but to the latter is suspended horizontally a key.

In the Southeast sits the *Scribe*, decorated as the other officers, but with a pen suspended horizontally to his jewel.

All the Brethren must wear the apron and jewel of the Order. The latter must be tied with or have a rose of yellow ribbon worn on the left side of the coat suspended to a button-hole.

4

The *Apron* is of white leather, edged with yellow, within which is a border of bright pink. The flap, yellow silk, with the rising sun embroidered or painted thereon. In the area of the apron is the representation of the Cubic Stone, surrounded with a circle of yellow, edged with red, on which must be the following letters: *H. T. W. S. S. T. K. S.* In the centre of the cube may be the private mark of the individual.

The *Jewel* must be of silver gilt, or of gold, but it ought to be of the latter; of a circular form, with the same letters engraved on it as are on the apron, the private mark in the centre. It should have on the top of it the Past Master's Jewel.

In the centre of the Lodge must be three *Orders* placed in a triangular form; within them, a Pedestal about two feet high, a yellow cushion, a Bible thereon, shut, gilt square and compasses, and the officers' jewels lying thereon.

In a book, generally that containing the By-laws, the members, on signing their names, must record their marks, and once having adopted one a member must never change or alter it.

FACSIMILE

TO OPEN.

R∴ O∴ Bro. Junior Minor, pray what is your duty in this Lodge?

Jun∴ M∴ To prepare everything which may be necessary for the Brethren to proceed to labor; to see that there are no idlers nor eavesdroppers about the Temple.

R∴ O∴ Be pleased, my Bro∴, to do your duty.

[The Junior Minor goes to the door, and strikes four, and gives orders to the Tyler to do his duty. He lights the Orders, opens the Bible, fixes the square and compasses, delivers to the several officers their respective Jewels, and then returns to his place.]

R∴ O∴ Pray, my Brother, why do you place yourself at the right of the Worshipful Senior Warden?

Jun∴ Minor. To render him all the assistance he may require, and convey his wishes round the Lodge when so directed.

R∴ O∴ Where is the Senior Minor's place in the Lodge?

Jun∴ Min∴ Near the Respectable Overseer.

R∴ O∴ Why in that situation, my Brother?

Sen∴ Min∴ By being near your person, Respectable Sir, I shall be the better able to receive your orders, and convey them where necessary, and to discharge such other duty as you may require of me.

R∴ O∴ Thank you, my Brother. Where is the Junior Warden's place?

S∴ M∴ In the South, Respectable Sir.

R∴ O∴ Why there, my Respectable Brother?

Jun∴ Warden. As the immutable laws of nature require a portion of rest after labor, and as Masons have set hours for refreshment, the Junior Warden is placed in the South to observe the great Luminary at meridian; to call off the Brethren from their toil, and be attentive that they return in due season to their duty; to introduce the Candidate and give him instruction.

R∴ O∴ Where is the Worshipful Senior Warden's place?

Jun∴ Warden. In the West, Respectable Sir.

R∴ O∴ For what purpose is your situation in the West?

Sen∴ Warden. The day being closed with the setting of the Sun in the West,

6

the Senior Warden is there placed to close the Lodge; to discharge the workmen after their labor is finished, and fulfill a text in Scripture.

R∴ O∴   Be pleased to explain that text, my Brother?
S∴ W∴   Let not the wages of the hireling abide with you all night.
R∴ O∴   Where is your Respectable Overseer's place?
S∴ W∴   Everywhere, but more particularly in the East.
R∴ O∴   Why there, my Worshipful Brother?
S∴ W∴   As the resplendent Orb of Light, directed by the Grand Architect of the Universe, rises in the East to open and illumine the day, so should the Respectable Overseer be situated in the East, to open his Lodge, diffusing knowledge and instruction to the Brethren, or direct so to be done.
R∴ O∴   What is the time of the day?
S∴ W∴   The Sun is rising.
R∴ O∴   As the sun is rising, it is time to pursue our labors. Proclaim, my Worshipful Brothers Senior and Junior Wardens, that I am going to open a Master Mark Mason's Lodge.
S∴ W∴   [Rising.] Brethren, to order! [The Brethren rise.] Our Respectable Overseer is going to open a Master Mark Mason's Lodge. Be silent and attentive.

[The Junior Warden repeats the same.]

R∴ O∴   By the power vested in me, I proclaim this Master Mark Mason's Lodge duly opened, in the presence and in the name of the G∴ A∴ of the Universe. Let me exhort you, my dear Brethren, to attend strictly to the duties which are attached to your several situations. Let a due observance of our Laws and the General Regulations of our Mystic Rites be punctually and assiduously attended to, that Friendship and Harmony may prevail among us!

[He then strikes 1, the Senior Warden 2, the Junior Warden 3, and the Brethren 4.]

PRAYER.

O, Lord God, Supreme Architect of the Universe, in mercy look down upon the few here assembled before *Thee!* Inspire us with a due reverence for Thy most holy and sacred name! Enkindle in our hearts the pure spirit of Brotherly Love and Charity for all mankind. May we be cemented to each other by every moral and social virtue! Endue us with a competency of thy Divine Wisdom, and enable us to regulate our conduct agreeably to the true principles of Masonry, that we may thereby be fully enlightened in its Sacred Mysteries; and grant that as this meeting has so happily commenced, it may be conducted with Order and close with Harmony and Friendship. Amen!

7

RECEPTION.

[The Treasurer goes to the Candidate in the ante-chamber, and divests him of all offensive and defensive weapons, and of all metals. He places in his left hand a hod, with some imperfect stones and a cubic stone. He then knocks on the door distinctly 1, 2, 3 and 4.]

[The R∴ O∴ strikes *one*, and says:]

R∴ O∴ Brother Junior Warden, be pleased to see what occasions the alarm.

[The Junior Warden goes to the door, knocks 2, and demands:]

J∴ W∴ Who is it that alarms in that mysterious manner?

Treas∴ [Answering without.] Bro. A . . B . . , a Past Master, who has faithfully labored in the mystic art, now comes to claim, as a reward for his services, the honor of beng admitted a Master Mark Mason.

J∴ W∴ By what means does he expect to obtain it?

Treas∴ By the name he bears, and by virtue of a Pass-word.

J∴ W∴ What name does he bear?

Treas∴ A Giblimite.

J∴ W∴ What is his Pass-word?

Treas∴ Giblim.

J∴ W∴ Is he duly qualified to receive that favor?

Treas∴ He is. I answer for him.

J∴ W∴ Is he well and properly prepared?

Treas∴ He is.

J∴ W∴ Wait until I obtain permission to admit him.

[He returns to his seat and strikes 3.]

R∴ O∴ Pray, my Brother, what occasioned that mysterious alarm at the door?

J∴ W∴ The zealous Bro. A . . B . . , Worshipful Past Master, solicits the honor of being admitted a Master Mark Mason.

R∴ O∴ What are his claims and qualifications? Has he given you any *Word* or *Token?*

J∴ W∴ He has, Respectable Sir. He has given me the pass-word, and calls himself a Giblimite.

R∴ O∴ Is he well vouched for, and is he duly prepared?

J∴ W∴ He is, Respectable Sir.

R∴ O∴ Let us, my dear Brethren, applaud the zeal of our worthy Brother, who has faithfully discharged his duty, and now comes to claim his reward.

[The Brethren all strike with their hands four times.]

8

[The Senior Warden goes to the door, takes the candidate by the Past Master's Grip, and leads him to the foot of the Pedestal, facing the East.]

R∴ O∴ Pray, my Bro∴, what brings you hither?

Candidate. My zeal for the Craft, and to obtain the reward for my services.

R∴ O∴ What services have you rendered the Craft?

Cand∴ I have wrought in preparing stone for the building, and have now brought some to finish the most sacred place.

R∴ O∴ Are your materials suitable for the purpose for which you intend them?

Cand∴ I have prepared them agreeably to the best of my ability.

R∴ O∴ Go, my Brother, to the Worshipful Senior Warden in the West, and let him examine them.

[The Candidate is conducted to the Senior Warden, and the Junior Warden takes his place. The Senior Warden tries the stones by the square. Such as are imperfect he takes with both hands, and says:]

S∴ W∴ My dear Brother, these stones do not answer the purpose for which you intended them. We must therefore heave them over. This cubic stone is well adapted, and shows you to be a workman. Go, my Brother, convince the brethren that you are a Giblimite. Bro∴ J∴ W∴, be pleased to instruct our Bro∴ how to travel.

[The Candidate is then conducted four times round the Lodge, with the stone in his right hand. On the first round he gives the sign of the Entered Apprentice; the second time, the Fellow Craft's; the third, the Master's; and the *fourth* time, he stops at the Senior Warden's, facing the East, and takes 1, 2, 3 and 4 steps, which brings him to the Pedestal.

R∴ O∴ My dear Bro∴, I feel infinite satisfaction in rewarding your merit by initiating you into the mysteries of Mark Masonry. Are you willing to be obligated agreeably to the tenets of our Mystic Rites?

Cand∴ I am.

R∴ O∴ My dear Bro∴, in receiving this part of Masonry, as well as the Ineffable Degrees, you will be forcibly struck with the very great dissimilarity between these and the degrees you have already taken. When you were initiated into the first Symbolic Degree, called Entered Apprentice, you was sworn not to write, print, stain, carve, etch or engrave any part of the secrets or mysteries of those degrees. Under these impressions, my Bro∴, you will no doubt be somewhat surprised that we deliver this, as well as the Sublime Degrees, from manuscripts. It is therefore necessary to give you some explanation of this difference.

9

Masonry was founded in those dark and rude ages when civilization was yet in its infancy, and the arts and sciences shed but few and imperfect rays across the gloom of Barbarism. Mutual wants and necessities impelled our primæval Brethren to seek for mutual aid and assistance. Diversity of talents, inclinations and pursuits rendered each dependent, in some measure, upon the genius or exertions of another. Thus society was formed, and as a consequence, men of the same habits and pursuits associated more intimately together, not only with the view of mutual improvement and advantage, but from that natural impulse felt by congenial minds. In this manner societies were formed, as civilization began to extend through the world, and the minds of men became enlarged from the contemplation of the works of nature.

The arts and sciences were cultivated by the most ingenious of the people. The contemplation of the stellar system, as the work of an Almighty Artist, and the attributes of their God, gave rise to religion and the science of astronomy.

The measurement of land, and the division and marking of their property, gave rise to Geometry, and these to the society into whose mysteries you now desire to be instructed.

If we should look upon the Earth and its productions, the Ocean with its tides, the coming and passing of day, the starry arch of Heaven, the seasons and their changes, the life and death of man, as being merely accidents in the hand of Nature, we must shut up all the powers of judgment, and yield ourselves to the darkest folly and ignorance.

The august scene of the planetary system, the day and night, the seasons and their successions, the animal frame, the vegetation of plants, all afford us subject for astonishment; the greatest, too mighty, but for the hand of a Deity, whose works they are; the least, too miraculous, but for the wisdom of their God. It is no wonder, then, that the first instructors of our society, who had their eye on the revelation of the Deity from the earliest ages of the world, should hold the sciences hallowed among them, whereby such lights were obtained by man on the discovery of the great wisdom of our adorable Creator in the beginning.

This institution, which was originally founded on the mysteries of Religion and Science, is now maintained by us on the principles of lending mutual aid to each other, as well as to preserve our adoration to the Almighty Artist, and to improve our minds with the principles of science. How should we be able to discover the Brethren of this family, but through such tokens as should point them out from other men?

Language is now provincial, and the dialects of different nations would not be comprehensible to men ignorant and unlettered. Hence it became necessary to

10

use an expression which should be cognizable to people of all nations. So it is with Masons. They are possessed of that universal expression, and of such remains of the original language, that they can communicate their history, their wants and prayers to every Bro∴ Mason throughout the globe; from whence it is certain multitudes of lives have been saved in foreign countries when shipwreck and misery had overwhelmed them; when robbers had pillaged, and when sickness, want and misery had brought them even to the brink of the grave. The discovery of being a Brother hath stayed the savage hand of the conqueror, lifted in the field of battle to cut off the captive; it hath withheld the sword imbrued in carnage and slaughter, and subdued the insolence of triumph, to pay homage to the Craft.

Such, my Brother, being the importance of our profession, the utmost caution was necessary to prevent the mysteries and privileges from falling into the hands of, and being used by, the unworthy.

The more sublime and Ineffable Degrees being still of higher importance, and containing the real secrets and principles of the Mystic Institution, were to be guarded in a more particular manner, both from the knowledge of the world and from those who may be unworthy of receiving them.

It was ordained that the three first or Blue Degrees (which are only symbols of the Sublime and true Degrees of Masonry) should be committed to memory, that it might be thereby known, from the manner in which a Symbolic Mason discharged the duties of these preparatory degrees, whether he was capable of being trusted with the real and important secrets of the Craft.

Again, the histories of Masonry, as contained in the higher degrees, give an accurate and authentic detail of occurrences found only in the Records and Archives of the Sublime Institution, and which are so lengthy that they fill many volumes, which it would be impossible to commit to memory, unless the whole of our lives were dedicated to it. It is for these reasons, my Brother, that this part of Masonry, into which you are about to be initiated, will be delivered to you from manuscript.

Do you now feel any repugnance at taking a further obligation, which will bind you more intimately to the Order?

Cand∴ I feel no repugnance. An anxious desire animates my breast, and urges me to solicit to be admitted as one of the Elect.

R∴ O∴ Approach, then, my dear Brother, to the altar erected to the name of the Eternal God, and in His presence contract your obligation.

[The candidate is then desired to kneel at the foot of the pedestal, his left hand on the Holy Bible, and his right on his left breast, and in this position takes the following

OBLIGATION:]

I, A . . B . . , do most sincerely promise and swear, in the presence of the Grand Architect of the Universe and before this respectable assemblage of Brethren, never to reveal, directly or indirectly, the secrets or mysteries of Mark Masonry, to any but such as shall be duly and lawfully entitled to receive the same; nor be present when it is given, but in a regular constituted Lodge of Master Mark Masons. And I do furthermore swear that I will obey all summonses, and answer immediately in person all regular marks which may be sent to me, if not prevented by sickness, imprisonment, or some other unavoidable cause; that I will never pledge my mark but in the utmost distress, and not even then but with the determined intention of redeeming it as soon as it shall be in my power; that my eyes, ears and heart shall ever be open to see, hear and commiserate the distresses of my Bro∴ Mark Mason, and grant him such relief as my situation in life will admit of, without injuring myself or family. And I do furthermore swear that I will observe and obey all orders and decrees of the Grand Council of Princes of Jerusalem, and the laws and regulations of this Lodge, as long as I shall be a member of the same. To all this I promise and swear with sincerity and truth; and should I fail in this my solemn obligation, I ardently wish to be eternally disgraced as a man of honor, and despised as a Mason, and be hunted from society as unworthy of existence; that my neck and heels be tied together, and I be cast on a dunghill, to perish and rot, and my bones be mingled with the rubbish. *So help me God.*

[He kisses the Bible, the R∴ O∴ takes him by the Past Master's grip, his left hand under his elbow, and says:]

R∴ O∴ My dear Bro∴, with extreme pleasure I raise and hail you as a Master Mark Mason. May you ever cherish and practice the virtuous principles of the Mystic Profession! Permit me to invest you with the apron of this Order. The Jewel, on which will be engraved your mark, you will no doubt take an early opportunity of procuring, as no Bro∴ can appear here without it. Go, my Bro∴, to the Junior Warden, and he will instruct you in the signs, token and words.

[The Junior Warden gives him the following signs, token and words; after which, he is placed near the R∴ O∴:]

1st Sign. Both hands on the neck, alluding to the penalty which will be suffered for a violation of the obligation; that is, that your neck and heels shall be tied together and your body be thrown on a dunghill, and there left to perish.

2d Sign. The fingers of both hands interlaced and raised to the left shoulder, as if heaving something over it, alluding to those materials which were not properly prepared, and which were thrown over the left shoulder among the rubbish.

Token. Take each other by the right hand, and clinch the fingers, which forms the cube, and is the emblem of the Order. It should remind us that our actions should be formed on the equal scale of justice and propriety.

1st Pass-word. Giblim or Stone Cutter.

2d Pass-word. Joppa. The materials which were prepared in Tyre were sent on floats and landed at Joppa, from whence they were conveyed by land to Jerusalem.

Hailing Sign. The thumb of the right hand bent on the palm, the palm upwards; *i. e.*, the method which is used by Mark Masons when they introduce their hands through the square hole to receive their wages.

Answer to the Hailing Sign: Touch the eyes, ears and heart, alluding to this passage in the obligation: That my eyes, ears and heart shall ever be open to see, hear and commiserate the distresses of my Bro∴ Mark Mason.

Sign of Reproof. Extend the left hand, and place the right on the left breast, being the position in which a candidate takes the obligation.

CHARGE.

I congratulate you on being thought worthy to be promoted to this respectable part of Masony. Permit me to impress upon your mind this great and important truth: that as charity and benevolence render all who possess them amiable in the eyes of the world, and acceptable to the Deity, so is it particularly incumbent on you, as a Mark Mason, to practice them, who belong to an institution whose foundation is laid in those great bulwarks of society. The Institution to which you are now promoted will draw upon you the scrutinizing eyes of the world at large, but particularly those of your Brethren on whom this part of Masonry has not been conferred; and they are justified in expecting your conduct to be such as they may with safety and advantage imitate.

In the honorable character of a Master Mark Mason, it is more particularly your duty to guide with caution all your words and actions. Endeavor to let your conduct in society at large, as well as in the Lodge among the Brethren, be

13

such as may stand the test of the strictest scrutiny; that, like the cubic stone, it may bear the application of the Senior Warden's square, and not like the unfinished and imperfect work you brought in your hod, be rejected and thrown aside as unfit for the Masonic edifice.

While virtue is your ruling principle, my Bro∴, Hope will always find a residence in your bosom; for, should misfortune assail you, should your friends forsake you, should envy traduce your good name and malice persecute you, should you be despised by the proud and treated with scorn by the vainglorious, yet may you have confidence that among Master Mark Masons you will find a friend who will administer relief to your distresses and comfort you in your afflictions. Under the frowns of fortune keep this consolation in your mind: that he who has a due faith in the dispensations of his Beneficent Creator, and a becoming charity for his fellow creatures, will be sure of receiving that just reward which is the consequent attendant on good and virtuous actions.

HISTORY.

In the formation of this society religious as well as civil regulations were the basis on which our forefathers thought it expedient to place its foundation. They had experience that by religion all civil ties and obligations were compacted, and from thence proceeded all the bonds which could unite mankind in social intercourse. Hence it was they laid the corner stone of the edifice on the bosom of religion. Solomon, when he was about to build the Temple at Jerusalem, selected such men as were enlightened with the true faith, who, being full of wisdom and religious fervor, were the most proper to conduct the great work. As he had been blessed with the smiles of peace and prosperity from the moment he ascended the throne of Israel, he felt an ardent desire to cultivate the friendship and esteem of his neighbours, and to continue to himself the alliances which his father had enjoyed for many years. He was no doubt prompted by a circumstance which rendered a measure of this kind highly necessary. The kingdom of Judea did not furnish all the materials which were necessary to perfect an undertaking of such magnitude. He therefore sought the friendship of Hiram King of Tyre, whose dominions abounded in those articles which were necessary for the construction of the Temple. An opportunity was soon afforded him, in consequence of King Hiram having sent ambassadors to congratulate him on his accession to the throne and on his present happy circumstances. He then addressed the following letter to King Hiram of Tyre:

14

"Know thou, that my father would have built a Temple to God, but was hindered by wars and continual expeditions, for he did not leave off to overthrow his enemies till he made them all subject to tribute, but I give thanks to God for the peace I at present enjoy, and on that account I am at leisure and desire to build an house to God. For God foretold to my father that such an house should be built by me, wherefore I desire thee to send some of thy subjects with mine to Mount Lebanon to cut down timber, for the Sidonians are more skillful than my people in cutting of wood. As for wages to the hewers of wood, I will pay whatsoever price thou shalt determine."

The good King Hiram was pleased with that letter, and returned the following answer to Solomon :

"It is fit to bless God that he hath committed thy father's government to thee, who art a wise man, and endowed with all virtues. As for myself, I rejoice at the condition thou art in, and will be subservient to thee in all that thou sendest to me about; for when by my subjects I have cut down many and large trees of cedar and cypress wood, I will send them to sea, and will order my subjects to make floats of them, and to sail to what place soever of thy country thou shalt desire, and leave them there, after which thy subjects may carry them to Jerusalem. But do thou take care to procure us corn for the timber, which we stand in need of, because we inhabit on an island."

The two Kings renewed the alliance which had subsisted between Hiram and David, and became intimately attached to each other by friendship and personal esteem. King Hiram, to show his zeal, and manifest his ardent wishes of contributing all in his power towards completing an object of such exalted magnitude as the erection of an House to be dedicated to the worship of the only True and Living God, sent to King Solomom *Hiram Abiff*, who was the son of a widow of the tribe of Naphthali, a man peculiarly endowed with wisdom, and surprisingly skillful in the knowledge of the arts and sciences, and in all the branches of mechanics. He was pious and virtuous, kind and benevolent to all mankind. He was beloved and revered for the many excellent qualities which he possessed, and which gained him the esteem and confidence of his monarch. His counsel on the most momentous occasions was highly appreciated. Such was the general good opinion of him that he was surnamed "*Abiff*," from the word AB, (Father.) He was much attached to sculpture, and to those who possessed talents in that art. On his arrival at Jerusalem, King Solomon was so much

15

pleased with his understanding that he immediately committed the superintendence of all the works to his care. Hiram Abiff having so heavy a charge upon him knew that it would be impossible for him, alone, to direct and superintend such an immense number of workmen as were employed in the building. He therefore appointed overseers to the different classes. He was careful to select those whose characters were irreproachable, and in whom the utmost confidence could be placed. He was particularly attached to the "Stone Cutters" or "Giblimites," whom he formed into a body. As these consisted principally of overseers, it was their duty to procure from the Treasurer General such sums of money as were necessary to pay off the workmen over whom they presided. This was done in a chamber particularly appropriated to this purpose and at a particular hour.

To prevent confusion and imposition among the classes, the Giblimites were ordered to provide for themselves each a particular mark. When they went to receive their pay, they placed their mark under the thumb, which was bent on the palm of the hand. They then thrust their hand through a square hole, which had been made for the purpose, turned the palm upwards, raised the thumb, and showed their mark. Their wages were paid into their hand, which they drew out open with the palm upwards.

H∴ A∴, to distinguish this favored class of workmen, caused each of them to wear a medal, on which was engraved their particular mark or device. Above the mark was the compass, extended to sixty degrees, with the sun in the centre, as an emblem of their duty: that is, to rise with that luminary, to attend to their avocations.

As none were permitted to be employed in preparing materials for the Sanctum Sanctorum but the Mark Masons, the attachment of H∴ A∴ to this class of workmen created great jealousy among the rest of the workmen. They had often observed that at a particular hour the Mark Masters would go to a particular chamber of the Temple, and thrust their hand through a square hole, with something in their hand, and when they withdrew them they always brought out money.

This circumstance led some of them to watch for an opportunity of procuring a mark from some of the Mark Masons by some device or other, and an opportunity of the kind sometimes occurred from their neglect and inattention. They seized the opportunity, and thrust their hands in, but not knowing the mystic mode, they always paid dear for their villainy. The moment they felt the money in their hands they would close them and attempt to draw it out, which proved their fraud, when immediately a sharp-edged tool, which was suspended over the hole, fell, and severed their hand from their body, and they were immediately dis-

16

charged with this indelible mark of disgrace, to be execrated by all honest and virtuous men.

By this and a variety of other means did this great and good man regulate such an immense number of workmen without the smallest confusion; each knew the duty he had to perform, and did it cheerfully.

By his vigilance and attention was that glorious and superb model of excellence, the Temple of Solomon, erected; and by his ingenuity and labor was it enriched with the most precious and beautiful decorations, and all its utensils for the worship of God Almighty. But when he fondly anticipated the pleasure of seeing it consecrated, he was basely and cruelly assassinated!

After his death the eight letters were added to the Mark Jewel, to remind them of his being the founder of the order.

Having given the origin of this degree, I will now point out the use of it.

It is the lot of hamanity to be exposed to misfortunes, and happy are they who possess the means of communicating their wants and their wishes to those who feel an interest in affording them relief! The Master Mark Mason possesses those means, should he be overwhelmed by sickness or other misfortunes; should he be even locked up from the light of day and the blessings of society, in the cell of a dark and dismal dungeon, without one kind friend to whom he might communicate the anguish of his heart, to whom he might portray with paternal feeling the distress of his little family starving by his imprisonment. Perhaps he is even deprived of the means of writing to those who would assist him, if they knew but of his situation. His Mark is the Talisman, which renders writing needless.

He sends it to a Mark Mason, who instantly obeys the summons and flies to his relief, with an heart warmed by the impulse of Brotherly Love, and leaves no exertions untried to alleviate his misfortunes and to render him happy.

Such are the glorious advantages to be derived from the possession of this degree.

LECTURE.

R∴ O∴ My Worshipful Brother Senior Warden, are you a Master Mark Mason?

Sen∴ Ward∴ I am, and feel happy in having that distinguished favor conferred on me.

R∴ O∴ Pray, my Bro∴, where were you made a Master Mark Mason, and on what occasion?

FACSIMILE

17

Sen∴ Ward∴ I was made a Mark Mason in the middle of the Temple. H∴ A∴, our Respectable Grand Master, having been appointed by King Solomon chief Overseer over the workmen, and Inspector over all the work, finding the charge too great for one person to attend to, and direct the many thousands which were employed in the construction of the building, appointed the most skillful and pious masters to superintend the workmen, and report to him daily their conduct. He took charge himself of those who worked in the S∴ S∴, and was particularly attached to the Giblimites or Stone Cutters.

R∴ O∴ How were you prepared, and in what manner were you initiated into this part of Masonry?

S∴ W∴ I was divested of all metals, of all offensive and defensive weapons, with a hod in my left hand, and led by a brother, by the right, to the door of the Lodge.

R∴ O∴ What did you perceive on being brought to the door?

S∴ W∴ My conductor struck on the door 1, 2, 3 and 4 distinctly.

R∴ O∴ What answer did he receive?

S∴ W∴ I heard *one* loud knock in the inner part of the Lodge, and shortly after *two* upon the inside of the door.

R∴ O∴ What questions were asked you at the door?

S∴ W∴ Who it was that had given the alarm in that mysterious manner.

R∴ O∴ What answer made you?

S∴ W∴ My conductor answered for me, that I was a Master Workman, and had faithfully discharged the several duties entrusted to me; that I was a true Giblimite, and felt an anxious desire of being enrolled as a Mark Mason.

R∴ O∴ Had you your wishes gratified?

S∴ W∴ I had. My conductor vouched for me as one whose zeal, fervor, constancy and knowledge in the Mystic Art merited that confidence.

R∴ O∴ Did you gain admittance immediately?

S∴ W∴ No, Respectable Sir. After waiting some time, I was led in by the Junior Warden, who instructed me to take 1, 2, 3 and 4 steps towards the Respectable Overseer.

R∴ O∴ What was then said to you?

S∴ W∴ The Respectable Overseer demanded what brought me there. I answered, My zeal for the Craft, my knowledge in the art, my profession as a Giblimite, the warm desire I had to exert every faculty nature had endowed me with to perfect the grand work we had been employed in, which operated so powerfully and forcibly as to induce me to claim, as a reward for my past services, that con-

18

fidence which I perceived had been granted to other Brethren; and, to evince my zeal, produced the hod, with materials intended for finishing the Holy of Holies.

R∴ O∴ In what manner were your materials received?

S∴ W∴ Such as were well wrought, and adapted to the purpose, were retained; what were not, were hove over among the rubbish.

R∴ O∴ Who examined the materials?

S∴ W∴ The Worshipful Senior Warden.

R∴ O∴ What was the most material article you brought with you, and which was most approved of?

S∴ W∴ The cubic stone, most made use of in the Sanctum Sanctorum.

R∴ O∴ Why is the cubic stone most made use of in that part of the building?

S∴ W∴ As the cube is the most perfect figure, it is the most made use of in the S∴ S∴, that place being intended as the most sacred. It therefore required the most perfect work to make it suitable.

R∴ O∴ After your materials were approved of, how were you disposed of?

S∴ W∴ With the cubic stone in my hand, I was led four times round the Lodge, to convince the Brethren my work was perfect, and that I was justly entitled to the favor I solicited.

R∴ O∴ What was done to you, after you had performed this mysterious ceremony?

S∴ W∴ I was desired to approach the R∴ O∴ and contract my obligation.

R∴ O∴ Can you, my dear Brother, repeat that obligation? If you can do me that favor, it will not only serve to remind us of the solemn duties which we have imposed on ourselves, but also to bring to our recollection the honor we have enjoyed in being admitted to labor for the service of the Grand Architect of the Universe.

S∴ W∴ With cheerfulness, Respectable Sir, I will comply with your request.

[He rises and stands in the same position as when the obligation is first given. The Brethren also all rise, and stand with their left hand extended and their right on the heart.]

R∴ O∴ Thank you, my Bro∴! After taking this obligation, what instructions did you receive?

S∴ W∴ I was instructed in the signs, token and words of this part of Masonry.

R∴ O∴ Will you be so obliging, my Worshipful Brother, as to repeat them with their meanings?

[The S∴ W∴ repeats the signs, token, words, &c.]

R∴ O∴ Thank you, my Brother. What other information did you receive?

S∴ W∴ I was presented with the Apron and Jewel of the Order.

R∴ O∴ Pray what were the figures on the Apron and Jewel?

S∴ W∴ In the area of the Apron was the representation of the cubic stone, surrounded with a yellow circle, edged with red, on which were engraved these letters: H. T. W. S. S. T. K. S. The flap of yellow, with the rising sun on it.

R∴ O∴ Be so obliging as to explain the meaning of those letters and figures on the Apron?

S∴ W∴ The yellow represents the morning at sunrise, the time Masons should rise to follow their occupation. The Sun just emerging above the horizon indicates to Masons that they should be ready to attend him in his daily career with industry and labor. The red represents the setting sun when the labor of the day is finished, and Masons retire to offer up their orisons to the Great Architect. The circle is emblematical of the immensity of the power and glory of the Deity, without beginning and without end. He was, He is, and ever will be, the great and eternal God of Heaven and Earth. The cube represents the perfect harmony of the building, and it also shows the equality of Masons: that in a Lodge no distinctions are shown to titles, wealth or rank, but as the children of one parent we know of no pre-eminence but in virtue.

The letters bring to our recollection many events connected with the building of the house, which was erected and dedicated to the sacred name of God, and of the Perfect Artist, whose ingenuity and labor adorned the Temple: that is, Hiram of Tyre, the widow's son, sent to King Solomon. His piety and virtue, his unbounded knowledge of the mystic art, were so eminently displayed in all his actions that King Solomon, who was sensible of the many services rendered by that great man, and wishing to evince the high regard he entertained for him, caused a medal to be struck, which he oftentimes wore himself, with those letters on it. He ordered all the master workmen to wear one, particularly those who were appointed overseers; and after the melancholy event which took place at the finishing of the Temple, it was generally worn by every good Mason, who endeavored in this manner to show their veneration for their virtuous chief.

R∴ O∴ Permit me, my Respectable Brother, to revert to an expression you made use of: that when at the door of the Lodge, previous to your entering, your conductor struck on the door 1, 2, 3 and 4 distinctly. What does this allude to?

S∴ W∴ The *first* implies there is but one God, Eternal and Infinite. The *second* alludes to the most perfect created beings, our primordial parents. The *third* reminds us of the three great principles of Masonry, *Faith, Hope and Charity*. The *fourth* alludes to the four cardinal virtues, *Prudence, Temperance, Justice and*

20

Fortitude, which should be the governing principles in the actions of every Mason. The numbers, when added together, make *ten*, and allude to the Decalogue, the fundamental principles of religion.

TO CLOSE.

R∴ O∴ Worshipful Brother Senior Warden, how wears the day?

S∴ W∴ The Sun is just setting.

R∴ O∴ As the Sun is setting, what remains to be done?

S∴ W∴ To close the Lodge, fulfilling the text; that every heart may depart satisfied, and the Respectable Overseer enjoy those grateful sensations which are the attendants on good actions.

R∴ O∴ Worshipful Wardens, be pleased to declare my intentions that this Lodge be closed, and remain so, until the next regular meeting, except in cases of emergency, when the Brethren shall receive timely notice thereof.

S∴ W∴ Brethren attend. [All rise.] Our Respectable Overseer declares the business of the meeting to be over, the Lodge closed, and to remain so, until the next regular meeting, unless your attendance should be sooner deemed necessary, when you shall receive due notice thereof.

[The Junior Warden repeats the same, then he strikes 1, the Senior Warden 2, the Respectable Overseer 3, and all the Brethren 4.]

PRAYER.

O Sovereign God, Who sittest on the throne of mercy and governest with benevolence, deign to view our labors in the cause of virtue and humanity with the eye of compassion! Purify our hearts, and cause us to know and to serve Thee aright. Guide us in the paths of rectitude and honor. Rectify our errors, and enable us to practice the precepts of Masonry, that all our actions may be acceptable in Thy sight! Amen.

FINIS.

FACSIMILE

ROYAL ARCH EXALTATION.

FACSIMILE

The old ceremony of the Royal Arch is faithfully and fully set out in Carlisle's "MANUAL," (sent with this.) In 1835 the Royal Arch Degree was re-modeled and the following pages are evidently taken from some poor copy of the authorized present mode of working. As a whole it is pretty nearly correct—in all its essentials it is quite so—but in some of its language it is imperfect as not being STRICTLY in accordance with the speeches as now given. Still—for the purposes of comparison with the older work—it is sufficiently creditable to set an enquirer on the right track. Want of time, alone, induces me to send it so as to obviate the labour of writing that which would be identical in spirit but occasionally varied in diction. The passing of the veils are altogether abandoned. All the rest is in order.

☩ *MATTHEW COOKE, XXX°.*

I have erased, or notified in red ink, the most palpable inaccuracies.

FACSIMILE

The Honorable M. P. Sov. G. Com.,

BRO. ⨳ ALBERT PIKE, XXXIII°,

Southern Jurisdiction,

FROM HIS ADMIRING BROTHER,

✝ MATTHEW COOKE, XXX°, P. M., P. Z.

REPRINTS OF RITUALS OF OLD DEGREES

CEREMONY OF
EXALTATION.

———◦◦❊◦◦———

N. There is a report, M. E.

Z. See who seeks admission.

N. Without the door of this Chapter is Br. A. B., who has been regularly iniated into Masonry, passed the second, and in due time raised to the sublime degree of a M. M., and in that character, during twelve months and upwards, has made himself proficient therein, and has been intrusted with a test of merit, by which he seeks admission to this R. A. C.

Z. Do you vouch that he is in possession thereof?

N. I do.

Z. Then let him be admitted with all due caution, on the five ps. of f . . p.

[The Candidate is then admitted, and stands in the West.]

Z. Masonry being free in all its degrees, I demand of you, first, whether you now present yourself freely and voluntarily, uninfluenced by any unworthy motives, to participate with us in the mysteries of this supreme degree?

A. I do.

Z. Do you likewise seriously declare, upon your honour, that if admitted amongst us, you will abide by the ancient usages and customs of the Order?

A. I will.

Z. Then let the Can. k . . l while we implore a blessing of the Most High.

S. E. O, Almighty and Eternal Lord God, at whose command the world burst forth from chaos to perfection, the Protector of all who put their trust in Thee,

8

without whom nothing is strong, nothing holy, we, Thy unworthy servants, humbly implore Thee to look on this Convocation assembled in Thy Most Holy Name, and grant that he who kneels before Thee as a Candidate for the sacred mysteries of this Supreme Degree may so consider his present undertaking that he proceed not lightly in it, nor recede from it dishonourably, but pursue it steadfastly, ever remembering the object and intent of the Institution, obedience to Thy sacred laws. Grant unto us the knowledge of Thy truth, that Thou being our Ruler and Guide, we may so pass through things temporal, as finally not to lose the things eternal.

Z. In whom do you rely for support?

A. In the true and living God Most High.

Z. Let the Candidate be led round the Chap. and placed in the West. [Which is done.]

Z. As you seek to be admitted to the mysteries of this Sublime Degree, I must call on you to advance to the E., and to the sacred shrine, and that you will do by seven s . . s thrice h. and b . . g at the 3d, 5th and 7th, for be assured that every s . . p brings you nearer the ineffable name of the Deity. [Which is done.]

Z. You are now arrived at the crown of a vaulted chamber, from which you will remove two of the cape stones, and that you will figuratively do by pulling the cord or life line round your body three times for each stone. [Which is done.]

Z. Let the Can. be lowered into the vault, and be attentive while certain portions of the Scripture are read.

[E. then reads Prov. 2, ver. 1 to 9 inclusive, and 3d chap., ver. 13 to 25 inclusive.]

Z. You will now lean forward on your l . . t hand, and search round with the right.

P. S. It is found.

Z. What have you found?

P. S. Being deprived of light I am unable to say.

Z. Let the want of light remind you that man by nature is the child of ignorance and error, and as such would ever so remain under the darkness and shadow of death unless it had pleased the Almighty to call him to light and immortality by the revelation of His most Holy Word and Divine will. Arise, therefore, and wrench forth the third cape stone as before.

9

Z. Let the Candidate be again lowered as before into the vault, and be attentive to another portion of Scripture.

[Hag. 2, vs. 1 to 9 inclusive.]

Z. I now demand of you whether you are prepared and willing to take and enter into a solemn ob . . n to keep inviolate the secrets and mysteries of this order?

[To which, having assented, kneels on . . knee.]

OBLIGATION.

I, A. B., in the presence of the Most High, and before this Chap. of the supreme order of H. R. A. of Israel, regularly constituted and properly dedicated, of my own free will and accord, do hereby and hereon most solemnly and sincerely swear, that I never will divulge any of the secrets and mysteries belonging to this supreme degree, denominated the H. R. A. of I., to any individual whomsoever, unless it be to a lawful Compa. of the Order, whom I shall find to be such after due examination, or in the body of a lawful constituted Chap. regularly assembled. I furthermore do promise and swear that I will not dare to pronounce that sacred and mysterious N . . of the M. H. which now for the first time may be communicated to me, unless it be in the presence of two or more Coms. of the Order, or when acting in open Chap. as First Principal, under no less penalty than having my . . cleave to the . . , and my s . . s . . off, sooner than I would at any time knowingly or willingly violate the same. So help me Most High.

Z. In your present state, what are you most desirous of?

Can. Light.

Z. Let that blessing be restored in the West. [Which is performed.]

Z. I will thank you to read the scroll.

Can. In the beginning God created, etc.

Z. Such, my brethren, are the first words of that sacred volume, which contains the treasure of God's revealed will and word. Let us therefore praise and magnify His Holy Name for the knowledge of himself which he has vouchsafed unto us, and let us walk in that light which has shone around us. You may now retire with the P. S., and accompany him through a ceremony that will inform you how the sacred word was discovered. The s . . gs and Can. retire.

[A report is heard.]

N. [Rises and turning to the M. E. says:] There is a report.

10

Z. See who is there.

N. [Partly opens the door, and after ascertaining, says to the M. E. :] Without the entrance of the Chapter are three M. M. from B . . n.

Z. Let them be admitted.

Z. Whence come you ?

P. S. From B . . n.

Z. And your request ?

P. S. Having heard that you are about to rebuild the Temple of the Lord God of Israel, we have come up to sojourn amongst you, and to offer our services in that great and glorious undertaking.

Z. Before we can accept your services, we must inform you that on no account can strangers be permitted to assist in that most holy work. I demand more fully who you are ?

P. S. Brethren of your tribes and families.

Z. But are you descended from those who basely fled when the Holy City and the Temple were oppressed, or of that menial tribe left behind to till the land by the B. G.

P. S. We would scorn to be descended from those who fled when the Temple and the Holy City were oppressed; neither are we of that menial tribe left behind to till the land by the B. G.; but we are nobly born, and, like yourselves, descended from a race of patriarchs and kings. A., I. and Jacob were our forefathers. M. E., we are descended from the princes and rulers of Judah, who, for their sins and those of their forefathers, were led into captivity with their king Jehoachin by Nabuzaradan, captain of the guard of Nebuchadnezzar, King of Babylon, where we were to remain for seventy years, as foretold by the prophet Jeremiah; and then return to our native land and there dwell, our captivity having expired. In the first year of the reign of Cyrus, King of Persia, when it pleased the Almighty to inspire the mind of that young Prince to issue a proclamation, saying, All the kingdoms of the earth hath the Lord God of Israel given me, and hath commanded me to build Him a house in Jerusalem, which is in Judea: who are there amongst you of all His people, the Lord his God be with him, let him go up. We eagerly availed ourselves of his permission, and we are come up accordingly to offer our assistance in rebuilding the temple of the Lord God, who hath promised by the mouth of his prophet to establish there His name for ever, and give peace to the whole earth.

Z. We congratulate you on your noble ancestry, and recognize you as brethren of our tribes and families; it remains for us to enquire in what department of the building you seek to be employed.

11

P. S. Any to which your Excellency may appoint.

Z. Your humility is an indication of your merit, and we doubt not of your being qualified for offices of importance, but from the lateness of your application, as they are already filled, we therefore appoint you to prepare for the foundation of the most holy place, for which purpose you will be furnished with the requisite implements, strictly enjoining that should you discover any relics of the ancient structure, you will communicate it to none, but immediately report it to us sitting in council.

P. S. We cheerfully accept the trust reposed in us, and will endeavor to evince our gratitude by our zeal and fidelity.

Z. Go; and may the God of your fathers be with you and prosper your work.

[They retire. A report is given, when N., having ascertained the cause, makes the following address:]

N. M. E., without the door are three M. M., who have made a discovery.

Z. Let them be admitted.

Z. We understand you have made a discovery ?

P. S. Early this morning, on resuming our labour, we discovered a pair of pillars of exquisite workmanship; proceeding onwards we discovered six other pairs of equal beauty, and from their position appeared to us to have supported the roof of a subterranean passage, communicating with the most holy place; our progress being then obstructed by the fragment of the former structure, and having cleared them away, we arrived at what at first had the appearance of a solid rock, but accidentally striking it with the crow I remarked a hollow sound. I therefore hailed my companions, who, with the pickaxe, loosened the earth for some distance, which my companion with a spade cleared away, when we perceived that instead of a solid rock there were a series of stones in the form of a dome. Aware who was the architect of the former structure, and that no part of it had been constructed in vain, we determined to examine it, and for which purpose we removed two of the cap stones, when a vault of considerable magnitude appeared to view, and we determined on a descent. All being desirous, we cast lots who should. The lot, M. E., fell on me, and lest any noxious vapours, or other causes, should render my position unsafe, my companions fastened this cord or life-line round my waist, by which they could lower me into the vault or raise me out according to the signal I gave to my r . . t or l . . t hand companion. In this manner I descended through the aperture which we had made, and on arriving at the bottom I gave the agreed on signal, and my companions gave me more line, which enabled me to encompass the vault, and I felt something in the form of a pedestal of a column, and could also feel certain char-

12

acters thereon, but for the want of light I was unable to discover what they were. I also laid hold of this scroll, but from the same cause I was unable to read its contents; I therefore gave another preconcerted signal and was drawn up, and on arriving in the light of day we discovered from the first sentence of the scroll that it contained the volume of the Most Holy Law, which had been promulgated by our G. M. M. at the foot of Mount Sinai. This precious treasure stimulated our exertions still further; we increased the aperture by the removal of other stones, and I again descended into the vaulted chambers. The sun had now gained its altitude, and darted its rays of light more immediately into the aperture, and I then perceived a pedestal of pure virgin marble in the form of an altar of incense—that of a double cube. On the front thereof were engraven the names of the three Grand Masters who presided over the Sacred Lodge, and certain mystic characters engraved on its plinth, whilst a veil covered the face of the altar. Approaching with reverential awe, I lifted the veil, and beheld what I humbly conceived to be the sacred word itself. Having made this discovery, I replaced the veil on the sacred pedestal, and was again raised out of the vaulted chamber, and with their assistance closed the entrance, and I am now come to report to your Excellency.

Z. Give us the word you discovered.

P. S. That, Most Excellent, we would wish to decline, for we have heard with our ears, and our forefathers have declared unto us, that in their days, and in the old time before them, that it was not lawful for any but the H. P. to mention the name of the living God, nor him but once in every year, when he entered the holy of holies, and stood before the ark of the covenant, to make propitiation for the sins of Israel.

Z. We commend your pious caution, and will commission certain of our companions to examine and report to us the extent of your discovery.

[The sojourners now retire to the extremity of the Chap. with E. and N., and on their return, after having unveiled the pedestal, they, E. and N., address the M. E., and say it is correct.]

Z. Companions E. and N., divest them of the implements of labour, clothe them with the robes of innocence and truth, and instruct them to advance towards us.

[They are now clothed in white, and advancing, bow at every step, showing the reverential sign when in front of the Principals.]

Z. It is my duty to inform you that the Grand and Holy Chapter of R. A. Masons of Israel, in recompense for your zeal and fidelity, now call you to the

13

rank held by your great and illustrious ancestors. I first present you with this Jewel, the Square, in token of our esteem and approbation.

H. And I present you with this Ribbon, the Badge of our Order.

J. And I present you this Staff, to be borne by you as a sceptre, denoting power and royalty, which you will be ever entitled to bear, unless seventy-two of your elders be present, and we hereby constitute you princes and rulers; and to ennoble you yet more, receive you as companions of this august assembly or council, and if we find you faithful to your trust, will admit you by regular gradations to the full participation of our mysteries.

P. S. Thus invested and entrusted by your Excellencies and this grand assembly, we will endeavour to evince our integrity and zeal by a regular discharge of the duties of our exalted station.

ADDRESS OF THE THIRD CHAIR.

J. There are three epochs in Masonry which peculiarly merit your attention— the history of the First or Holy Lodge, the second or Sacred Lodge, and the third or Grand and Royal Lodge.

The first or Holy Lodge was opened Anno Lucis 2415, two years after the departure of the children of Israel from their Egyptian bondage, by Moses, Aholiab and Bezaliel, on consecrated ground, at the foot of Mount Horeb, in the Wilderness of Sinai, where the host of Israel pitched their tents and assembled to offer up their prayers and thanksgivings for their signal deliverance from the hands of the Egyptians. In this place the Almighty had revealed himself before, to his faithful servant Moses, when He commissioned him His high ambassador of wrath against Pharoah and his people, and of freedom and salvation to the house of Jacob. Here were delivered the forms of those mysterious prototypes, the tabernacle and the ark of the covenant; here were also delivered the sacred law, engraven by the hands of the Most High, with those sublime and comprehensive precepts of religious and moral duty, and here also were dictated by His unerring wisdom those peculiar forms of a religious and civil polity which, by separating his favourite people from all other nations, consecrated Israel a chosen people for his service. For these reasons we denominate this the first or Holy Lodge.

14

SECOND OR SACRED LODGE.

J. Solomon, King of Israel; Hiram, King of Tyre; and H. Abiff presided over the second or Sacred Lodge, opened Anno Lucis 2992, in the bosom of the holy Mount Moriah, under the very centre of the place where the solemn Sanhedrim was afterwards erected. On this consecrated spot Abraham proved his constructive faith by leading his only and beloved son a destined victim on the altar of his God. Here, on the threshing floor of Arunah the Jebusite, David offered the mediatorial sacrifice by which the plague was stayed; and here he received in a vision the plan of that glorious temple which was afterwards completed by his illustrious son; and in this place had God declared he would establish his most holy name, therefore we distinguish this the Sacred or Second Lodge.

THIRD OR GRAND AND ROYAL LODGE.

J. The Grand and Royal Lodge was holden at Jerusalem, and opened Anno Lucis 3469, after the return of the Israelites from captivity, under Zerubabbel, the prince of the people; Haggai, the prophet; and Joshua, the son of Josedech, the high priest. Now it was that the kingly power was restored in the person of Zerubabbel to the royal tribe of David, and the princely line of Judah; nor was there again any vestige effaced until the destruction of Jerusalem by the Romans under Titus, in the seventieth year of the Christian era, thereby verifying the prediction of Judah, in Egypt, that the sceptre should not depart from Judah, nor a lawgiver from beneath his feet, until Shiloah came to commemorate this restoration. It is called the Third, or Grand and Royal Lodge, and the resemblance in the Chapter before us represent those great originals that is in every regular R. A. Chapter. We acknowledge the representation of the Grand and Royal Lodge at Jerusalem in the persons of the three Principals, Zerubabbel, Haggai and J., whose names they also bear. The two Scribes represent Ezra and Nehemiah, the expounders of the sacred law, and attendants on the august Sanhedrim, by whose names they also are designated. Yourselves (addressing the three sojourners) represent the faithful sojourners by whom the secrets of the R. Arch were discovered, and for which they were honoured with a seat in the august assembly, composed of the rulers and elders of the people, represented by the rest of the Companions now present.

15

SYMBOLIC EXPLANATION.

H. The forms, symbols and ornaments of R. A. Masonry, as well as the rites and ceremonies at present in use amongst us were adopted by our predecessors at the building of the second Temple, as well to preserve in our minds the providential means by which the grand discovery was effected, as in our hearts the lessons of that exalted morality which, as members of this supreme degree, we are bound to practice. The form in which the Companions of every R. A. Chapter are arranged approach, as near as circumstances will admit, to that of the true catenarian arch. Thus we preserve the memorial of the vaulted shrine, in which the sacred word was deposited, which, from the impenetrable nature of the strongest of all architectural forms, we learn the necessity of guarding our mysteries from profanation by the most inviolable secrecy. It also strongly typifies that adherence to order, and the spirit of fraternal union, has given energy and permaneney to the constitutions of Masonry, enabling it to survive the wreck of mighty empires, and resist the destroying hand of time. And as the subordinate members of the catenarian arch naturally gravitate to the centre, or key stones, which compress or cement the whole structure, so are we taught to look up with reverence, and submit with cheerfulness, to every lawfully constituted authority, whether Masonic or civil regulation. The cape stones are represented by the three Principals of the Chapter, for, as the knowledge of the secrets contained in the vaulted chamber could only be obtained by the drawing forth of the three first of a series of stones, therefore the complete knowledge of this supreme Order can only be obtained by passing through those several offices. In this degree we acknowledge six l . . s. The three lesser together represent the light of the law and the prophets, and by their number allude to the patriarchal, mosaical and prophetical dispensations. The three greater representing the S. W. itself. These l . . s are placed in the form of an equilateral t . . e, each of the lesser intersecting the line formed by two of the greater, thus geometrically dividing the greater t . . e into three lesser t . . e on the extremities, which, by their union, form a fourth t . . e in the centre, all of them equal and equilateral. This symbolical arrangement corresponds to the mysterious T. H., or triple Tau, which forms two right angles on each of the exterior lines, and two others at their centre, by their union, for the three angles of each t . . e are equal to two right angles. This illustrates the jewel worn by the Companions of the Order, which forms, by its intersections, a given number of angles. These may be taken in five several combinations, and when reduced into their amount in right angles, will be found equal to the five platonic bodies which represent the four elements, and the sphere of the universe.

16

The ribbon worn by the Companions of the Order is a sacred emblem denoting light, being composed of two different or principal colours, with which the veil of the Temple was also interwoven. The same is further signified by its irradiated form; and in both these respects it has ever been considered as an emblem of royal power and dignity. The ensigns which the Companions bear on their staves were the distinguished bearings of the twelve tribes of Israel, and figurativaly of the peculiar blessings bequeathed to each by the patriarch Jacob, who, before his death, assembled them together for that purpose, as we find recorded in the 49th chapter of Genesis.

The principal banners are the standards of the leading tribes of the four divisions of the army of Israel, and unitedly bear a device of an angelic nature, under the combined figures of a man, a lion, an ox and an eagle—a man to represent integrity and understanding, a lion to personify strength and power, an ox to denote the ministration of patience and assiduity, and an eagle to display the promptness and celerity with which the will and pleasure of the Creator are ever executed. A detail of the tribes attached to each division, and names of their commanders, will be found in the 2d chapter of Numbers. The bearings of the sceptres denote the regal, prophetical, and sacredotal offices, which are now, and still ought to be, conferred in a peculiar manner, and accompanied with the possession of particular secrets. The B . . e, C . . s, and S . . e are considered as appropriate emblems of the three Grand Masters who founded the first Temple. The B. denotes the wisdom of King Solomon, the S. the power of Hir. of Tyre, and Com. the exquisite skill of H. A. But the truly speculative Mason regards them as the mysterious symbols of the wisdom, truth, and justice of the Most High. His wisdom is most amply exemplified in the S. V., which contains the records of His mighty acts, and in the treasure of His revealed will. His truth is as justly represented by the S., it being the acknowledged symbol of strength, and the criterion of perfection; and H. is impartial and unerring justice, which has accurately defined the limits of good and evil, assigning to each its due proportion of pleasure and pain, and is elucidated by the C . . s, which alone enables us to ascertain the limits of all geometrical forms, and to reduce our ideas of proportion and equality to a certain standard. The S . . d and T . . l are adopted by R. A. Masons to commemorate the valour of those worthy Masons who carried on the building of the second Temple, with a T . . l in their hands, and a S . . by their sides, that they might be ever ready to defend the holy city and sanctuary against the unprovoked attacks of their enemies, by which they have left a sacred and impressive lesson to succeeding ages, that, next to obedience due to lawful authority, is a manly and determined resistance to lawless violence—the first step to social duties.

17

The pickaxe, crowbar and shovel were the implements used by the sojourners to clear away for the foundation of the second Temple—the pickaxe to loosen the earth, the crowbar to take purchases, and the shovel to clear away the rubbish.

These we spiritualize thus: The sound of the stroke of the pickaxe reminds us of the sound of the last trumpet, when the graves shall be shaken, opened, and deliver up its dead.

The crowbar, being an emblem of uprightness, represents the erect manner in which the body shall arise on that awful day to meet its tremendous but merciful judge.

The mortal state in which the body is laid in the grave is powerfully impressed on our minds by the work of the shovel, so that when the rubbish of the body shall be properly disposed of, we, with holy confidence, hope the spirit will arise into immortal and eternal life.

MYSTIC EXPLANATION GIVEN BY THE FIRST CHAIR.

Z. The mystic knowledge of this degree comprehends the form and explanation of the sacred S . . s, the nature and import of the Holy W . . d, and the traditional ceremony used in sharing and communicating our secrets in R. A. Masonry. There are five S . . s, corresponding in number to the five points of fellowship, in which the M. Mason is instructed, and as those point out to us the relative duties we owe to each other, so do the s . . s of a R. A. Mason mark, in a peculiar manner, the relation we bear to the Almighty as creatures offending against His power, yet the adopted children of His mercy.

[Now follows the five s . . s, viz: First, the penal; second, the hailing or reverential; third, the penitential or supplicatory; fourth, the monitorial; fifth, the fiducial.]

THE FIRST OR PENAL SIGN.

Z. The penal s . . n marks our O. B., and reminds us of the fall of Adam and the dreadful penalty entailed by all his sinful posterity, no less than death, intimated by the action itself that the stiff neck of the disobedient shall be cut off from the land of the living by the judgment of God, even as the head is severed from the body by the sword of human justice, to avert which we are taught by the

18
REVERENTIAL OR HAILING SIGN

to bend with submissive resignation beneath the chastening hand of the Almighty, and at the same time to engraft His law in our hearts. In this expressive form did the Father of the human race first present himself before the Most High to receive the denunciation of His just and terrible judgment. It was also adopted by our Grand Master Moses. When the Lord appeared to him in the burning bush, Moses covered his face from the brightness of the divine presence, and laid his hand on his h . . t in token of obedience and salutation, which was afterwards accounted to him for righteousness.

THE THIRD, PENITENTIAL OR SUPPLICATORY,

may be considered as the parent of the reverential or h . . g sign, since it justly denotes that frame of mind and heart without which our prayers and oblations of praise would not obtain acceptance at the throne of grace, before which how should a frail and erring creature of the dust present himself unless with bended knees and uplifted hands, betokening at once his humility and dependence? In this humble posture did Adam kneel to God and bless the author of his being. Thus did he bend with contrite awe before the face of his offended Judge, to avert His wrath, and conciliate His mercy, and has transmitted the sacred form to his posterity forever.

THE FOURTH OR MONITORIAL SIGN

reminds us of the weakness of human nature, unable of itself to resist the powers of darkness, unless aided by that help which is from above. By this defenceless posture we acknowledge our own frailty, and confess that we can do no good or acceptable service but through Him from whom all good counsels and just works proceed, and without whose divine and special favour we must ever be found unprofitable servants in His sight; therefore adopting the manner of our ancestors and atoning priests by this form of contrition and humility,

THE FIFTH OR FIDUCIAL SIGN,

as if we would prostrate ourselves on the face of the earth, we must throw ourselves upon the mercy of our Creator and our Judge, looking forward with confidence to His gracious promises, by which alone we hope to pass through the ark of our redemption in the presence of Him who is the great I AM, the Alpha and Omega, the beginning and the ending.

Z. On the front of the pedestal are engraven the names of the three Grand Masters who presided over the building of the former Temple, viz: Solomon, King of Israel; Hiram, King of Tyre; and Hiram Abiff, and are meant to perpetuate their names, as well as to commemorate the proceedings during the erection of the former Temple. There is likewise a triple Tau, or letter T, a mark or character affixed to the summons of R. A. Masons, when summoned on other than usual occasions. The triple Tau, or letter T, is translated from the Hebrew, a mark or sign spoken of by Ezekiel, when he said to the man with the ink-horn, "Go thy way through the midst of the city of Jerusalem, and set a mark on all those who sigh and lament for the abominations thereof." By which mark they were saved from among those who were slain for their idolatry by the wrathful displeasure of the Host High.

In ancient times this mark was placed on the forehead of all those who were acquitted by their judges, as a proof of their innocence; and military commanders caused a T to be placed on all those who had escaped unhurt from the field of battle, denoting that they were in perfect life. The union of the three T's alludes to the grand tri-union of the Deity, by whom the horrific, gloomy, and unshaped chaos was changed into form and existence.

Z., (continues.) The w . . d you observe on the t . . e is the sacred word, which you have promised and S. never to divulge without the assistance of two or more R. A. M. lawfully congregated, constituted, and dedicated, which, as Principal of this Chapter, I am authorized to pronounce. It is in itself a compound w . . d, and its combination forms the word J. B. O. J. is the Chaldean name of G., signifying His essence of Majesty incomprehensible; it is also a Hebrew w . . d, signifying I am, and shall be, thereby expressing the actual future and eternal existence of the Most High. B. is an Assyrian w . . d, signifying Lord, or powerful; it is also a compound w . . d, from the proposition Beth, which signifies in or on heaven, or on high; therefore this w . . d means Lord in heaven or on high. O. is an Egyptian w . . d, signifying father of all; it is also an Hebrew w . . d, implying strength and power, and expressive of the omnipotence of the Father of all. Taking each together will read this, I AM, and shall be Lord in heaven, Father of all, in every age, in every clime adored, by savage and by sage; Jehovah, Jove, or Lord. The w . . d on the c . . e is the grand, awful, tremendous, and incomprehensible name of the Most High, signifying I AM, the beginning and the ending, which was, and is to come, the actual, future and all-

20

sufficient God, who alone has His living in and out of Himself, and gives to all others their being; that he was and shall be both what he was, and what he is, from everlasting to everlasting, all the creation being dependent on His mighty will. The c . . e typifies the omnipotent and Almighty Author of the universe, having neither beginning nor ending; it also calls to our remembrance the grand and awful hereafter, or futurity, where we hope to enjoy endless bliss and everlasting life. The characters which are placed on each angle of the D . . e are Hebrew, and particularly worthy of your attention. The Aleph, answering to our A, the Beth to our B, and the Lamed to our L; take the Aleph and the Beth, and they form the w . . d Ab, meaning Father, the Aleph and Lamed the w . . d Al, which means word; take the Lamed, the Aleph, and the Beth, they form the word Lab, meaning Spirit; take the Beth, Aleph, and Lamed, the word Bul, meaning Lord; take each a . . e of the t . . , they will form the following sentences—Father Lord, Word Lord, Spirit Lord.

The t . . e was, in the days of Pythagoras, esteemed as the most sacred of all emblems, and when any oath of more than usual import was to be administered, it was given on the t . . e, and when so administered none were ever known to have violated it. The ancient Egyptians called it the sacred number three, or number of perfection, and it was an object of worship amongst the ancients as the grand principle of animated existence, and they gave it the name of God, representing the animal, vegetable, and mineral creation; it was also called Avolet, that is to say, the soul of nature. The sacred delta is usually placed in the midst of squares and circles, indicating the vivifying principle, extending its ramifications throughout all created matter; it is therefore, denominated the great all, or summum bonum,

THE CLIMAX OF ROYAL ARCH MASONRY.

This sublime degree is the climax of Masonry, and is intimately blended with all that is near and dear to us in another state of existence. Our divine and human affairs are interwoven so awfully and so minutely in all its disquisitions. It has virtue for its aim, the glory of God its object, and the eternal welfare of man is considered in every point or letter of its ineffable mysteries. Suffice it to say that this degree is founded on the name of J . . h, who was from all eternity, is now, and shall be one and the same for ever, the being naturally existing of and for himself, all actual perfection originally in His essence.

FACSIMILE

21

This sublime degree inspires its members with the most exalted ideas of God, and leads to the exercise of the most pure and sublime piety; a reverence for the incomprehensible J . . h, the eternal ruler of the universe, the elemental life, the primordial source of all its principles, the very spring and fountain of all its virtues.

SCRIPTURE READING REFERRED TO AT PAGE 8.

"My son, if thou wilt receive my words, and hide my commandments with me; so that thou incline thine ear unto wisdom, and apply thine heart to understanding; yea, if thou criest after knowledge, and liftest up thy voice for understanding; if thou seekest her as silver, and searchest for her as for hid treasures; then shalt thou understand the fear of the Lord and find the knowledge of God. For the Lord giveth wisdom: out of his mouth cometh knowledge and understanding. He layeth up sound wisdom for the righteous: he is a buckler to them that walk uprightly. He keepeth the paths of judgment and preserveth the way of His saints. Then shalt thou understand righteousness, and judgment, and equity; yea, every good path.

"Happy is the man that findeth wisdom, and the man that getteth understanding. For the merchandise of it is better than the merchandise of silver, and the gain thereof than fine gold. She is more precious than rubies; and all the things thou canst desire are not to be compared unto her. Length of days is in her right hand; and in her left hand riches and honour. Her ways are ways of pleasantness, and all her paths are peace. She is a tree of life to them that lay hold upon her, and happy is every one that retaineth her. The Lord by wisdom hath founded the earth; by understanding hath he established the heavens. By his knowledge the depths are broken up, and the clouds drop down the dew."

SCRIPTURE READING REFERRED TO AT PAGE 9.

"In the seventh month, in the one and twentieth day of the month, came the word of the Lord by the prophet Haggai, saying, Speak now to Zerubbabel, the son of Shealtiel, governor of Judah, and to Joshua, the son of Josedech, the high priest, and to the residue of the people, saying, who is left among you that saw this

22

house in her first glory? and how do ye see it now? Is it not in your eyes in comparison of it as nothing? Yet now be strong, O Zerubbabel, saith the Lord; and be strong, O Joshua, son of Josedech, the high priest; and be strong, all ye people of the land, saith the Lord, and work; for I am with you saith the Lord of Hosts; according to the word that I covenanted with you when ye came out of Egypt, so my spirit remaineth among you; fear ye not. For thus saith the Lord of Hosts, Yet once it is a little while, and I will shake the heavens, and the earth and the sea and the dry land. And I will shake all nations, and the desire of all nations shall come; and I will fill this house with glory, saith the Lord of Hosts. The silver is mine, and the gold is mine, saith the Lord of Hosts. The glory of this latter house shall be greater than that of the former, saith the Lord of Hosts; and in this place will I give peace, saith the Lord of Hosts."

TO CLOSE THE CHAPTER.

The M. E. asks if there is anything to offer for the benefit of the Chapter. After ascertaining there is not, he says, We do agree, in love and unity, &c., which is repeated by the Companions. He then gives one knock with his sceptre, which is followed by one each by H. and J. The M. E. then gives another, making together four, and says to the Principal Sojourners: The labours of the evening being ended, you have my commands to close the Chapter.

P. S. In the name of the Most High, and by command of the M. E., I close the Chapter until——

Each Comp. salutes the Volume of the Sacred Law, ending with the M. E. Z.

One of the Past Z's comes forward and says: Nothing remains, &c., the same as in Craft Masonry, repeating fidelity four times.

FACSIMILE

WIGAN RITUAL

OF

THE EARLY GRAND ENCAMPMENT.

REPRINTS OF RITUALS OF OLD DEGREES

FACSIMILE

Presented to his dear friend and Brother, the Ill. Bro. ☩ Albert Pike, M. P. Sov. G. Com. XXXIII° Southern Jurisdiction,

BY

☩ MATTHEW COOKE, XXX°, P. M., P. Z.,
England.

FACSIMILE

How I Came by this Ritual.

Five years ago I delivered a Lecture on Templary and Free-Masonry, (see accompanying card of admission,) and several Sir Knights gave me all the information they could, believing the matter to be of considerable interest. In this way the working book of the Priory of Ayr, (Scotland,) was sent me to copy, and very curious it is as a hybrid ritual, embracing points of both the Chivalric and Masonic Rites.

Sir Knight John Yarker also sent this, but as it is so closely written I could not read from it, and, therefore, copied it out afresh, so that I retain a copy of it, and he had made his copy, (this one,) from a copy made by Sir Knight P. L. Bold, of this ritual preserved at Wigan, in Lancashire, bearing date A. D., 1801, and professing to be but itself a copy of a more ancient manuscript.

Of course my "Masonic Press" had not then been published, and when Sir Knight Yarker contributed those papers to it on the Manchester Encampment, (the Jerusalem,) he alluded to this ritual.

Now he has republished the same under the title of "Notes on the Temple," &c., (sent herewith.) Page 25 will tell all he knows of his ritual; but here you have it in his own hand as a copy from a copy from another copy of older date: and that is how it came into the hands of

☩ *MATTHEW COOKE, XXX°.*

THE ORDER OF HIGH KNIGHTS TEMPLAR consists of twenty-one members, assembled in Grand Chapter and Royal Encampment. The Grand Master or Captain General is the head, with Captains commanding, Standard Bearers, &c. At all positions (processions) are carried a sword and scabbard, with a blue silk cushion fringed with black. Each Knight a broad ribbon across the breast, hanging down the left side, tied with a ribbon in a bow knot, with the Star of the Order on the left breast. At the bottom of the ribbon or scarf hangs a short sword or dagger; also, the image or picture of St. John hangs pendant to a blue silk ribbon at the middle of the breast. The habit and ensign of the Order are: A marble girdle, cup, star and garter and cross. The Cross or Star of the Order is made of blue silk twist, with gold, irradiated with beams of blue. The Knights of the Order are esteemed clearly the greatest military order in the world.

The manner of electing a Knight of this Order is, when the Grand Master or Captain General, with the consent of the whole, desire to install a candidate, he draws a Letter on which is the Seal or Cross of the Order, which is sent to the candidate, as follows:

CONCLAVE OF ――, A. D. 1801.

We, the Captain General, &c., &c., of the Grand Encampment of the Most Noble, Holy, Invincible and Magnanimous Order of High Knights Templar, at our Castle, Conclave or Encampment, in ――――, Commanding, to A. B. send greeting: For the zeal and fidelity you have shown in our rights in Masonry, we have elected you to become one of this Order. Therefore we require and command you to repair to us at our Castle, Conclave or Encampment aforesaid on ――day, the ―― day of ――, A. D. 1801, at ―― o'clock, to be installed and receive the Ensigns of the Order.

Given at, &c., &c.

Signed: A. B., *Captain General.*

OPENINGS, &c.

C. G. to G. M. The Grand Master's place in the Encampment?

G. M. At the south angle.

C. G. His business there?

G. M. To marshal the Knights according to the order of the Captain General and accompany them to the battle.

C. G. to the H. Priest. The High Priest's place in the Encampment?

H. P. In the West.

C. G. Why in the West?

H. P. Because the Sanctum Sanctorum or Holy of Holies was placed in the west end of the Tabernacle, so is the High Priest placed in the west end of the Encampment to make atonement for the sins of the people.

C. G. The Captain General's place in the Encampment?

H. P. At the right angle.

C. G. His business there?

H. P. To put the Knights in battle array and lead them forth to fight against all Jews, Turks and Infidels, and the enemies of the Holy Christian religion.

C. G. In the name of $\triangle$ I pronounce this, &c., &c.

Almighty and everlasting God, who of Thy great goodness did send thy faithful soldier and servant, St. John of Jerusalem, to prepare the way of Jesus Christ, our blessed Redeemer, grant that we, by his imitation, may constantly speak the truth, boldly rebuke vice and vanquish our enemies, both of body and soul, and be crowned with eternal glory; and grant, O Lord, that as we are baptised into the death of Thy blessed Son, our Saviour Jesus Christ, who for our sakes was contented to be betrayed and given up into the hands of wicked men, and to suffer death upon the cross, so by continual mortifying our corrupt affections, we may be buried with Him, and that through the grave and the Gate of Death we may pass to our joyful resurrection thro' His merits, who suffered, died and was buried, and rose again for us, Thy dear Son Jesus Christ. Grant, O Lord,

8

that this candidate for the mysteries of our blessed Saviour's birth, passion, death and resurrection and ascension, may ever hold fast to the profession of a Christian, and boldly fight under the banner of Christ, and become a true, faithful and valiant Knight Companion amongst us. This we beg for the sake of Thy dear son Jesus Christ. Amen.

THE CHRISTIAN ARMOR.

Read Ephesians, 6 c. 10 to 18 vv—

"Be strong in the Lord, and in the power of His might," &c., &c.

Q. Worthy Knights of the Order of St. John of Jerusalem, please to attend to the introduction and explain the ceremonies of your installment. Where was you prepared to be a Knight Companion of the Order of St. John?

A. In a room adjoining a Royal Encampment of Knights of St. John, called Knights Templar.

Q. How was you habited?

A. As a pilgrim, with sandals on my feet, a mantle round my body, a girdle round my waist, a cap on my head, a scrip on my back, and a staff in my hand.

Q. How got you admission into a Knights Templar Encampment?

A. By IIIII distinct knocks and a pass-word.

Q. What was said to you from within?

A. A poor pilgrim from afar.

Q. From whence come you?

A. From the wilderness of Judea.

Q. Where are you going?

A. To the Temple of the Holy Sepulchre of Christ at Jerusalem.

Q. What are you going there to do?

A. To pray for the pardon of my sins and the sins of the people.

Q. In whom do you believe?

A. I believe in God the Father, the Creator of Heaven and Earth, and of all things visible and invisible, and in Jesus Christ, the only begotten Son of God, begotten of his Father before all worlds, God of God, Light of Lights, very God of very God, who, for as men and our salvation, came down from Heaven and was made man, was crucified, dead and buried, rose again and ascended into Heaven; and I believe in the Holy Ghost, the Lord and giver of life, who proceeded from the Father and the Son, who, with the Father and Son together, is worshipped and glorified.

Q. What was then asked you?

A. How I expected to gain admission.
Q. Your reply?
A. By the benefit of a pass-word.
Q. Did you give that pass-word?
A. I did.
Q. Give it to me.
A. I. H. S. V. (In hoc signo vinces.)
Q. Did you then enter the Royal Encampment?
A. No; I was ordered to wait till a report had been made to the Captain General, Captains Commanding, and the rest of the worthy Knights of a candidate's approaching; after which, I was ordered admittance.
Q. How did you enter?
A. By having a rough saw placed on my naked forehead.
Q. How was you then disposed of?
A. I was brought to the Captain General, who asked me if I was the candidate he had been apprised of, to which I answered I was.
Q. What confirmation did you give him of being so?
A. I delivered him my scrip, or invitation, as a confirmation, on which he ordered me to kneel down and receive the benefit of a prayer.
Q. What did the Grand Master or Captain General then do?
A. He read or repeated to me the Christian armour.
Q. How was you then disposed of?
A. I was led five times around the Royal Encampment, the worthy Knights guarding and defending, with their faces inward.
Q. Did any one oppose you?
A. Yes, the Captain General.
Q. How did you pass him?
A. By a second pass-word.
Q. Give it to me.
A. G . . . . . . (Golgotha.)
Q. What was you then desired to do?
A. I was ordered to kneel, with my face toward the East, my right hand on the Bible and sk., where I received the first part of the Kt. Templar's obligation.
Q. Please to repeat it.
A. I, A—— B——, &c., in the presence of the M. E. Grand Master, the Captain General, and the rest of the Knights present in this Royal Encampment of Knights Templar, dedicated to the Most Holy, Glorious and ever blessed Trinity,

10

Father, Son and Holy Ghost, three persons in one God, do hereby, &c., &c., &c., that I never will reveal the part of a Kn't. Templar to any one of the inferior degrees, except it be to a true, &c., or in an Enc. of Knts. Templar.

Q. After you had received the first part of your obligation, what was then done with you?

A. My staff was taken from me, and I was presented with a sword, my right hand still on the Bible and sk., I received the second part of my obligation.

Q. Please to repeat it?

A. I do also, &c., that I will answer and obey the sacred signs and summonses when given to me by a Brother Companion Knight Templar, or sent to me from the Grand Master or Captain General of a Knight Templar's Encampment, and that I will keep all my Brother Companion Knight Templar's secrets as my own, murder and treason excepted, and that I will not draw my Brother Knight Templars blood in anger, or cause it or suffer it to be done if in my power to prevent it, nor defame his good character, but will defend his cause, person and good name to the extent of my power. I also swear that I will defend the Royal Encampment of Knights Templar as much as lies in my power.

Q. After you had received the second part of your obligation, what did the Grand Master or Captain General do with you?

A. He raised me from that humble position, and told me he could do no more for me until I had taken a part of what I had so lately promised, viz: guarding and defending the Royal Encampment.

Q. How was you then disposed of?

A. I was led a second time around the Royal Encampment, the worthy Knights guarding and defending, with their faces outward.

Q. What was then commanded you?

A. I was commanded to kneel in the same manner as before, my right hand on the B. and sk., when I received the last part of my obligation.

Q. Please to repeat it?

A. I do, &c., that I will defend the Temple and Sepulchre of Christ at Jerusalem and the Holy Church in religion against all Turks, Jews and Infidels, and the enemies of the Gospel, as much as lies in my power, and that I will never be an apostate therefrom. All this I do, &c., under the penalties of having my head cut off and brought to the Grand Master or Captain General of a K. T. Enc. in a charger, as St. John's head was brought to King Herod, then to be sawn in two and my brains taken therefrom and put in an urn, and the S . . that cohabited with this B . . be inflicted on me if I violate my K. T. ob. So help me God and keep me steadfast therein.

11

Q. What was then done with you?

A. The Captain General dubbed me a Knight of the Order of St. John of Jerusalem or Knt. Templar, saying unto me: Your name, which was heretofore A. B, shall be no longer A. B., but Sir A. B. "In the name of the Holy Trinity, I dub, create and confirm thee a Knight of the Order of St. John of Jerusalem, the true and faithful soldier of Jesus Christ. Be faithful unto death and thou shalt receive a crown of life.

Q. How was you raised?

A. By the equal. triangle.

Q. What was then desired of you?

A. To draw my sword in defence of the Temple and Sepulchre against all Turks, Jews, Infidels and the enemies of the Gospel.

Q. What was you further ordered to do?

A. Extinguish a light and kindle another.

Q. Who did that extinguished light represent?

A. Judas Iscariot, who, after he had betrayed his Lord and Master, the light of his faith, departed from him, and his memory, should be detested by every Christian.

Q. Who did the newly kindled light represent?

A. Matthias, who was chosen by lot to fill up the place amongst the twelve disciples caused by the loss of Judas Iscariot.

Q. What was then explained to you?

A. The Cross of the Order, which I was told was the jewel of a Knt. Templar; also, the letters I. H. S.—Jesus Hominum Salvator, or Jesus the Saviour of men—which I was told was the mark of a Knt. Templar summons.

Q. What did you next receive?

A. The signs of a Knt. Templar.

Q. What are they?

A. 1st, the Penal Sign; 2d, the Defending Sign; 3d, the Agony Sign; 4th, the Nailing Sign; 5th, the Crucifixion Sign; 6th, the Bloody Sign; 7th, the Deadly Sign; 8th, the Ascension or Grand Sign.

Q. What was next given to you?

A. The grip or word of a Knt. Templar.

Q. How was you next disposed of?

A. I was ordered to traverse Bros Land seven times round the Captain, the rest of the worthy Knights in company.

Q. What did the Captain General then say to you?

A. He told me it was the usual custom for worthy Knights to be courteous

12

to strangers, and supposing I had traveled far, they had provided some refreshment for me, on which he presented me with a glass of liquor, telling me to drink to the immortal memory of S. K. I., H. K. T., H. A. B. and St. John of Jerusalem, the faithful soldier and servant of Jesus Christ.

Q. After you had drank to the immortal memory of these great personages, did the Captain General invest you with anything?

A. He invested me with a star and garter or scarf, saying: To the Great Omnipotent, and in memorial of St. John of Jerusalem, wear for thy renown this noble garter as a symbol of this illustrious Order, never to be forgotten or laid aside, whereby thou mayest be admonished to be courageous, and having undertaken a part against the enemies of Christ Jesus, our Lord and great redeemer, thou mayest ever stand firm and fast to it, and valiantly and safely conquer through the Cross. Amen.

Q. What was you next invested with?

A. The image of St. John, the Captain General saying unto me: Wear this, Sir A. B. Arrayed with the image of St. John of Jerusalem, the faithful soldier and servant of Jesus Christ, by whose imitation you may ever pass through both prosperous and advantageous adventures, and having vanquished the enemies both of body and soul, thou mayest not only receive the reward of this transient combat, but be crowned with a palm of eternal victory through the merits of Jesus Christ, who was dead and was buried and rose again for thee. Amen.

Q. What did you next receive?

A. A white stone, which the Captain General told me would be further explained. Rev., 2 c., 7 and 17 vs.; 3 c., 5 and 21 vs.; 21 c., 7 vs.

Q. After you had been thus installed, what did the Captain General or the High Priest explain unto you?

A. The emblems of the Order.

Q. What are they?

A. 1st, the Equilateral Triangle, in the centre of which is represented the all-seeing eye; 2d, the image of St. John of Jerusalem, the faithful soldier and servant of Jesus Christ, holding out the cup of salvation to all true believers in him; 3d, the Scull with the Cross-bones, with this motto, In Hoc Signo Vinces; 4th, the Sword and Sceptre; 5th, a Star; 6th, a Ladder of five steps resting on the Holy Bible; 7th, an Hour-glass and Scythe; 8th, an Urn; 9th, the twelve Great Lights; 10th, a White Stone; 11th, the Holy Tomb on Mount Zion; 12th, Porch belonging to the High Priest, on which is a cock; 13th, the Cross on Mount Calvary, with an ascent of five steps.

Q. What does the △ represent?

13

A. The trinity in unity—Father, Son and Holy Ghost—being co-equal, co-eternal and co-existent.

Q. What is signified by St. John holding out a cup of salvation to all believers in Christ Jesus.

A. It signifies the water of eternal life, which is fully offered to all through repentance, faith in Jesus Christ and the promises of God.

Q. What does the emblem of the Cross, with the skull and cross-bones and the motto, "In Hoc Signo Vinces," signify?

A. That by virtue of the Cross of Christ we conquer death and all our spiritual enemies through Jesus Christ our Lord.

Q. What do the sword and sceptre represent?

A. The sword of faith and the sceptre of righteousness.

Q. What does the star represent?

A. The star which appeared in the east to the four Eastern Magi or Wise Men, by which the promised Messiah or King of the Jews was born.

Q. Was that star ever foretold?

A. Yes, by the magician Balaam, when he was sent for to curse the Israelites, but God would not suffer him to curse them, and he prophesied and said, "There shall come a star out of Jacob,* and the sceptre shall rise out of Israel, out of Israel shall come he that shall have dominion, (Jacob.)

Q. Give a further description of this star?

A. When the time was accomplished that a Saviour should be born to redeem mankind, there appeared a Star in the East, which, from its magnitude and brightness, excelled in its appearance all the other stars in the heavens. It appeared in the middle region of the air, and went straight forward from the east to west, and pointed out the way for the wise men to go to Judea and pay adoration to the young child.

Q. Who did the wise men first apply to concerning the young child?

A. To King Herod, saying, Where is he that was born king of the Jews, for we have seen his star in the east, and are come to worship him? which, when Herod heard thereof, he was troubled, and all Jerusalem with him.

Q. Did Herod make any enquiries respecting the young king?

A. Yes; he gathered all the chief priests and scribes, and demanded of them where Christ should be born, and they answered him in Bethlehem of Judea, for it was written by the prophets, "And thou Bethlehem of Judea art not the least among the provinces of Judea, for out of thee shall come a governor that shall rule my people Israel."

---

*Numbers, xxiv., 17, 19 v.

14

Q. Did Herod call the wise men to him after this information ?

A. He called them privately, saying unto them, Go and search diligently for the young child, and when you have found him bring me word again that I may come and worship him also ; but at the same time he intended to murder him.

Q. What did the wise men then do ?

A. They departed, and lo the Star which they had seen in the east appeared a second time, and went before them till it came and stood over the place where the young child was, at which they rejoiced with exceeding great joy.

Q. What did the wise men then do ?

A. They went and worshipped him, and presented unto him gifts, gold, frankincense and myrrh.

Q. Why did they present unto him frankincense and myrrh ?

A. They had a mystical meaning, and designed to signify their acknowledgment both of the divinity, royalty and humanity of our blessed Saviour.

Q. Explain it ?

A. The incense was given to him as a God, the gold (myrrh ?) as a mortal man, whose body was to be embalmed therewith.

Q. Did the wise men return to Herod ?

A. They departed into their own country another way rejoicing.

Q. When Herod found himself deceived by the wise men what did he do ?

A. He fell into a violent rage, and resolved to effect by cruelty what he could not do by policy. He sent out his soldiers, and made a bloody massacre of all the children that were found in the city of Bethlehem and the neighboring towns that were two years of age and under, expecting in the general slaughter he should dispatch the young prince whose power he so much dreaded.

Q. How was the young prince preserved from his cruelty ?

A. God sent an angel to Joseph to inform him of Herod's design, and to order him to retire into Egypt with him and his mother, and there to continue till further notice.

Q. Was any other infant preserved from the bloody massacre ?

A. Yes, St. John the Baptist, the harbinger, herald and faithful soldier and servant of Jesus Christ.

Q. Whose son was he ?

A. The son of Zacharias, a priest whom Herod put to death between the porch and the altar of burnt offering for refusing to disclose the place of his son's abode, which was the wilderness of Judea.

Q. How was Zacharias' death discovered ?

A. When every one was ignorant of his murder, a certain priest, thinking he

15

stayed too long, entered the Temple and found him dead, and his blood congealed upon the ground, and at the same time hearing a voice that it should never be wiped out until his avenger came.

Q. How did God punish that bloody tyrant?

A. He afflicted him with the most painful and loathsome diseases, being smitten by God for his many iniquities in horrid pain and torment.

Q. What does the five steps resting on the Holy Bible allude to?

A. To the five different degrees or steps in Masonry, all of which have the Holy Scriptures for their groundwork or foundation.

Q. How do you apply them?

A. The three first steps allude to the three degrees in Craft Masonry, the fourth step to the degree of Royal Arch, and the fifth step to the illustrious Order of St. John of Jerusalem, in which we take a solemn O. B. to defend the Holy Sepulchre of Jerusalem and the Christian religion against all opposers of the gospel, and having fought the good fight of faith, there is laid up for us a crown of righteousness, which the Lord will give us in that day when the secrets of all hearts shall be revealed.

Q. What does the hour-glass and scythe represent?

A. The hour-glass represents the alloted period of human life.

Q. What does the urn represent?

A. It represents the hidden manna which Christ has promised to give to eat thereof, all those who overcome the temptation of the world, the flesh and the devil.

Q. What does the white stone allude to?

A. It alludes to the Greek and Roman custom of judges making their absolution by giving a white stone of innocence into the prisoner's hands, and if guilty a black stone. Pontius Pilate, contrary to his inclination, but compelled by the Jews, gave unto Christ a black stone in token of his condemnation. A white stone given by Christ, figuratively speaking, denotes a full pardon and glorious reward.

Q. What do the twelve great lights represent?

A. The twelve disciples of Christ, the twelve great lights of the Christian church. One of them was extinguished and destroyed to represent Judas Iscariot.

Q. Explain the Lamb on Mount Zion?

A. The Holy Lamb on Mount Zion is an emblem of innocence, and a type of our Lord Jesus, for we read that he was brought as a lamb to the slaughter, and as a sheep before his shearers is dumb, so opened he not his mouth; also, when Jesus went into the wilderness of Judea to be baptised of St. John, his great fore-

16

runner, John being divinely informed that he was the promised Messiah, cried out to his followers, "Behold the Lamb of God, which taketh away the sins of the world!" Further, he was the great Paschal Lamb, who was sacrificed for the sins of men that the divine vengeance of his Heavenly Father might be appeased.

Q. Explain the emblem of the cock in the porch of the High Priest's palace?

A. When our Saviour was eating the last passover with his twelve disciples, he signified that one of them should betray him, meaning Judas Iscariot. He also told them that all men should be offended with them because of him, for it was written, "I will smite the shepherd, and the sheep of the flock shall be scattered abroad." To which Peter replied, "Though all men shall be offended, yet will I not be offended, but am ready to go to prison and to death." Our Lord then said unto Peter, "Before the cock crow thou shalt deny me thrice." Peter answered him again and said, "Though I should die with thee, yet will I not deny thee." Judas Iscariot was gone from them, and covenanted to deliver him up to the Jews for thirty pieces of silver. Our Lord and the other eleven disciples withdrew themselves to the garden of Gethsemene, where they used to repair for retirement and devotion. Jesus retired from them three times, praying unto his Father that if it was possible the cup of His divine wrath might pass away from him whose black ingredients filled him with horror and amazement. Nevertheless in this he submitted himself entirely to His divine pleasure, and an angel was sent to comfort him. Immediately after Judas Iscariot came with a band of armed men and kissed him. Then they laid hands on him and led him away to the palace of the High Priest. Peter followed afar off, and it being cold weather the servants made a fire in the hall, and Peter sat down with them, and while he was warming himself one of them looking earnestly upon him said, "Thou certainly was with Jesus of Nazareth," but Peter denied it, and said he knew nothing of the man. Some time after another came and said unto Peter, "Surely thou art one of this man's disciples, and art a Galileean," but Peter denied with an oath, saying he never was with him, neither did he know him. Peter then returned to the porch to evade any further questions respecting Jesus and himself, when a damsel came to him and said, "Surely thou art one of Jesus of Nazareth's disciples, for thy speech betrayeth thee," on which he began to curse and to swear, saying he knew nothing of him; and immediately the cock crew, and the Lord turned and glanced a look on Peter, which brought to his remembrance the saying of Jesus, "Before the cock crow thou shalt deny me thrice;" and ever after, whenever he saw or heard a cock, he remembered his own sin and unworthiness in denying his Lord and Master.

Q. What does the ascent of the five steps to the cross allude to?

A. To the five agonies of Jesus Christ.

Q. Explain them?

A. First. His bitter agony and suffering in the garden of Gethsemene; for having withdrawn himself from his disciples, he went there to pray, and being in agony he prayed so fervently that the sweat which fell from his face was as if it were great drops of blood falling to the ground. 2d. His being laid hold of as a thief and a murderer, and forsaken by all his disciples. 3d. His being cruelly scourged by Pontius Pilate, and then delivered to the Jews to be crucified. 4th. Their placing on his head a crown of thorns, smiting him with a reed and the palms of their hands, and bowing the knee and worshipping him in derision, and loading him with the transverse beam of the cross; but fearing he would die before they had completed their cruelties in crucifying him, they laid hold of Simon of Cyrene, whom they compelled to carry the cross after Jesus to the place of execution. 5th. His being nailed to the cross with two malefactors, where he hung for the space of three hours in the most exquisite torture, being reviled, mocked and insulted by the chief priests, rulers, common people, passengers, and even one of the malefactors who was crucified with him.

Q. Did the other malefactor also insult Jesus?

A. No, for he reproved his companion for insulting the innocent, and while he himself was receiving the great reward of his crime, upbraided a person who suffered unjustly and undeservedly. Then looking on Jesus with a noble reliance and most wonderful faith, he entreated him to retain some remembrance of him when he came into his kingdom. To which Jesus made him this precious promise of speedy felicity, "To-day shalt thou be with me in Paradise."

Q. Why was Jesus crucified between two malefactors?

A. The more to mortify and insult him, and to cover their murder with a shield of justice by executing the guilty with the innocent.

Q. Was any particular prophecy concerning him fulfilled?

A. There was, for it was written of him that he was numbered among the transgressors.

Q. Was there not another particular prophecy concerning him at that time accomplished?

A. There was this: They parted his garments amongst them, and for his vesture, or coat, they did cast lots, because it was without seam, woven from top to bottom, and would have been spoiled by parting it.

Q. Did Jesus say anything to his friends who beheld his sufferings while upon the cross?

18

A. He said, "Daughter of Jerusalem, weep not for me but for yourself and for your children." He then foretold the destruction of the City and the many miseries which soon after befel the Jews.

Q. Did not Jesus pray for his enemies?

A. While they were nailing him to the cross he prayed and said, "Father forgive them, for they know not what they do."

Q. Did the Jews give him any further insult?

A. Yes, when he said "I thirst" they gave him vinegar mixed with gall, that it might be more horrid and unpleasant, and when he had tasted thereof he would not drink, but said, "It is finished," and he cried with a loud voice and bowed his head and gave up the ghost, commending his spirit into the hands of his Heavenly Father.

Q. About what time of the day was this?

A. About the sixth hour, which is high twelve or noon with us.

Q. What happened at that time?

A. There was darkness over all the earth for the space of three hours, the sun was darkened, the earth did quake, the rocks rent, and the graves were opened, and the bodies of many saints arose and appeared unto many; and when Jesus gave up the ghost the veil of the Temple was rent in twain from the top to the bottom.

Q. Did the soldiers inflict any more wounds on Jesus?

A. One of them pierced his left side with a spear, from which issued blood and water.

Q. Did they break any of his bones?

A. They did not, but they broke the bones of the two malefactors who were crucified with him, which fulfilled what had been said concerning him, "A bone of his shall not be broken, and they shall look on him they pierced."

Q. Was the darkness at Christ's death the effects of an ordinary eclipse of the sun?

A. It was not, for an ordinary eclipse of the sun can never happen except the moon is about the change, whereas at Christ's death it was full moon, for the Jewish feast of the passover was always celebrated at full moon; and the total darkness occasioned by natural solar eclipses never continued above twelve or sixteen minutes, whereas the darkness at Christ's death continued for three hours, and was universal. It is recorded that Dionisius, the Arcopagite, was at that time in Egypt studying astronomy, and knowing that that supernatural darkness was the effects of some supernatural cause exclaimed, "Either the world is at an end or the God of Nature suffers."

Q. To what do you ascribe that extraordinary alteration in the face of nature?

A. It was produced by the Divine power in a manner not to be accounted for from natural causes, but it was peculiarly proper while the Sun of Righteousness was withdrawing its beams from the land of Israel and from the world. It was a miraculous testimony by God to Christ's innocence, and it was a full emblem of his departure and its effects.

Q. Why was Christ crucified and not put to death in a more easy manner?

A. Because crucifixion was the most dreadful, ignominious and painful of all deaths, so scandalous that it was inflicted as the last mark of detestation upon the vilest of people, murderers and robbers, provided they were slaves, too.

Q. How was the execution performed?

A. The person was nailed to the cross as it lay upon the ground, through each hand, extended to its utmost stretch, and through both the feet together. The foot of the cross was then thrust with a violent shock or jog into a hole prepared in the earth to receive it, which disjointed the body, whose whole weight being upon the nails, which went through the hands and feet, till the person expired by the extremity of pain.

Q. Where was Christ crucified?

A. At a small hill to the west of Jerusalem, called Mount Calvary or Golgotha, signifying the place of a skull, because part of the Mount bore a resemblance to a human skull, and because the bodies of malefactors were exposed to ravenous birds and beasts, and the Mount frequently strewed with skulls and bones.

Q. Was Christ's body exposed to ravenous birds and beasts after being taken down from the cross?

A. No, for Joseph of Arimathea, a rich man and a private disciple of Jesus, went openly to Pilate, and begged the body, which he embalmed and laid in a new sepulchre cut out of the rock near the place where Christ was crucified, where never before man lay, and near the spot where the first was buried, fulfilling another prophecy, "He made his grave with the rich in death," although he suffered as the vilest and most infamous among men.

Q. What were the water and the blood which flowed from Christ's side emblems of?

A. Water was the emblem of Christ's purity, and blood the evidence of his

20

fortitude and patience, and both signified the two Christian sacraments—baptism and the supper of the Lord.

The foregoing faithfully copied from a ritual belonging to Sir Knight Thomas Lonsdale Bold.

✠ JOHN YARKER, Jr

FACSIMILE

K. T.

FACSIMILE

THE ENGLISH RITUAL

FOR

KNIGHTS TEMPLAR:

Transcribed, verbatim et litteratim, for the Honorable M. P. Sov. G. Com.,

BRO. ☩ ALBERT PIKE, XXXIII°,

Southern Jurisdiction.

BY

☩ *MATTHEW COOKE, XXX°,*

Past Grand Organist to the Grand Conclave of Knights Templar and St. John of Jerusalem,

AND

Past Organist, and (Past) Master of the Ceremonial to the Sup. G. Council of the XXXIII° for England and Wales, &c.

Mr. MATTHEW COOKE,—a Member of the Newspaper-Press Fund (formerly one of the Children of Her Majesty's Chapels Royal,) a Contributor to numerous Periodicals, Newspapers and Reviews; Compiler of "The Clerical Directory;" late Sub-Editor of "The Literary Gazette," and "The Freemasons' Magazine:"—Transcribes Old Documents; Collates MSS. or Printed Books; Institutes Searches on Literary and Genealogical Matters; Verifies References; Makes Indexes; Scores and Copies Ancient Music; Catalogues Libraries; Executes Fac-Similes; Prepares Authors' Manuscripts for the Press; Makes Extracts from The British Museum, Public Offices, or University and College Libraries.

Terms and other Information can be obtained of him (by Post) at 25 Mayland Road, Shepherd's Bush, London, W. England.

REPRINTS OF RITUALS OF OLD DEGREES

"Copy of the Ritual agreed to at the Grand Conclave held on the 11th day of April, 1851, and recommended for adoption by the Order."

OPENING THE ENCAMPMENT.

Eminent Commander. Sir Knights, assist me to open this Encampment. [Sir Knts. all rise, with drawn swords in their right hands.] Sir Knt. Second Captain, what is the first care of a Knt. Templar?

2nd Capt. To see that the Encampment is properly guarded.

E. C. Direct that duty to be done.

2d Capt. Sir Knt. Captain of the Lines, see that the Encampment is properly guarded.

Capt. of Lines. [On the door.] ♪♪♪♪♪♪

Equery, (without.) [On the door.] ♪♪♪♪♪♪

Capt. of Lines. Sir Knt. 2d Captain, the Encampment is properly guarded.

2d Capt. Eminent Commander, all is secure.

E. C. Sir Knt. 1st Capt., what is the next care?

1st Capt. To see that none but Knights Templar are present.

E. C. To order, Sir Knts.

[All stand with swords in their right hands, the points resting in their left palms, and the sword being held, diagonally, across their bodies.]

E. C. Sir Knt. Registrar, call the muster-roll.

[Registrar calls over the names of members, each one present answering "Here."]

E. C. Let us now deposit our arms at the foot of the cross, and implore the blessing and protection of the Holy Trinity.

[Each one places his sword, before him, on the floor, the handle towards himself, the point towards the sepulchre.]

6

Prelate. Let us pray. Merciful Redeemer of perishing mankind, who hast promised that Thou wouldst be in the midst of those who assemble in Thy holy name, look down upon us, Thy servants, with an eye of tender compassion, and so direct us, this day, that all our labours may be begun, continued, and ended in Thee, affection to our companions, protection to the distressed, and obedience to our Order. Amen.

E. C. Sir Knt. 2d Capt., the situation of the Capt. of Lines.

2d Capt. Within the entrance of the Encampment.

E. C. His duty?

2d Capt. To see that the sentinels are regularly placed at the outposts, that the Encampment may be safely guarded without, as well as within.

E. C. Let him resume his arms and duty. [He takes up his sword and goes to his place.] Sir Knt. 1st Capt., the situation of the Expert?

1st Capt. In the West.

E. C. His duty?

1st Capt. To assist the E. C. and 1st and 2d. Capts. in the performance of our Rites and Ceremonies.

E. C. Let him resume his arms and duty. [He does so.] Sir Knt. 2d Capt., your situation in the Encampment?

2d Capt. In the northwest angle of the Encampment.

E. C. Your duty?

2d Capt. To see that all commands of the E. C. or 1st Capt. are obeyed in the north column.

E. C. Resume your arms and duty. [That done.] Sir Knt. 1st Capt., your situation in the Encampment?

1st Capt. In the southwest angle of the Encampment.

E. C. Your duty?

1st Capt. To receive reports from the 2d Capt.; to forward them without delay to the E. C., and to see that the Knts. are arranged under their respective banners.

E. C. Are they so arranged?

1st Capt. To the best of my knowledge.

E. C. Resume your arms and duty. [That done.] Where is the E. Commander's place?

1st Capt. At headquarters, in the East.

E. C. His duty?

7

1st Capt. To open the Encampment in form; to issue his commands for its regulation, and to close it when he may deem it convenient.

E. C. Sir Knts., resume you arms. [All those who have not done so previously, do so now.] Sir Knts., our Encampment being thus formed, I, in the name of the three scriptural offices of Christ our Prophet,† Christ our Priest,† and Christ our King,† declare it duly opened.

[As the E. C. pronounces each of these names he, and all present, salute. The salute is by raising the pommel of the sword level with the left breast, drawing it *smartly* across to the right breast, carrying it, *quickly*, up to the forehead, and thence down to the navel. This forms a passion cross. The sword is held completely upright the whole time.]

E. C. ♩♩♩♩♩♩ [Repeated by 1st and 2d Capt., Capt. of Lines and Equery, all one after the other.]

CLOSING THE ENCAMPMENT.

E. C. Sir Knts., assist me to close the Encampment. [All rise.] Sir Knt. 2d Capt., what is the constant care of a Knt. Templar?

2d Capt. To see that the Encampment is properly guarded.

Capt. of Lines, (on door.) ♩♩♩♩♩♩

Equery, (without.) ♩♩♩♩♩♩

Capt. Lines. Sir Knt. 2d Capt., the Encampment is properly guarded.

2d Capt. Eminent Commander, all is secure.

E. C. Sir Knt. 1st Capt., the next care?

1st Capt. To see that the Knts. appear to order as Knts. Templar.

E. C. To order, Sir Knts. [All stand to order.] Let us deposit our arms at the foot of the Cross, and implore the blessing of the Holy Trinity. [That done.]

Prelate. Let us pray. O merciful God, grant Thy holy protection and salutary blessing to this Encampment. Enlighten its rulers with the rays of Thy brightness, that they may always see the just ways of our heavenly Captain, and may, by His example, induce the companions committed to their charge so to follow through the wilderness of temptation that, having overcome the enemies of Thy holy name, they may arrive at the heavenly Jerusalem, armed with the shield of faith and the breast-plate of righteousness, through Jesus Christ our Saviour. Amen.

E. C. Sir Knts., resume your arms. [That done.] Our labors being finished, I, in the name of the three scriptural offices of Xt. our Prophet,† Xt. our Priest,† and Xt. our King,† declare this Encampment duly closed.

[At † all present salute.]

E. C. ♩♩♩♩♩♩ [Repeated one after the other by 1st Capt., 2d Capt., Capt. of Lines, and Equery, without.]

INSTALLATION.

FIRST PART.

[An alarm (trumpet call) is sounded without.]

Capt. Lines. Sir Knt. 2d Capt., there is an alarm at the outposts.

2d Capt. Ascertain the cause of the alarm.

Capt. of Lines. [Opens door and sees the Candidate being prepared. Closes it and says:] Sir Knt. 2d Capt., a stranger is endeavoring to penetrate our lines.

2d Capt. E. C., a stranger is endeavoring to penetrate our lines.

E. C. Be cautious, and see who the intruder is.

2d Capt. See who comes.

Capt. of Lines. [Opens door and enquires of Equery, without.] Who comes here?

Equery. Companion (X. Y. Z.,) a pilgrim on his travels, weary and fatigued, having heard of this Encampment of Knts. T., is anxious to take refuge therein, and, if possible, to be admitted to the privileges of the Order.

Capt. of Lines. What recommendation does he bring?

Equery. The sign and word of a Royal Arch Mason.

Capt. of Lines, (to Cand. outside.) Show me the sign and communicate the word. [Cand. gives the reverential sign and the word by which R. A. Companions reveal themselves to each other.] Wait while I report you to our Eminent Commander. [Closes the door, salutes, and says:] Eminent Commander, beyond the outposts is Companion (X. Y. Z.,) a pilgrim, (&c., same as before.)

E. C. What recommendation does he bring?

Capt. of Lines. The sign and word of a Royal Arch Mason.

E. C. Let him be admitted with caution.

[The Knts. stand to order. The Candidate, habited as a pilgrim, with a rude cross for a staff, blue gown, hat with a cockle-shell in front, bag, with a water bottle in it, slung across his shoulders, is admitted and received by the Expert, who conducts him to the 2d Capt., and he, presenting the point of his sword to the Candidate's breast, asks:]

2d Capt. Who are you that dares to penetrate thus far into our Encampment.

Expert, (prompting or at times answering for the Candidate.) Companion (X. Y. Z.,) a pilgrim on his travels, (&c., as before.)

2d Capt. What recommendation do you bring?

Cand., (prompted by Expert.) The sign and word of a Royal Arch Mason.

2d Capt. Show me the sign and communicate the word.

[The Cand. gives the sign and word, and is thereupon conducted by the Expert to the 1st Capt., who challenges him as the 2d Capt. had just done. Then the Expert conducts him to the foot of the sepulchre, and (softly) directs him to salute the E. C. with the sign, and at the same time give the word of a R. A. Mason. That done]—

E. C. Welcome, in the name of J∴ Rest yourself and partake of bread and water, the staff of life; the only refreshment we can at present afford you.

[The Pilgrim (or Candidate, both terms being used indiscriminately,) is seated in the West, and the Expert hands him bread and water. The Knts. all seated in their stalls. After be has partaken of both he rises, and the]—

E. C. says: Pilgrim! you have sought refuge in our Encampment, and de-

10

sire to be admitted to the privileges of the Order; let me, therefore, demand of you, On whom, in the hour of danger, do you rely?

Cand., (prompted by Ex.) On God.

E. C. And in whom do you put your trust for eternal salvation?

Cand., (prompted by the Ex., in all cases, being understood.) In our Blessed Saviour, Jesus Christ.

E. C. Can you give me any proof of your sincerity?

Cand. I am ready to undertake any task, however perilous, which may entitle me to admission, under your banner, as a soldier of the cross.

E. C. Then, as a proof of your faith, I enjoin you a seven years' pilgrimage. This you will, figuratively, perform by proceeding round the Encampment seven times. Sir Knts., guard your Encampment.

[The E. C. and his two Capts. remain at their respective stations. The other Knts. stand round the sepulchre, to order, facing outwards. The Ex. conducts the Cand. round the Encampment, preceding him, with a drawn sword in his hand. After the third round the Ex. and Cand. halt in the West.]

2d Capt. E. C., the pilgrim having performed three years of his pilgrimage, and having evinced great zeal and fidelity, I have to request that you will remit the remainder of the term.

E. C. Sir Knt. 2d Captain, I readily attend to your request, and remit the remainder of the term. [The Knts. resume their stalls.] To order, Sir Knts.

[The Cand. standing in the West, with the Ex. on his left, the Prelate reads one of the three following prayers or the lesson from Scripture:]

Prel. Let us pray. Merciful Lord God of heaven and earth, who hast protected this Thy servant through a long and dangerous pilgrimage, and hast inclined his heart to dedicate the remainder of his life to Thy holy service, grant, we beseech Thee, that he may constantly adhere to those pious resolutions; that he may heartily detest all the sins of his former life, and may, henceforward, with a firm resolution, shun all occasions of offending Thee, O Great Emanuel! And may at last arrive at the conclave of the heavenly Jerusalem. Amen.

Or, verses 1-16 of ii chapter of St. Paul's Epistle to the Hebrews,(a.)

Or,

Let us pray. Grant, O Lord, that this Candidate for the mysteries of our Lord and Saviour's Birth, Life, Death, Resurrection and Ascension may ever hold fast the profession of a Christian: may boldly fight under the banner of the cross as a faithful knight and soldier of our Blessed Master, and may become a true com-

---

(a)The Scriptural extracts are not written here in full, to save trouble. So, where such occur, the texts are quoted by chapter and verse.

panion amongst us. This we beg for the sake and in the name of thine only Son, our Lord and Redeemer. Amen.

[This properly belongs to the Knt. of Malta degree. It contains five passwords of that Order, but was incorporated when we ceased to work it separately. Now, however, that it is being worked again by itself, this prayer has been restored to its legitimate place. But as I am giving the authorized working, according to the last revision, in 1851, I did not feel justified in omitting it, although, in practice, we now no longer use it, except in the S. John of Jerusalem.]

Or this:

O Emanuel! our great and heavenly captain, look down, we beseech Thee, on this Encampment of Thy devoted servants, and impart Thy holy spirit to the Candidate now before Thee, that he may be worthy of Thy acceptance and salvation. Amen.

E. C. Let the Pilgrim now approach the holy sepulchre, and, bended on both knees, enter into a solemn engagement, placing both hands on the holy gospel. [The Ex. directs the Cand. to kneel at the foot of the sepulchre, and place his hands, open, on the New Testament, the 1st chapter of the gospel according to St. John being the portion exposed. The 1st and 2d Capts. leave their stations, and, standing on each side of the Cand., cross their swords upon the backs of his hands.] To order, Sir Knts.

Prelate, (or E. C.) Pilgrim! you will repeat your Christian and surnames, and say after me. "I, (X. Y. Z.,) in the name of the holy and undivided Trinity, and in the presence of the Knights here assembled, do hereby and hereon most solemnly and sincerely promise and swear, never to reveal the secrets of a Knight Templar to any one beneath that degree, unless it be to a candidate for the same in a lawful Encampment of Knights Templar, and then, only, whilst acting as a regularly installed Commander. I furthermore solemnly promise that I will faithfully defend, and maintain, the holy Christian faith against all unprovoked attacks of its enemies. That I will not shed the blood of a Knight Templar in wrath, unless it be in the just wars of sovereign princes, or States, but, on the contrary, will defend him, even at the risk of my life, when or wheresoever his life, or his honor, may be in danger. That I will, to the utmost of my power, protect the near and dear relatives and connections of a Knight Templar, and, if possible, prevent all harm, danger, or violence to which they may be exposed. Lastly, I do most sincerely promise to be obedient to the supreme authorities of the country in which I do, or may, reside, and strictly to observe, and maintain, the ancient laws and regulations of the Order, and the statutes of the Grand Conclave of England and Wales; and to answer and obey, so far as lies in my power,

12

all summonses sent to me, the same being duly marked. To all these points I swear fidelity, without evasion, equivocation, or mental reservation of any kind, under no less a penalty than the loss of life by having my head struck off and placed upon a pinacle or spire; my skull sawn asunder, and my brains exposed to the scorching rays of the sun, as a warning to all infidels and traitors. So help me Christ, and keep me steadfast in this my solemn obligation."

E. C., (alone.) You will seal that solemn obligation seven times, with your lips, on the Holy Gospels. [That done.] Arise, a novice of our Order. [Cand. rises.] Let the Novice be divested of his pilgrim's habit and assume the garb of a soldier of the cross.

[The Ex. takes off the pilgrim's habit, and puts on the Cand. the various portions of the Christian armour, as the Prelate mentions them in reading.]

[Prelate reads verses 10-17 of 6th chapter of St. Paul's Epistle to the Ephesians.]

E. C. Being now armed as a soldier of Christ, you are prepared to enter on a warfare of seven years. But I must request you, first, to make those professions which your sainted predecessors have made. You will repeat after me,—suiting the action to the word,—

"I draw my sword in defence of the holy Christian faith."

[Does it and sheaths it.]

"I draw my sword in defence of all Knights Templar."

[Does it and sheaths it again.]

"I draw my sword in defence of the near and dear relatives and connections of Knights Templar."

[Does it and sheaths again.]

E. C., (alone.) You are now about to proceed on a seven years' warfare, and, as you may be occasionally stopped and subjected to an examination as a soldier enrolled under the banner of the cross, I shall now entrust you with the sign(a) and word(b) of a crusader, whereby you will gain confidence and support. [Gives the pass-sign and word of a crusader.] Thus prepared, you may proceed on your crusade, which you will, figuratively, perform by proceeding seven times round the Encampment, and be prepared to defend yourself with your sword. Sir Knts., to order.

[Sir Knts. stand to order under their respective banners. The Expert conducts the Novice round the Encampment, going to the north side. At each round the Novice is stopped and challenged(c.) In the East by the Past E. C., in the S. W.

(a)The salute as before. (b)Golgotha. (c)This consists in each one striking his sword, as if to attack him, when he wards off the blow with his sword, makes the sign, gives the word, and is allowed to pass on.

13

by the 1st Capt., in the N. W. by the 2d Capt. To each of whom he gives the sign and word of a crusader. After he has been stopped for the third time by the 1st Capt., the E. C. is thus addressed:]

1st Capt. E. C., the Novice has zealously prosecuted the campaign up to the present time. Is it your pleasure to remit the remaining portion?

E. C. Most willingly I remit the remaining four years of probation as a crusader.

[The Exp. conducts the Novice to the foot of the sepulchre.]

E. C. With the point of your sword you will assist the Sir Knt. Expert to unveil the cross, and you will then notice the scroll at its foot,(*a*.) [That done.] *Whenever that mark, which is formed from the initials of the Latin inscription placed over our Saviour, at His crucifixion, it will be your imperative duty, in accordance with your obligation, to obey it.* If unavoidable circumstances render your personal attendance impossible, you will then, by letter, explain the cause of such inability to the Commander by whom the summons has been issued.

[The following portion of the charge may be given, or omitted, at pleasure:]

Pilgrim! now a Novice of our Order, the ceremonies in which you are now engaged are calculated deeply to impress your mind, and, I trust, will have a long and happy effect upon your future character. You were first, as a trial of your faith and humility, enjoined to perform a seven year's pilgrimage. It represented the pilgrimage of life, through which we are all passing. We are all weary pilgrims, looking forward to that asylum where we shall cease from our labours and be at rest forever. You were then directed, as a trial of your courage and constancy, to perform seven years of warfare. It represented to you the constant warfare, with the lying vanities and deceits of this world, in which it is necessary for us always to be engaged. You are now about to perform a year of penance, as a further trial of your humility. It is also a trial of that faith which will conduct you safely on the dark gulph of everlasting death, and land your enfranchised spirit in the peaceful abode of the blessed. Let the emblems of life and death, which lie around, remind you of the uncertainty of your earthly existence, and teach you to be prepared for the closing hours of your mortal life. And rest assured that a firm faith in the truths revealed to us will afford you consolation in the gloomy hour of dissolution, and insure your ineffable and eternal happiness in the world to come.

(*a*)   *So in Mss.

14

[When the foregoing portion of the charge is omitted, the ceremony must begin again here:]
You are now to undergo one year of mortification and penance. You will, therefore, take that skull in your left hand, and one of those small lighted tapers in your right hand, and, banishing all worldly thoughts, and mentally invoking the blessing of heaven on your undertaking, you will, figuratively, perform one year of penance by walking, slowly, round the Encampment, keeping your eyes steadily fixed on the emblems of life and mortality in your hands. To order, Sir Knts.

[The Knts. stand to order. The Ex. hands the Novice the skull and lighted taper, upon which the latter proceeds slowly, by himself, once round the Encampment. A solemn dirge may be played here. When the Novice has returned to the West, he stands facing the E. C.]

E. C. You will now repeat after me these imprecations: "May the spirit which once inhabited this skull rise up and testify against me if ever I wilfully betray my obligation as a Knight Templar." Seal it with your lips seven times on the skull. [He does so, and the Exp. takes the skull from him and replaces it on the sepulchre.] "May my light also be extinguished amongst men as that of Judas Iscariot was, for betraying his Lord and Master, and as I now extinguish this light, if ever I wilfully betray my obligation as a Knight Templar." [The Novice blows out the light, and the taper is replaced, but NOT relighted by the Expert.] You will now retire to meditate on the ceremony you have just passed through, and prepare yourself for the honour of Knighthood. But, in order to enable you to gain re-admission, I will entrust you with the casual sign and grand pass-word of the Order.

[Prelate reads verses 1, 2 and 3 of the 8th chapter of Isaiah.]

E. C. The casual sign is given thus,(a.) The grand pass-word is contained in the portion of Scripture which has just been read to you by the Reverend Prelate. It is considered a type of the Redeemer, and, in the Hebrew language, it signifies, "In making speed to the spoil He hastens the prey."

[The Novice salutes and retires.]

(a)With the right hand pluck a hair from the left whisker and throw it over the left shoulder. The answer to it is to reverse it by using the left hand to the right whiskers.

END OF PART I.

15
INSTALLATION.
PART II.

Equery, (without.) ♪♪♪♪♪♪

Capt. Lines. Sir Knt. 2d Capt., there is a report.

2d Capt. E. C., there is a report.

E. C. See who seeks admission.

Capt. of Lines. [Opens the door, sees, closes it, returns and says:] Our new Companion in arms.

E. C. Admit him.

[The Novice is admitted, and the Expert takes him to the 2d Capt., to whom he shows the casual sign and gives the grand pass-word. Then he is taken to the 1st Capt., where he does likewise. He is then placed in the West, facing the E. C.]

E. C. Our new Companion will now attend to a portion of the Holy Scriptures, which the Reverend Prelate will read.

[Prelate reads verses 1 to 17 (always inclusive wherever mentioned in this ritual) of the 2d chapter of the 1st Epistle of St. Peter.]

E. C. Sir Knt. Expert, let the cup of memory be presented to our new Companion in arms. [The Ex. presents a cup of wine to the Novice.] Worthy brother, at your first admission you were refreshed with bread and water. We now invite you to refresh yourself with the cup of memory, which you will dedicate to seven distinct libations. To order, Sir Knts. You, my new Companion, will now repeat after me:

I. "To the memory of Moses, Aholiab and Bezaleel, the three Grand Masters who presided over the Holy Lodge."
[The Expert tells the Novice to drink.]

II. "To the memory of Solomon, King of Israel; Hiram, King of Tyre; and Hiram Abiff, the three Grand Masters who presided over the Sacred Lodge."
[Drinks.]

III. "To the memory of Zerubbabel, prince of the people; Haggai, the prophet; and Joshua, the son of Josedech, the high priest, the three Grand Masters who presided over the Grand or Royal Lodge."
[Drinks.]

16

IV. "To the memory of St. John the Baptist, the forerunner of our Lord and Saviour, Jesus Christ."
[Drinks.]

V. "To the memory of St. John the Evangelist, who finished, by his learning, what the former had commenced by his zeal."
[Drinks.]

VI. "To the pious memory of all those valiant Knights who sealed their faith with their blood under the banner of the cross."
[Drinks.]

VII. "To all Knights Templar wheresoever dispersed over the face of earth and water."
[Drinks the remainder. After which the Knts. resume their stalls.]

E. C. You will now attend to another portion of Scripture, which the Reverend Prelate will read.

[Prelate reads verse 17 of the 2d chapter of Revelations. The Expert then advances to the Novice with a drawn sword in his hand.]

E. C. Worthy brother! it was customary, at the period of the institution of our Order, for each Novice to be required to sign his name, with his blood, on the northeast corner of the mystical stone, before he could obtain the sacred word which it enshrines. Are you prepared to sign your name on the stone which is now presented to you?

[The Exp. presents the stone, and asks, "From what part of your body shall I draw blood with this sword?" After ascertaining that the Novice is willing to conform to the custom, he addresses the E. C. thus:]

Expert. Eminent Commander, the Novice is prepared to sign.

E. C. Worthy brother! accepting your ready acquiescence as a sufficient proof of devotion to our Order, we dispense with the observance of the custom further than to require you to moisten the pen with your lips, and write your initials with it on the stone. [The Novice signs his initials on the stone. The Exp. then shows him the word(a,) and presents him with a small stone(b) as a memorial and pass voucher.] You will carefully preserve that memorial, for should you at any time wish to gain admission into a Knt. Templar's Encampment, you will, on presenting that stone and explaining the circumstances under which you received it, be at once recognized and admitted as a companion of our Order.

(a)The stone is a perfect cube. One part of it fits in to the other. At the bottom of the cavity is written the word "Emanuel." (b)The Exp., in giving this small stone, directs the Novice to hold his hand at the point of the Ex.'s sword, whilst the latter slides the small stone down the blade, and lets it drop thence into the Novice's palm.

17

Approach, brother, and receive the highest honor I can at present bestow upon you. [The Novice is conducted to the East. The E. C. descends from his throne; the standards are raised, and the Novice kneels before the E. C., who gives him the accolade, thus:] In the name of the Holy, Blessed and Glorious Trinity, and by the authority vested in me as Knt. Commander, I make thee a Knight of the Holy Temple. [Here, striking the Novice on the left shoulder with his sword.] Be loyal, brave and free. Arise, Sir Knt. (Helps him up.) [The Chamberlain then presents the E. C. with the Novice's ribbon, star of the Order and mantle, all of which he brings upon a cushion, and the E. C. invests the Novice with each at its proper place.] Wear this ribbon, the ensign of our Order, and this star, an emblem of the reward which the Great Captain of our salvation has promised to those who conquer in His name. Even the emblem of Himself, He being the bright morning star, whose rising brought health and salvation to mankind, and light to those who sat in darkness and in the shadow of the valley of death. Bear this ever in mind, and continue his faithful soldier unto death. We clothe you also with this mantle of pure white, ennobled with the red cross of the Order. I will now entrust you with the grand word(*a*,) grand grip(*b*) and grand sign,(*c*.)

[After which, the Exp. conducts the new Knight to his stall, and the Heralds make proclamation.]

1st Herald. Sir Knts. of the Order of the Temple! Our brother and companion, Sir Knt. (X. Y. Z.,) is this day installed a Knt. of our illustrious order.

2d Herald. Long life, honor and prosperity to our newly-installed Knt. Companion, Sir Knt. (X. Y. Z.,) to our Most Eminent and Supreme Grand Master, the Grand Officers, and all other Knts. of the Order.

[The Sir Knts. salute thrice, and the new Knt. returns the salute from his stall.]

E. C. I will now explain to you the symbols of our Order. [The Exp. conducts him to the foot of the sepulchre.] The three Great Lights, placed at the angles of the equilateral triangle, represent the three favorite Apostles of our Saviour, viz: Peter, James and John, of whom the last-mentioned was the most beloved, for, leaning on our Saviour's bosom, he received those instructions which he communicated so faithfully to the other disciples. The nine smaller lights, distributed equally between those already noticed, are emblematical of the nine other Apostles, of whom the one, represented by the taper extinguished by you, betrayed his Lord and Master. You may now re-light the taper. [That done.] So may our Saviour lift upon you the light of his reconciled countenance and

---

(*a*)Emanuel. (*b*)Reciprocally cross both arms and interlace the fingers of all four hands. (*c*)That of the crucifixion. The feet crossed, arms extended, and the head inclined to the left shoulder.

18

keep you from falling! The skull, the emblem of mortality, is placed at the foot of the cross. These two, collectively, remind us of the place called, in the Hebrew, "Golgotha," into which Simon, of Cyrene, was constrained to bear the cross on which our Saviour was crucified. The skull also reminds us of the fate of one Simon, of Syracuse, who was admitted into our illustrious Order, but violated his obligation by betraying his trust to the infidels. They, although they profited by the treason, despised the traitor, and caused his head to be struck off, which they sent, in a charger, to the Grand Master of the Templars, who ordered it to be placed on the top of a pinnacle or spire, the skull to be laid open and the brains exposed to the scorching rays of the sun as a warning to all others. It is in allusion to this circumstance that the penal sign(a) of a Knt. Templar had its origin. The lamb, the dove and the cock are sacred symbols of the Order. The first is emblematical of the Paschal Lamb, slain from the foundation of the world. The Dove, of the Almighty Comforter, which descended, in that bodily shape, on Jesus Christ at His baptism, whereby His divine mission was indicated to St. John, the Baptist. The Cock is the monitor of the Order. For as his crowing heralds the morn, so let it, at that still hour, call to your remembrance our duties as Knights Templar, and remind us to ask, thus early, for assistance to perform them throughout the day. May we ever welcome that sound as a friendly caution, and not have reason to fear it as the periodical memento of a broken vow.

(a) The hand applied to the forehead as if sawing the head open. (Now discontinued.) The thumb raised from the fist and the lower jaw resting upon it. (Now used.)

END.

FACSIMILE

GRAND MAITRE ECOSSAIS,

OR

SCOTTISH ELDER MASTER

AND

Knight of St. Andrew,

BEING

THE FOURTH DEGREE OF RAMSAY

OR OF

La Regime Reforme on Rectifie of Dresden.

From an old MSS. in English, without name or date, found by me in the Archives of the Supreme Council at Charleston, S. C.

ALBERT PIKE.

REPRINTS OF RITUALS OF OLD DEGREES

GRAND MASTER ECOSSAIS.

FORM OF THE LODGE.

The Grand Master is styled *High Exalted*. He is seated in the East, at the head of a table covered with green cloth. Over his head is suspended a blazing star, with the letter G in the centre thereof. On his right are seated the Grand Secretary and Grand Treasurer; on his left the Grand Orator and Grand Master of Ceremonies. The two Grand Wardens are seated in the West, and all the Knights sit around the table.

The Lodge must be lighted by seven large lights—two in the East, two in the West, one in the South, one in the North, and one in the centre of the table.

CLOTHING, &c.

The *Apron* is white, lined with green. On the flap are embroidered or painted a Death's Head and Cross Bones, over a Cubic Stone, and in the middle of the Apron a Blazing Star, with the letter G in its centre.

4

The *Order* is a broad green Watered Ribbon, worn from the left shoulder to the right hip, to which is suspended the Jewel.

The *Jewel* is a Saint Andrew's Cross of gold, or silver gilt, enameled. The *Thistle* is between the points suspended to the collar.

FACSIMILE

TO OPEN.

[The Grand Master, from the chair, addresses the Brethren as follows:]

Gr∴ M∴ Most honorable Knights and Brethren, I have resolved this day to open, in the name of the Almighty Grand Architect of Heaven and Earth, this our High and Exalted Lodge. That we may propose, consider and undertake something for the good of mankind in general and this our Honorable Order in particular, do ye who are present Exalted Scottish Knights and my dear Brethren arm yourselves with 4 towards the Scottish Chair, to enable this our assembly carefully with me to weigh everything, that we may never resolve or undertake anything for which we may have cause to repent. First let your knightly firmness assist me in opening the Scottish Lodge.

G∴ M∴ What is the duty of the Grand Senior Warden in opening the Scottish Lodge?

G∴ S∴ W∴ [Rising and drawing his sword.] To see that this Grand Lodge is utmostly secured, and that it may so remain.

[The High Exalted orders the Gr∴ S∴ W∴ to do his duty in every point, which he does by going out and examining if all things are in proper security. When he returns, he stands behind his chair, with a drawn sword in his hand, and makes his report to the Grand Master.]

G∴ M∴ Bro. J∴ G∴ W∴, how many compose our Exalted Scottish Lodge?
J∴ G∴ W∴ [Rising and drawing his sword.] Four.
G∴ M∴ How many do four and three make?
J∴ G∴ W∴ They make seven complete.
G∴ M∴ What does the number seven signify?
J∴ G∴ W∴ It is the noblest and most complete of numbers.
G∴ M∴ How does the wind blow?

6

J∴ G∴ W∴ From the four quarters of the globe.

G∴ M∴ Bro. Gr. Secretary, is everything prepared and in readiness for the opening of the Grand Scottish Lodge?

G∴ Secy∴ [Rising and drawing his sword.] Yes, Most Exalted Grand Master, everything requisite for that grand and solemn undertaking is in readiness.

G∴ M∴ What weather is it?

G∴ Sec∴ A most glittering, starred sky.

G∴ M∴ What is the hour?

G∴ Sec∴ It is high midnight.

G∴ M∴ Grand Scottish Masters, Exalted Knights and my Brethren, I declare this Lodge to be opened, and every Brother will conduct himself accordingly.

S∴ G∴ W∴ Noble Knights and Brethren, let us not forget the duty we owe towards our Most Exalted Grand Master.

[The Knights all rise, drawing their swords, pass them to their left hands, take off their hats with their right, and salute the Grand Master, all together, taking the cue from the Gr. Master of Ceremonies, by lowering the points of their swords, bowing their heads very low, then putting on their hats, sheathing their swords, and giving the common Scottish sign. Then each returns to his place.]

ORDER OF RECEPTION.

[A Blue Master's Lodge is first opened, and the proposed Candidate is then vouched for; after which the Lodge is closed and the Candidate led out.]

[The Grand Master of Ceremonies goes out and directs the Candidate to wash. His shoes are then taken off, and he is blindfolded. Four raps are given at the door, which is opened to him by the J∴ G∴ Warden, who, as the Candidate enters, throws over his neck a gold colored rope with *four* knots on it.]

[The knots must be so made that with one pull they will all be loosened, and during the opening of the Lodge the Candidate lies on the ground.]

7

[After the Candidate has entered with the ceremony above described, he is placed between I∴ and B∴, and then the Most Exalted speaks as follows:]

G∴ M∴ My Brother, do you desire to become a Grand Scottish Mason?
Candidate. I do most cordially.
G∴ M∴ I must inform you that your aim is a very lofty one. Are you perfect in the common Blue Master's Degrees?
Cand∴ I am.
G∴ M∴ Then give the signs, tokens and words to the S∴ G∴ Warden.

[He gives them.]

G∴ M∴ My dear Brother, since you have proved your knowledge of your duties in the Blue Master's Degrees to our satisfaction, I will now instruct you in the mysteries and duties of the Scottish Masters, provided you have confidence to go through the same.

An Elder Scottish Master is of a high Priestly Order, my Brother, by means of the large circumference of his duties. His work is Heaven's, and far different from that of the Blue Master, or Master of the three lower degrees, wherein you have been until now but a Common Master, and by which you have been only taught to venerate the God-Head, under His name of the Most Great, Most Wise and Almighty Architect of the Universe. An Elder Scottish Master pays to the Almighty God a more profound and heartfelt veneration. That due veneration was taught by the Teacher and Promulgator of our Holy order when he said, "Those who truly worship Him, do worship Him in spirit and in truth;" and again, "They shall be unto me my people, and I will be unto them their God." The first-mentioned veneration is common to all men and Brethren, as dictated by common sense; but the latter belongs only to those who wholly dedicate their hearts to be the dwelling places of the great, merciful God, the Grand Architect of the Universe: and it alone is practiced among true Scottish Masters. Will you now, my dear Brother, adhere to your old way of worship, or do you resolve to enter upon the veneration in spirit and in truth, and henceforward to be instructed and directed in the doctrine professed by the Grand Scottish Masters?

Cand∴ I do most cordially so resolve.

G∴ M∴ Have you, during your Blue Mastership, duly and faithfully observed the following articles:

1st. Have you paid due veneration to the Most High, Most Wise and Mighty Architect of Heaven and Earth?

Cand∴ I always have.

8

2d. Have you improved yourself by fleeing from vice and practicing virtue?
Cand∴ I have.

3d. Have you studied the works, fruits of the industry of the wise, and their profitable precepts?
Cand∴ Most carefully.

4th. Have you at all times lived peaceably among the Masters and defended their prerogatives against rebellious craftsmen?
Cand∴ I have to the utmost of my power.

G∴ M∴ My dear Brother, I am happy to find you worthy to be received amongst the Elder Masters; but I must first ask if you have resolution and fortitude enough to go through their holy work; for it is more exalted than that to which you have been used, and greatly differs from it. Until now you have used the Square and Compass for the purposes of ordinary Geometry and right-lined and right-angled Mathematics, and for drafting exact designs for architects; but in Scottish Masonry they are put to quite another use.

Hitherto you have worked only on isolated and exoteric edifices, and made but an imperfect draft of our world; but by the Scottish work you will attain the most brilliant and splendid results, and grasp the plan of the whole universe. Will you most sacredly and solemnly promise and swear to keep the mysteries of Scottish Masonry, that may be confided to you, in everlasting silence, and that you will not directly or indirectly disclose or communicate them, or any part of them, to the Brethren of the Blue Order, or to any one in the world beside who is not entitled to the same?

Cand∴ I do most willingly consent to all these injunctions, and do most solemly promise to observe them.

> [Then the G∴ M∴ orders the Gr∴ Junior Warden to lead the Candidate out of the Porch, into the Outer Court of the Temple, thence into the Temple or Sanctuary, and thence into the Sanctum Sanctorum, and thence to conduct him to the three Golden Basins.]

> [The Jun∴ Warden leads him four times round the Lodge, and each time as the Candidate comes in front of the altar, the Gr∴ Master gives from the chair the four Scottish raps and also the common sign, which is repeated by all the Brethren.]

> [After the first four knocks the G∴ M∴ says:]

G∴ M∴ O! how great and glorious is the presence of the Almighty God, which gloriously shines from between the cherubims!

FACSIMILE

9

[After the second four:]

G∴ M∴ We adore Thee, Great and Mighty Jehova, who existeth from eternity! Glorified be Thy great and mighty name, for ever and ever!

[After the third four:]

G∴ M∴ How adorable and astonishing are the rays of that glorious light that sends forth its bright and brilliant beams from the Holy Ark of alliance and covenant!

[After the fourth:]

G∴ M∴ Let us with the deepest veneration and devotion adore the great source of life, that Glorious Spirit who is the most merciful and beneficent Ruler of the Universe and of all the creatures it contains!

[After this the Candidate is led to the altar, where he kneels on both knees and takes the following:]

OBLIGATION.

I, A . . B . ., of my own free will and accord, do most solemnly swear, in this most sacred and holy Temple, in the presence of the most brilliant and glorious rays, diffused by the Most Puissant, Most Merciful, and Most Terrible Almighty God and Grand Architect of the Universe, and before this Right Worshipful and Exalted Chapter assembled, of Grand Scottish Masters and valiant Knights of Saint Andrew, that I will always hail, forever conceal and never reveal any part or parts of the mysteries of the Scottish Masonry which I am now to receive, or shall at any time hereafter be instructed in, to any of the Brethren of the Blue Order of St. John's Lodge, and still less to a profane, or to any person in the world besides. I do furthermore swear that I never will give this degree and Order of Scottish Master and its mysteries to a Brother singly by myself, unless duly and properly authorized so to do; and the person to whom the same shall be given must be duly qualified for it, by having regularly and lawfully passed through all the preceding high degrees of Sublime Masonry, and at least having regularly served as Master of the chair in a regular constituted Lodge of the Order of St. John.

All this I sincerely and solemnly promise, with a steady resolution to keep the same; and in failure thereof I invoke that all curses may be fastened on my soul, so that I may be an everlasting example of a wretch, accused to all mankind in

10

future ages. I promise further to redouble my zeal and friendship towards my Brethren, and more particularly towards my Brother Scottish Masters; that I will heartily and sincerely love them; that I will assist them with my counsel, support them with my purse, even should it be attended by a probability of the loss of my property, honor or life, so far as shall be in my power and be consistent with my own and my family's preservation. So God maintain me in equity and justice to persevere steadfastly in the same. Amen! Amen! Amen!

[After which the candidate is reconducted to the West, and placed between the two Grand Wardens, when the High Exalted Grand Master says to him:]

G∴ M∴ My dear Brother, do you now desire to see that great and glorious light of the Temple?

Cand∴ I am most desirous.

[Upon this the G∴ J∴ W∴ removes the bandage from his eyes, and he beholds the glories of Solomon's Temple. He particularly sees the rays of the flaming star which hangs over the head of the Gr∴ Master of Solomon's chair, who says to him:]

G∴ M∴ Do you see, my dear Brother, the glorious light which so brightly and brilliantly shines from between the cherubims of the Ark of the Mercy Seat?

Cand∴ I do see with joy the most glorious light.

[Upon this the Grand Master advances to the newly admitted Brother with a drawn sword in his hand, all the Brethren at the same time drawing their swords. He then says to him:]

G∴ M∴ My Brother, this sword, and those of all the Scottish Knights, shall deprive you of your life in any part of the globe in case you should prove a wretch so wholly devoid of conscience as to disclose or discover the least of the mysteries of the Scottish Knights; but I can assure you that, so long as you are constant and true to your promises and obligations, all the valiant Knights shall stand by you and protect you, and extricate you from all impending danger, even at the risk of their own honor, property and life; and that their swords will defend you as long as you remain virtuous, true and steadfast to your trust and obligation, and prove yourself a true as well as a valiant Knight; and that they will punish you whenever you prove otherwise. I congratulate you upon the exalted rank and honorable degree at which you have arrived; and may the GREAT JEHOVA assist you to persevere in your most solemn and sacred engagements, so that you may in every point and particular fulfill them!

[After this, the newly initiated Brother is taught to make the *four* Scottish Steps, viz: from West to South, thence to East, thence North, and thence to West again, which is afterwards fully explained to him on the tracing-board.]

[Then the Master of Ceremonies gives him the following signs, token and words:]

1ST SIGN. This is called THE COMMON SCOTTISH SIGN. It is to carry your hand, half clinched, to your left hip, as if to draw your sword, and from that position draw your hand up to your throat, as if ripping open your belly.

2D SIGN. This is called THE GRAND SCOTTISH SIGN. It is to bring your hands across your forehead, in the form of a St. Andrew's cross, the right hand uppermost, the fingers extended, and forming a square with your thumbs. Then bring them in that position under your chin, at the same time clinching your fingers, which represents a death's head and cross bones.

TOKEN. Put your right hand to the other's neck, he doing the same, and each his left hand to the other's arm pit, doing as if you would raise each other.

PASS-WORD. GABAON, meaning a river or spring.

SACRED WORD. JEHOVA; the grand and ineffable name of the Grand Architect of the Universe.

A Knight of St. Andrew, to make himself known to another, takes his sword or dagger in his left hand in such manner as if he was going to give a back-stroke, crossing at the same time his right hand over it, in the form of a St. Andrew's cross, and holding it upwards, as if he were holding a working tool.

[N. B. The first part of the Grand Scottish Sign alludes to the Priests in the Temple, who always put their hands to their foreheads, the fingers and thumbs extended, as if to keep off the rays, whenever they gave the benediction. This ceremony is still in use in the Synagogues.]

[Then the Grand Master invests him with the Apron, and at the same time explains to him the mystery and meaning of the Green Colour, viz: that a Scottish Master must, in all his works and undertakings, put his trust in Almighty God, and that from Him alone success is to be hoped for. He then places a *Naked Sword* in his left hand and a *Trowel* in his right, in such positions that they form a St. Andrew's cross, the sword being held as if the Brother were going to give a back-stroke or thrust; this sign signifying that

12

the Knights of St. Andrew, having waged their wars against the Saracens with their swords in their hands, they also aided and protected the workmen, who had always the working tool in one hand and the sword in the other.]

[Then the Grand Master girds the sword upon the Candidate, and he is placed between the Gr∴ Wardens, while the Grand Master gives him the explanation of the Tracing Board before him.]

EXPLANATION.

Grand Master. It is well known to you, my dear Bro∴, that to the High Priest in Solomon's Temple, the Temple, the Porch, with its outer courts, and the Sanctuary and *Sanctum Sanctorum*, were open; and as you are now a Grand Scottish Master, and of course of the Order of the High Priesthood, you also have free access, not only into the Porch, outer limits and Sanctuary, but even to the Sanctum Sanctorum, which is the secret place of your labours. You see also the whole before your eyes. Consider first the consecrated outer court and the two pillars. They are now shattered and broken, the meaning of which you shall know hereafter. Behold now the Sanctuary and the *Sanctum Sanctorum*, in which was nothing save the Ark of Alliance and Covenant, wherein were the two tables containing the Ten Commandments; and the Rod of Aaron, that blossomed, lay on the outside before it. This Ark of Alliance, which was the mercy seat, was flanked by two cherubim, one on each side of it, between which the God-head revealed Himself to the High Priest in a stream of fire under a thick cloud, and thence delivered his oracles. That Ark, which is represented before you in the painting, serves a Knight of St. Andrew as an emblem, teaching him to adore the Invisible and Eternal Jehova, and at the same time signifies that a Knight of St. Andrew ought always to have the law of the Eternal God engraved on his heart, and should never contemplate, undertake or do anything contrary to its precepts. You must, my dear Brother, as a Grand Scottish Master, hereafter adore the Deity, under the name of JEHOVA, the great and holy name, with all your heart and with all your mind; and that adoration and veneration, being of the spirit, must greatly surpass the common veneration for ADONAI. You see here as emblems the Brazen Sea and Blazing Star. They were not found in the Temple, but are hieroglyphic emblems belonging to the Scottish work. The 7 dots which you perceive there do not signify the combinations by sevens in our Order, which is their meaning in the lower degrees of the Blue Order of St. John, but they allude to the physical characteristics of the seven different metals; and when you

13

find other stars added to the Seven Planets, they symbolize other mineral substances besides those represented by the Seven Planets, which are the only Solomonian metals. The secret knowledge of the Grand Scottish Masters, as you may already have surmised, relates to the combination and transmutation of different substances; whereof that you may obtain a clear idea and proper understanding. You are to know that all matter and all material substances are composed of combinations of three several substances, extracted from the four elements, which three substances in combination are ⊖ Salt, △ Sulphur, and ⌒△ Spirit. The first of these produces solidity, the second saltness, and the third the spiritual, vaporous particles. These three compound substances work potently together, and therein consists the true process for the transmutation of metals. To these *three* substances allude the three golden basins, in the first of which was engraved the letter M∴, in the second the letter G∴, and in the third nothing. The first M∴ is the initial letter of the Hebrew word מלח, which signifies *Salt ;* and the second, G∴, of the Hebrew word גפרית, which signifies *Sulphur ;* and as there is no word in Hebrew to express the vaporous and intangible *Spirit*, there is no letter found in the third basin.

These three basins were found in the time of the Crusades or Holy Wars, concealed in a square, hollow corner-stone, by four Elder Masters from Scotland; and in memory of them, all the Elder Masters are called Scottish Masters to this day.

With these three principal substances, you may effect the transmutation of metals, which must be done by means of the five points or rules of the Scottish Mastership. The first Master's point shows us the Brazen Sea, wherein must always be rain water, and out of this rain water the Scottish Masters extract the first substance, which is ⊖, *Salt*, which salt must afterwards undergo a sevenfold manipulation and purification before it will be properly prepared. This sevenfold purification is symbolized by *the seven steps of Solomon's Temple*, which symbol is furnished us by the First Point or Rule of the Scottish Master; wherefore you will now set your foot on the same.

After preparing the first substance, you are to extract the second, △, out of the purest gold, to which must then be added the purified or celestial ⊖. They are to be mixed as the art directs, and then placed in a vessel in the form of a ship, in which it is to remain, as the Ark of Noah was afloat, 150 days, being brought to the first damp, warm degree of fire, that it may putrefy, and produce the mineral fermentation. This is the second point or Rule of the Scottish Masters; wherefore you will now, for the second step, set your foot on *the Ark of Noah.*

The multiplying the substance thus obtained is the third operation, which is done

14

by adding to them the Animate Volatile Spirit, which is done my means of the Water of the Celestial ☿, as well as by the ☿, which must be daily added to it, very carefully and strictly observing to put neither too much or too little; inasmuch as, if you add too much, you will destroy that growing and multiplying substance, and if too little, it will be self-consumed and destroyed, and shrink away, not having sufficient substantiality for its preservation. This third point or Rule of the Scottish Masters gives us the emblem of the *Building of the Tower of Babel*, used by our Scottish Masters, because, by irregularity and want of due proportion and harmony, that work was stopped, and the workmen could proceed no further; wherefore, my Brother, you must, for the third step, set your foot upon the Tower.

Next comes the fourth operation, represented by the Cubical Stone, whose faces and angles are all equal. As soon as the work is brought to the necessary point of multiplication, it is to be submitted to the third degree of Fire, wherein it will receive the due proportion of the strength and substance of the metalic particles of the Cubical Stone; and this is the fourth point or Rule of the Scottish Masters; wherefore, my Brother, you must, for the fourth step, set your foot upon *the Cubical Stone*.

Finally we come to the fifth and last operation, indicated to us by the Flaming Star. After the work has become a duly proportioned substance, it is to be subjected to the fourth and strongest degree of fire, wherein it must remain 3 times 27 hours, until it is thoroughly glowing, by which means it becomes a bright and shining tincture, wherewith may be changed the lighter metals, by the use of one part to a thousand of the metal; wherefore as this *Flaming Star* shows us the fifth and last point of the Scottish Master, you must now, my Brother, for the fifth and last step, set your foot upon that Star, whereby you have completed the four steps of a Scottish Master.

These four different steps which you have taken are only ceremonial; but you should pass practically through the five Points or Rules of the Master, and by the use of one part to a thousand transmute and ennoble metals. You may then in reality say that your age is a thousand years, which age we can at present give you by ceremonial only.

This great and noble art was, in the time of Solomon, and thenceforward until the Crusades, confined to the brotherhood. At first it chiefly flourished at Jerusalem, but after our enlightened and most respectable and honored Grand Master Hiram was murdered by three vicious and villainous Fellow-Crafts, it was entirely forgotten there. That unhappy event is represented by the two overthrown and broken pillars, the bases of which, and part of each column, is still standing, but

FACSIMILE

15

the residue of each column, with the capitals, chapiters and architraves, is missing. This gives us also to understand that not only are the foundations of the Divine Ark solidly laid, but the superstructure thereon has been raised to a considerable height, and it only remains to find out the due measure and proper height of exaltation.

Learn, my Brother, from all this, that in whatever art or work your inclination may lead you to engage, if you desire to be an expert Scottish working Master, you must devote yourself to the accumulation of real physical knowledge, that thereby you may become familiar with the principles and practical processes of Chemistry.

So will you become more expert and dexterous in the use of the true Square and Compass, which you also see on the Tracing Board, and therewith build up an edifice of practical knowledge, that will fit you to proceed to the loftiest investigations of Philosophy.

Finally, my Brother, you have still in sight a sad emblem of the tragical fate of our Respectable Grand Master Hiram, to wit: the rope placed around your neck at your entrance, and which you have worn for the honor and the immortal memory of that enlightened and noble Grand Master. I will, as a remuneration, shortly invest you with a more brilliant and glittering decoration.

Note, also, the grave in which our Respectable Grand Master is buried in the most holy and consecrated quarter of the Temple, while his memory is embalmed and preserved forever in the inmost heart of every Scottish Master, Kinght of St. Andrew.

And learn finally, that through the great zeal and valor which they displayed during the Crusades, the Scottish Masters became associates of the Knights of St. Andrew, were honored with the decoration of the Thistle, and made members of that most ancient and honorable Order, pre-eminent for its fiery enthusiasm, with all the formalities required. With that honour of Knighthood, I now propose to invest you, as a reward for your valour, virtue, fervor and constancy.

[The newly initiated Brother kneels down on a perfect square. The Grand Master draws his naked sword twice across his back, marking a St. Andrew's cross, and says, while two other swords, crossed on his back in the shape of St. Andrew's cross, are held there during the investiture :]

FORM OF KNIGHTING.

G∴ M∴ 1st. I create you Knight of the Holy Order of THE GREAT JEHOVA.

16

2d. I create you Knight in the name of our noble Grand Master Hiram Abiff.

3d. I create you Knight of the Noble and Honorable Order of St. Andrew.

4th. I create you Knight in the name of the Grand Worshipful Scottish Elder Lodge, and in the name of the whole body of Knighthood over the surface of the two Hemispheres.

> [At every knighting, thus conferred, the Grand Master strikes him with his sword on the forehead, twice, making a St. Andrew's cross, and all the Brethren stand round him with their swords drawn. Then the Grand Master raises him and kisses him four times; after which, he invests him with the Order and Jewel, and says: "I decorate you, my dear Brother, with the Order of Hope and Perfection."

> [Then follows the consecration. The Grand Master puts both his hands on the head of the newly created Knight, and says:]

CONSECRATION.

G∴ M∴ The Lord bless thee and keep thee! The Lord make his face shine on thee and be gracious unto thee! The Lord lift up his countenance upon thee and give thee peace! Amen!

> [This benediction, pronounced in a solemn tone, is the same as is still practiced in the Synagogues on their festivals by the Cohens or Priests, descendants of Aaron.]

> [After this, the newly initiated Brother makes himself known to all the Knights, by giving them the signs, token and words. Then the Grand Orator delivers the following moral oration:]

ORATION.

To us, my Brother, as Grand Scottish Masters, the whole Temple is open, and by our undertaking the whole work thereof is completed. By this you see our great pre-eminence over the Masters of the Blue Order of St. John's Lodge, who are permitted to serve only in the Sanctuary or Middle Chamber of King Solomon's Temple.

17

You see here the three divisions of the Temple, namely: the *Outer Court*, the *Sanctuary*, and the *Sanctum Sanctorum*, signifying the three principles of our Holy Order, that directs to the knowledge of morality, and teaches these most practical virtues, that ought to be practiced by mankind. Therefore the seven *Steps* which lead up to the outer court of the Temple are the emblems of the sevenfold light we need to possess before we can arrive to the height of knowledge, in which consist the ultimate limits of our Order.

Next to this we come to the *Mosaic Pavement*, which reminds us that men, in their nature rude and unpolished, present themselves in many different aspects as they are driven hither and thither by disappointment, sorrow and imperfection; as this mosaic pavement has been so put together by the skill of the artist, that the colours and arrangements vary as it is looked at from one point of view or another.

We see also our two pillars, I∴ and B∴, which signify *Strength* and *Establishment;* but they are mutilated and disfigured, because they have lost their capitals by the death of our Most Respectable Grand Master Hiram.

We come now to the Tableau, which is divided lengthwise by three lines, and the signification whereof we are to learn and understand. Beginning at the right we find the *Tower of Babel*, which we are well aware was an absurd undertaking by men foolishly fearful of the Almighty God. It serves as an emblem that we should never entertain notions too high and exalted, but should, in all our undertakings and works, use the greatest foresight and consideration, being most careful and circumspect not to act against the will and holy ordinances of the Great and Mighty JEHOVA: that we may not, like those inconsiderate builders, find in our works our ruin and our graves. Truly we find consolation in the branch of acacia upon the grave of our Most Respectable Grand Master Hiram Abiff for the errors committed by those who preceded us; but it must not, by the sense of security it gives, induce us to enter upon evil undertakings, fit only to be classed with their's.

The *Moon*, upon the painting, is a cold body of herself, and so brings nothing forth by her own warmth; and thus is a symbol to us of the insufficiency of man's exertions without the Divine assistance.

The double injury to the beauty of our Order by the mutilation of its *pillars* symbolizes the severe blow it sustained by the tragical end of our Most Respectable Grand Master Hiram Abiff, which unhappy event each Scottish Master remembers with the most acute sorrow, and the whole Order laments it; for he very ardently laboured for the firm establishment of the Order of the Great and Mighty Jehova.

On the left, passing the mutilated pillar B∴, you see *the Ark of Noah*. This

18

signifies the wonderful preservation and establishment of our Order under a thousand dangers and difficulties; the preservation of Noah and his family being more miraculous than that of our Godly Forefathers.

The *Cubical Stone* signifies the perfection of our Order, as it is the most regular of bodies, having all its sides, faces and angles equal. So, too, is our Order perfect in its regularity, unanimity and harmony, and the sacredness of the ties that bind us together.

Further on is a drawing of the *Temple*, the most noble and elegant structure that ever existed, planned by the Almighty God himself, and which He, in the most especial manner, honored with His glorious presence as a high testimonial of His favour: that presence which we represent as ever with us in our assemblies.

The *Sun* signifies the former glory of the Temple, the fame whereof was spread abroad among all the nations.

The *Pillar I∴*, which signifies the *establishment* of our Order, has likewise suffered severely. But the base and much of the column still remains as perfect as ever, and the Sun, the most magnificent of the Heavenly Bodies, stands vertically above it.

Observe now the middle way, on which we pass over the *Mosaic Pavement*, between B∴, the *strength*, and I∴, the *establishment* of the Order, to the *Brazen Sea*, in which we are symbolically to purify ourselves from all pollutions, from all faults and wrongful actions, as well as those committed through error of judgment and mistaken opinion, as those intentionally done; inasmuch as they equally prevent us from arriving at the knowledge of true wisdom. We must thoroughly cleanse and purify our hearts, to their inmost recesses, before we can rightfully contemplate that *Flaming Star*, which is the emblem of the divine and glorious *Shekinah*, before we may dare approach the Throne of Supreme Wisdom.

The *Ark of the Covenant*, wherein formerly the Tables of the Law were deposited, serves to remind us that our hearts are now the proper depositories of those laws, and that upon them they ought to be ineffaceably engraven.

That Divine Wisdom has remained undiminished among our Order, even in the periods of its greatest depression.

This is symbolized by the middle way, on which there is no spot to mar its brightness or remind us of our past afflictions. For God loves his Order, and has ever protected it; and whenever its destruction has seemed impending and inevitable, and he has suffered it for the time to be depressed, it has only been that He might afterwards raise it again in greater glory.

19

LECTURE.

Ques∴ Are you a Grand Scottish Master?

Ans∴ I am; the whole Worshipful Brotherhood acknowledge me as such; and I am perfectly acquainted with the letters M∴ and G∴

Ques∴ Where was you received a Scottish Master?

Ans∴ In the Sanctum Sanctorum, under the Acacia.

Ques∴ How did you come there?

Ans∴ Through the Porch, Outer Court and Sanctuary.

Ques∴ After you was received and brought to light what did you see?

Ans∴ A Brazen Sea.

Ques∴ Of what use is that Brazen Sea?

Ans∴ That the Scottish Masters may wash and purify themselves therein, as the Priests and Levites did, who were obliged to wash themselves before they could enter the Temple.

Ques∴ What more did you see?

Ans∴ Three Golden Basins, in the first of which was the letter M∴, in the second the letter G∴, and in the third nothing: and which three basins the Scottish Elder Masters found in the ruins of the Temple, in the times of the Crusades.

Ques∴ Did you see nothing else?

Ans∴ Yes; I saw the Ark of the Covenant, wherein were deposited the Tables of the Law.

Ques∴ What does all this signify?

Ans∴ That the Scottish Masters must keep the laws of God in their hearts, in order that they may have a covenant with him.

Ques∴ Did you see anything besides?

Ans∴ I saw also a Flaming Star.

Ques∴ What does it signify?

Ans∴ The holy presence of Almighty God.

Ques∴ What Brethren did you see in the Temple?

Ans∴ The Apprentices and Fellow-Crafts in the Outer Court, the Masters in the Sanctuary, and the Elder Masters in the Sanctum Sanctorum.

Ques∴ Is that all that you saw there?

Ans∴ No; I saw other things also, which I and all the Grand Scottish Masters keep in our hearts.

Ques∴ How old are you?

20

Ans∴ A thousand years.
Ques∴ How many pillars has a Scottish Lodge?
Ans∴ Four: Two broken and mutilated, and two overturned and thrown down.
Ques∴ What do they signify?
Ans∴ That the Temple is in ruins.
Ques∴ What is the hour?
Ans∴ The break of day.

TO CLOSE.

G∴ M∴ Most Honorable Knight and Brother Senior Grand Warden, as we are about to suspend for the present these our Holy Labours, which we carry on through the assistance of the Almighty Grand Architect of the Universe, and have concluded to close this Grand Scottish Lodge, I must ask you if our Holy Knightly labours have been so conducted as to entitle us to praise and honour.

Sen∴ Gr∴ War∴ High Exalted Grand Master and Honorable Knight of St. Andrew, this most Right Worshipful assembled Lodge of valiant Knights and Brethren, upon the honour of each, most respectfully thank you for your highly commendable zeal, industry and prudence, so perfectly exemplified in the work of this present assembly. Your uprightness, impartiality, courtesy and brotherly kindness have inspired us with the greatest personal regard and affection, and will forever bind us to you. In your knightly demeanor and bearing, we see beautifully exemplified the theory and precepts of our Order. Our desires are fully satisfied. We ask no more than that you, Most Exalted Knight and Grand Master, may never cease henceforward to assist us with your good counsel and example, and superintend our future Knightly labours, that we may be enabled to transmit to our successors, unimpaired, the true bases of our Order and the correct practice of its work.

Jun∴ Gr∴ War∴ The wonderful secrets which the Scottish Knights and Brethren discovered, in exploring the ruins of the Temple at Jerusalem, made

21

the discovery of the true use thereof important; and that we may always make proper use of the same, the Knights and Masters of this Exalted Scottish Lodge pray the Most Excellent Grand Master that our labour and diligence may be aided by his great wisdom and foresight, so that we may be enabled to make further discoveries, and through Wisdom, Strength and Beauty never fail in carrying out the excellent purposes of our Holy Masonry.

Gr∴ Secy∴ We most heartily thank our Most High Exalted Grand Master for holding this Lodge. We are all unanimously resolved to be regulated and governed in everything by his will and pleasure. Let us now, my Brethren, not omit our duty toward him, by four times four, with all the knightly honours due to his exalted station, thus anew pledging him our allegiance. My Brethren and Exalted Knights, assist me therein!

[All the Knights rise, and clap with their open hands 4 times 4. Then they take off their hats with their left hands, and draw their swords with their right, raising their hands up, the hilt in front of the forehead, and then lowering the point to the ground together, taking the time from the Grand Master of Ceremonies. They then make a low bow, and remain standing. The Grand Master then draws his sword, and returns the compliment, and says:]

G∴ M∴ My dear Brethren and Exalted Knights, I am glad to find that you are not slow to perform your duty. It is not to me these honours are due, but to the Mighty Grand Architect of the Universe, whose precepts and holy laws we practice in our holy assemblies. To Him all homage is due. Let the fear of His mighty name be ever present with you! His Laws be ever engraved on your hearts. Endeavour, so far as possible, to imitate his goodness. Be forgiving and merciful to your enemies, benevolent and bountiful to your friends and fellow-creatures. Do unto every one as you would be done by, and thereby do honour to His holy name. Blessed be that great and mighty name, for ever and ever! Amen! Retire, my Brethren, in peace and friendship, and practice the virtues you have here been taught. This Lodge is closed.

[The Brethren put on their hats, sheathe their swords, applaud by once 4, and give the Common Scotch Sign.]

END.

The manuscript from which the foregoing Degree is copied is evidently translated from the French, as appears by the constantly recurring mistakes in the meaning of French words, done into most execrable English. There are many omissions, and many passages are absolutely without any meaning. I have corrected these defects as far as has been in my power; so that this copy is not by any means a literal one, but the whole substance of the original is preserved.

The SALT spoken of, as that word was used by the Alchemists, was NITRE. They used, as the three principle substances, that SALT, SULPHUR and MERCURY. Ragon says: "The Salt is the attribute of the FATHER, the Sulphur that of the SON, and the Mercury that of the HOLY SPIRIT. From the action of these three, results the Triangle in the Square; and from the Seven Angles of these, the DECADE or perfect number."

ALBERT PIKE, XXXIII°.
Sov. Gr. Ins. Gen'l.

IT WAS WELL SAID: *Alchimia est ars, cujus initium larborare, medium mentiri, finis mendicare.* The Hermetic Philosophers furnished this key of nature: "From all material substances ashes is made; from ashes is extracted salt; from the salt we separate water and mercury, and from the mercury we make an elixir or quintessence."

So the body or substance to be operated on is reduced to *ashes* to clear it of all its combustible portions; to *salt*, to separate it from these that are terrestrial; into *water*, to be purified; and into *spirit* to become a quintessence.

There is properly but one Salt, but it is divided into three sorts, to form the principle of bodies: *nitre, tartar* and *vitriol*. All the others are compounded from these. From the vapors of these salts mercury is formed. Of mercury and sulphur are formed, in the earth, all minerals.

The Philosopher's Stone was imagined to contain certain proportions of nitre, sulphur and mercury proper to produce transmutation of metals, with the action of *electricity*, when they should reach a state of fusion. *Electricity* is the *spirit* of the foregoing degree.

24
FROM RAGON'S ORTHODOXIE MACONNIQUE.

PAGE 116.

Regime Reforme on Rectifie de Dresde.

This Regime was based upon the Templar system of Ramsay. The Ritual of initiation is divided into two parts: The External Order, comprising the three symbolic degrees; and the Internal Order, composed of three degrees, forming a religious system based on chivalry. These two Orders are connected by an intermediary degree, the Maitre Ecossais de Saint Andre, in which candidates are selected for the Beneficent Knights of the Holy City. This is their nomenclature:

Exterior Order . . . . $\begin{cases} 1° \text{ Apprentice.} \\ 2° \text{ Companion.} \\ 3° \text{ Master.} \end{cases}$

Intermediary Degree . . . . . . 4° Scottish Master of St. Andrew.

Interior Order . . . . $\begin{cases} 5° \text{ Equestrian Chapter.} \\ 6° \text{ Novice.} \\ 7° \text{ Knight.} \end{cases}$

This Regime produced divers directories, styled Ecossais, which had a particular denomination and a magestral see, exercising, each in its jurisdiction, a pretended Masonic supremacy.

Bordeaux had the Directory of Occitania, 2d Province.
Lyon   "   "   " Auvergne, 3d   "
Strasbourg "   "   " Burgundy, 5th "

These three distinct establishments, united by the same principles, the same doctrine, and the same Masonic forms, were entitled the French Langue. They corresponded with Chambery, which had the Directory of Italy or Austrian Lombardy. Many French Provinces, among others Alsace, Franche-Comte, Dauphine and Provence, counted many Lodges constituted by these Scottish Directories.

FACSIMILE

EXPLANATORY.

There are in the Archives of the Grand Lodge of Louisiana a great number of Rituals and other Manuscripts, which came to the old Grand Lodge of that State many years ago, from French Lodges in the State that had ceased working. Among the Rituals are several, copied by some one person with care, pains and neatness, in one and the same fashion of arrangement and execution, in a peculiarly neat and plain handwriting, always uniform and accurate; mostly from original Rituals certified by the Bro∴ Achille Huet de Lachelle.

Among these are the Rituals of Mark-Mason, Royal Arch and Past Master, which are here translated, the original paging and the characteristics of the manuscript being in all substantial respects preserved, especially as regards the underscoring in red ink and the braces (accolades) in the margin; and the translation being as literal as possible.

In the Tableau of the feast of St John, 5801, "*of the Brethren who compose the Resp∴ Lodge of St. John of Jerusalem, under the distinctive title of La Réunion Désirée, regularly constituted by the Gr∴ O∴ of France, the 17th day of the 3d Masonic month of the year of the True Light, 5784, at the O∴ of Port-au-Prince (now Port Republicain*")—(*au Port Republicain, de l'imprimerie des ff∴ Gauchet, Lagrange &c' e*") I find registered, as honorary officer and free Affiliate, "*Achille Huet de la Chelle, former Sénéchal du Petit-Goave, and there residing, born at Paris, M∴ E∴ T∴ G∴*"

And in the Tableau for the same year of the Lodge *La Réunion des Cœurs,* "*of the Ancient constitution of York, regularly constituted at the O∴ of Port Republicain, on the 18th day of the 10th Month, 5789,*" of which GERMAIN HACQUET, Notary Public, born at Paris, and aged 40 years, R∴ A∴ R∴ †∴ P∴ du R∴ S∴ and Dep∴ G∴ Insp∴ was Venerable, and JOSEPH CERNEAU, Merchant Goldsmith, born at Villeblerin, aged 37 years, R∴ A∴ R∴ †∴ was keeper of the Seals and Archives,—I find, among the Deputies near other Lodges, "ETIENNE FOURTEAU, *resident of Jérémie, Deputy of the*

2

Resp∴ L∴ No. 47, near the Respectable L∴ La Réunion des Cœurs, at the Or∴ of Jérémie, R∴ A∴ R∴ †∴ P∴ du R∴ S∴. He will be spoken of hereafter. The copy of this Register in my possession is authenticated by the autograph signatures of the Bros∴ Hacquet and Cerneau: and nearly all the members were R∴ A∴ (Royal Arch Masons.)

The certificates of the Bro∴ Huet de Lachelle to the Rituals were of different dates, from 1796 to 1801. That to the Ritual of Rose Croix d'Heredom de Kilwining is in these words:

"We, Achille Huet de Lachelle, [Wisdom] Ecuyer Sénéchal du Petit Goave, Grand Master of the Grand and Sublime Chap∴ Provincial of Heredom of Kilwining, having its See at the Little Goave, Island of Santo Domingo, under the distinctive title of le St. Esprit, undersigned, do certify unto all whom it may concern, that the course of Reception of R∴ C∴ †∴ hereinbefore by us transcribed, literally conforms to the original, which has been expedited to us as Provincial Gr∴ Master, by the Grand Lodge and Sublime Chapter, chief of the Order of Heredom of Kilwining of Edinburg."

"In testimony whereof, we have in the margin caused the seal of our arms to be impressed in black wax, and have signed these by our names, surnames, characteristics and qualities.

"At the Orient of Arcahaye, this 26th day of the 8th month, of the Masonic year 5796.

HUET DE LACHELLE, [SAGESSE.]
Prov∴ Gr∴ Master."

And the Ritual in my possession, of *Le Vrai maçon, Grade Philosophique*, written entirely by himself, has his seal in black wax, and is certified by him as Provincial Grand Master, on the 18th day of the 4th month, 5796.

In his introduction to the degrees of Rose Croix Heredom of Kilwinning he gives the following account of his connection with Masonry in Santo Domingo: "Until in 5788, the colony of Santo Domingo had no regular Chapter of Rose Croix. Those that existed had been founded by Brethren who may in good faith have believed themselves regular Rose Croix, but in fact were not so.

"The M∴ Illustrious B∴ Buttet, who had constituted most of these Chapters, and among others that of the Little Goave, of which I was an officer, was himself convinced of the irregularity of our working in this degree, after our correspondence with the Grand Lodge of the Grand and Sublime Order of Heredom of Kilwinning at the O∴ of Rouen.

FACSIMILE

3

"We received the first column from this Grand Lodge of France, in the Masonic year 5787.

"We then resolved, as good Masons, to regularize ourselves, and the more certainly to attain that, we addressed ourselves to the Grand Lodge of France, which had instructed us, and offered us its services.

"During the long time required for a correspondence at two thousand leagues distance, the Ill.·. Bro.·. Buttet abdicated the government of Masonry, and sent his demission as well to the Illustrious Provincial Lodge, as to the respectable Lodges of its own correspondence.

"I was elected Provincial Administrator, as his successor, and the Bro.·. Radoux, ex-Venerable of Lodges, a Mason distinguished by his age, his labors, and his virtues, still living, I obtained of his modesty his consent to accept the Presidency of the Chapter.

"We applied to the chief of the Order, through the Gr.·. Lodge at Rouen, and requested that the Bro.·. Domenique Laurent Radoux might be selected for President and Gr.·. Master of the Chapter, and he failing, the Bro.·. Achille Huet de Lachelle, and in my default again, the Bro.·. Joseph Laurent Landelle. These precautions appeared to be necessary in so sickly a a country, and the event showed that our precaution was wise.

"We obtained, in 5788, our Constitutions as Grand Lodge of the Royal Order of Heredom of Kilwinning, from the Sovereign Chief of the Order.

"The Bro.·. Radoux was appointed Grand Master; in his default, I was; and in mine, the B.·. Kt.·. Landelle.

"When we received these powers, the Bro.·. Radoux had died in France, and I found myself, in accordance with the appointment, the first Provincial Grand Master. I received at the same time the ceremonial of reception, and the secret instructions, but the original charter, the book of the laws, and the decorations of the knights had been lost at sea.

"I advised the Lodges of the Colony of the powers that I had received, and tendered them such services as duty required; but at the same time I informed them of my losses at sea; that I had duplicated my orders, and that I would not proceed to work until what I had ordered should have come to hand.

"Then the troubles of the Revolution came, and my correspondence, as well with the chief of the Order as with the Provincial Chapter of France, was wholly broken off.

"Nevertheless, Jeremie being one of the places in the Colony that suffered least, Masonry flourishing there, the Scottish Lodge, composed of at least fifty members, many of whom were Past Masters, I deemed it advisable, for the propagation of the Royal Art, to establish a Chapter at that Orient.— The Venerable Bro∴ FOURTAUD, founder and ex-Venerable of that Respectable Lodge, was the person whom I appointed President of the Chapter, which took the name of '*la Triple Unité des Cœurs.*' I accepted the Honorary Presidency, and affiliated nearly all the Members-Knights with the Sublime Provincial Chapter, of which I was the Grand Master.

"The Sov∴ Chapter of Jeremie did me the favour to take the seal of my arms as the seal of the Chapter.

"On the 29th day of the 5th month, 5796, I also regularized, at Baltimore, in Maryland, the Chapter *La Verité*. It had been founded long before by a Bro∴ Martin, and had worked for a long time, under the belief that it was regular, but becoming convinced of its error, as that of the Petit Goave had, it made application, after we had done so, to the Chief of the Order, to obtain letters of constitution. The Chief of the Order, by one of his columns, had advised us of this, and requested us to regularize that Chapter. The Bro∴-Knight Taveau, Second Light of that Temple, was affiliated by us in our Chapter, and was empowered by us to take the oath of these Officers-Knights, and to regularize them for us, in the name of the Chief of the Order."

As will be seen by the Ritual of Mark Mason, the Bro∴ Huet de Lachelle copied that Ritual from the Book of "*the Bro∴ Fourt∴*" This Bro∴ Fourtaud or Fourteau, was, as we have seen, the Representative, in 1801, of the Lodge Reunion des Cœurs, at Port-au-Prince, near the Lodge of the same name at Jeremie, and he was then a Prince of the Royal Secret. He had been Master of the Lodge there, before de Lachelle received his commission from France, which was before the beginning of the French Revolution. It is not in the least probable that he obtained the Ritual of Mark Mason or Royal Arch from the United States. It more probably came to him from Kingston; and as there were nineteen or more Royal Arch Masons, in 1801, in the Lodge *Réunion des Cœurs* at Port-au-Prince, that degree must have been worked there for some time.

The Rituals of Mark Mason and Royal Arch are without date; but the fact that the former was copied from the Book of the Bro∴ Fourtaud carries its date back even prior to 1796.

In the Bulletin of the Grand Orient of France, No. 22, for July, 1849, p. 85, is the following:

FACSIMILE

5

"In 1783, took place the constitution of the Lodge *Réunion Désirée*, O∴ of Port-au-Prince, by the G∴ L∴ of France . . . . . In 1788, the same authority founded, at Jacmel, the Lodge *le Choix des hommes*, the Lodge and Chapter *Des Freres réunis*, and at Jérémie the Lodge *Saint Jean de Jérusalem* . . . . .

"The Grand Orient of France founded also, at Port-au-Prince, in 1788, La Reunion des Cœurs . . . . .

"In 1788, the Royal Grand Lodge of Heredom and of Kilwinning, in Scotland, granted Constitutions to the Chapter of the *Saint Esprit*, Valley of the Petit Goave.

"A Provincial Grand Lodge of Santo Domingo, and a Grand Chapter of Heredom and of Kilwinning, were established in the Island, and M. HUET DE LA CHAPELLE, Civil Judge and Lieutenant of Admiralty, at the Petit Goave, was the Grand Master of it."

. . . .

"The whites, so violently and inhumanly expelled from Santo Domingo, went to Cuba, New Orleans, and New York." [Also they went to Charleston, Portsmouth, Virginia, and Baltimore.] "Those who went to Cuba, founded on that Island two Lodges, *la Concorde* and *la Perseverance*, which they carried with them, in 1809, to New Orleans. Those who settled at New Orleans founded there, in 1807, a Lodge under the title of *La Réunion Désirée*; and those in New York assisted in founding, in 1797, the Lodge *l'Union Française*."

Also the refugees founded *la Candeur*, at Charleston; *la Sagesse*, No. 2660; at Portsmouth, (chartered by the Gr∴ Orient of France, and of which I have printed tableaux of 1794 and 1795.) and a Lodge and Chapter of the Royal Order of Scotland, at Baltimore.

REPRINTS OF RITUALS OF OLD DEGREES

FACSIMILE

> Rite Ancien
> Maçonnerie D'York.
> ᵐᵉ∴ Grade, Mark Maçon
> &
> ᵐᵉ∴ Grade, Royale Arche.

REPRINTS OF RITUALS OF OLD DEGREES

INDEX

FOR THE DEGREE OF MARK MASON.

Arrangement of the Lodge, ... 1
Titles of the Brethren, ... 2
Opening of the Works, ... 2
Signs, batteries of the Opening of the Lodge, ... 4
Receptions of several Candidates, ... 5
Journey of Candidate
- 1 8
- 2 9
- 3 10
- 4 11

Oath of the Candidate, ... 13
Mode of putting the Lodge at Refreshment, ... 14
Mode of resuming Labor, ... 15
Explanation of the Medal, ... 16
Discourse of the Degree, ... 18
Signs,
- 1st of Order, ... 15
- 2d of Adhesion, ... 15
- 3d of Assistance, ... 16

Words,
- Sacred, ... 15
- Pass, ... 15

Grip of the Degree, ... 16
Catechism of the same, ... 20
Closing of the works, ... 20

FACSIMILE

B

INDEX

FOR THE 2D APARTMENT OF THE SAME DEGREE IN THE OTHER PART.

Titles of the Brethren, ... 24
Opening of the Lodge of Perfection, ... 24
Entrance of the Candidate into the Temple, ... 25
Oath of the Candidate in this Apartment, ... 29
Discourse, ... 30
Closing, ...

PAST MASTER, ... 53

INDEX

FOR THE DEGREE OF ROYAL ARCH.

Apartments,
- 1st 32
- 2d 32
- 3d 32
- 4th, or Sanctuary, ... 32

Order of Places of the Brethren and their Decoration, ... 35

Reception of the Candidate
- 1st, Apartment and its Oath, ... 36–37
- 2d, Apartment, ... 38
- 3d, Apartment, ... 39
- 4th, Apartment, ... 40

Opening of the Chapter, ... 35
Grip, ... 44

Words,
- Sacred, ... 44
- Of Merit, ... 44
- Pass, ... 45

History of the Degree, ... 45
Closing of the Chapter, ... 51

Signs,
- 1, Of Order, or of the Skull, ... 43
- 2, Of the Staff, ... 43
- 3, Of the Leprosy, ... 43
- 4, Of Recognition, or of the Water, ... 43
- 5, Of Admiration, ... 44

Grand Order and Jewels, ... 34

REPRINTS OF RITUALS OF OLD DEGREES

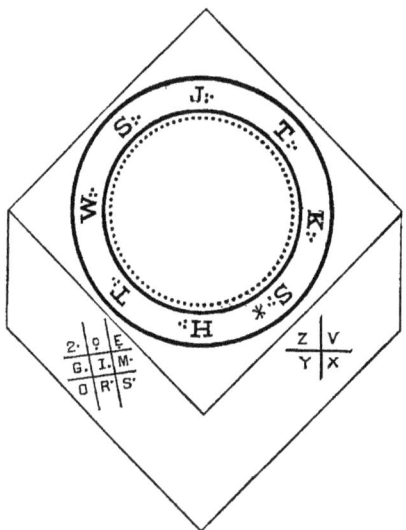

MARK MASON.

5th Degree of the Masonry of York, Ancient Rite.

For a Brother to be received in this degree, he must have attained the 3d degree of the Ancient Rite, and have been accepted, and have been accepted herein by ballot, without any negative vote.

If the ballot is favorable to the candidate, he will be informed of it in the ante-room, and be prepared for his reception as follows:

Preparation of the Candidate in the Chamber of Reflection.

This Chamber of Reflection, in which the candidate is placed, should be as dark as possible; his hair is dishevelled, his shirt turned down around his waist, in short breeches, without shoes or stockings, a cord around his neck, and deprived of all metalic substances.

Arrangement of the Lodge.

The hangings are of any color that may be preferred: while blue is most appropriate. As to lights, if the hall is not large, sixteen candles suffice;— but there must not be less: and if with sixteen the light is not sufficient, they may be increased to 19, 21, or 23. In the middle of the Lodge will be placed a small altar; of the form given on the preceding page, in the [2] centre of which will be a round stone, of considerable thickness, and of white marble, on which two circles will be drawn, between which will be cut the letters of the medal of the degree:

Hiram, Roi de	Thir	Vent	Envoyer	Jabulum	Au	Roi	Salomon
H∴	T∴	W∴	S∴	J∴	T∴	K∴	S∴
Hiram	Tyre	will	send	Jabulum	to	King	Solomon

1 . . . (1)

2 . . . (2)

On the altar will be placed a poniard, a Bible, a square, a compass, and three stars, two toward the South, and one toward the North. If there are large candle-sticks, these are to be added, and placed around the altar.

———•◆•———

MEDAL.

Titles of the Brethren.

The Grand Master, *Very Wise.*
The First Warden, } *Venerable.*
The Second Warden, }
The other brethren
Two Deacons, who sit, one by the side of the Grand Master, and one by the side of the First Warden.

OPENING.

Qu∴ Second Deacon, what is your duty in the Lodge?
Ans∴ It is to ascertain whether the Lodge is well tyled.
Well, First and Second Deacons, ascertain that.

[3] When the two Deacons have done so, the First says to the Very Wise, that the Lodge is well tyled. When the Very Wise, addressing himself to the First Warden says:

Qu∴ Venerable First Warden, what is the first care of the Warden in Lodge?
Ans∴ It is to ascertain whether all our Brethren are Mark Masons.
Ascertain that, my Brethren!

The two Wardens repair to their respective columns, and demand of each Brother the Sacred Word, which is given them accompanied with the Sign of Order (See page 15 *marg.*) This finished, they return to their places, and the Very Wise sends his Deacon to the two Wardens, to receive from them the Sacred Word, which he forthwith takes to and gives to the Very Wise, and returns to his place near him; and then the Very Wise asks him:

Qu∴ Brother First Deacon, what is your place in Lodge?
Ans∴ Behind you, Very Wise, or at your right if you permit it.
Qu∴ Why there, my Brother?

FACSIMILE

3 . . . (3)

Ans.˙. To bear your orders to the Venerable Wardens or to any other Brother of the Lodge, if you desire it.
Qu.˙. Brother Second Deacon, what is your place in Lodge?
Ans.˙. Behind the First Warden, or at his right if he permits it.
Qu.˙. Why there, my Brother?
Ans.˙. To bear his orders wherever it may seem good to him.
Qu.˙. Brother Treasurer, where is your place?
Ans.˙. Very Wise, it is in the South.
Qu.˙. Why, my brother?
Ans.˙. To account to the Lodge wherever it may be required of me.
Qu.˙. Brother Secretary, where is your place?
Ans.˙. Very Wise, it is in the North.
Qu.˙. Why there, my Brother? [4]
Ans.˙. To be ready to obey the orders of the Orient, and to register the works of the Lodge.
Qu.˙. Venerable First Warden, where does the Master station himself?
Ans.˙. Very Wise, in the East.
Qu.˙. Why, my Brother?
Ans.˙. The Sun rising in that quarter to light the world, so the Very Wise stations himself there to give light to the workmen of the Lodge.
Qu.˙. Venerable First Warden, where is your place in the Lodge?
Ans.˙. In the West of the Temple, Very Wise.
Qu.˙. Why is that, my brother?
Ans.˙. Very Wise, it is that I may there execute your will.
Qu.˙. Venerable Second Warden, what is your place in Lodge?
Ans.˙. In the South or West, Very Wise.
Qu.˙. Why is that, my Brother?
Ans.˙. To set the workmen at work, when you order it.
Qu.˙. Venerable First Warden, what is the hour?
Ans.˙. Very Wise, the Sun begins to appear.
Brethren, First and Second Wardens, announce to the respectable workshop that my intention is to open the Lodge of Mark Mason.

The 3 Signs of Apprentice, Fellow and Master.

The First Warden makes the announcement upon his column; the Second afterwards on his: which done, the First Warden announces it to the [5] Very Wise, ✶, who immediately raps 8 eqnal raps . . . . replied to by the Warden by four equal raps also . . . . and by the Second

4 . . . (5)

Warden by four others . . . . . at the last of which raps, all the Brethren rise and come to order (in what manner, see page 15) give the usual acclamation (See page 16), and then the signs of Apprentice, Fellow and Master (A): followed by that of Mark Mason, and the plaudits of the same, by 4 equal raps . . . . . , which done, each sits down.

Then the Very Wise directs the reading of the engraved plate of the last marks, upon the draft of which, each Brother has the right to offer remarks, which are acceded to, if it is found to be proper.

(*Note.*) That there must be a Book of Gold, specially belonging to this degree, about a fourth part of which is appropriated to recording the names and ages of the Brethren, and the device which each adopts; but it is not necessary to make mention in it of the degrees which one may have above this.

Then the Master says:

Qu.·. Venerable First Warden, what purpose has brought us together here?

Ans.·. Very Wise, it is the verification of the work of the Brethren who demand increase of wages.

Reception of a Candidate.

At the moment when the candidate is about to be announced at the door of the Lodge, to make his entrance, he is made to take with the two first fingers and the thumb of his right hand, the other fingers closed, a stone as large as he can carry, he being prepared as indicated on the first page (*Sign* 3.)

[6] (A) THE SIGNS.

Of Apprentice : . . . . thumb raised, forming with the other fingers, closed, a square.

Of Fellow : . . . . . thumb raised, forming with, &c., a square . . . . left, at height of . . . . fingers together, and thumb separated, forming square like the other hand.

Of Master : with the thumb, the other fingers together . . . . and raise the two hands above the head, the fingers spread apart.

Mark Mason : The index and medius of the right hand behind the ear.

5 . . . (6)

Continuation of the Reception.

Immediately after the announcement upon the columns has been completed, the Tiler raps with four equal knocks at the door . . . . without opening it, which announces to the Brother Terrible, who is in the ante-room with the Candidate, *that he can enter; if the Brother to be received is ready.* If he is so, the Bro.˙. Terrible will reply to these raps by seven, that is to say, as a Master . . . . which are replied to by the Tiler with 4 . . . . who, immediately after giving them, goes and informs the Second Warden that *one raps at the door of the Temple as a Master.* He in his turn will inform the First Warden, and he the Very Wise, who will say:

See who the indiscreet person is who dares thus to disturb our labors.

The Second Warden transmits this order to the Tiler, who immediately [7] repairs to the door, opens it, and after having ascertained who it is, closes it, re-enters, and goes and informs the Second Warden, in a low voice, who says aloud to the Very Wise:

It is (one or two) Master or Masters, who demand increase of wages.

The Very Wise says:

Cause them to be asked their names, their age, as Masons, their religion and their profession.

The Second Warden transmits this order to the Tiler, who goes to the door, opens it, and complies with the order, in such manner that the Secretary may have time to write the detail of the works. Then he re-enters, and in a low voice communicates to the Second Warden the responses of the Candidate, who in his turn transmits them to the Very Wise, who then says:

Well, permit them to enter the Temple.

The Second Warden repeats this order to the Tiler, who at once executes it. They enter, the Bro.˙. Terrible preceding them, who leads them directly to the Second Warden, and causes one of them to give four equal raps . . . . . upon the left shoulder of the Second Warden, who says to him:

What do you desire?

To which he replies:

That our work may be verified, so that we may obtain increase of wages.

The Second Warden says to him:

Go and prefer your request to the Brother First Warden.

They go to the First Warden, and stand in front of him. One of them raps 4 on his left shoulder, and he, in the same manner, sends them on to the Very Wise. He descends to the lowest step of the throne, and one of

6 . . . (8)

the Candidates makes the same request of him, in the name of the others, [8] and in the same manner as it was made to the two Wardens, which done, the Grand Master sends them to the West of the Temple, ascends to his throne, and then addressing the Candidate, says:

What do you desire?
To make new progress in Masonry, if you find us worthy of it.

The Very Wise, then addressing himself to the Second Deacon, who is near the First Warden, says to him:
Cause these Candidates to make their first journey.

1st Journey of the Candidates.

The Second Deacon, going before the Candidates, causes them to halt first before the Second Warden, who, after having passed the plumb over the work which one of them presents to him, says to them:
This work is defective.

The Deacon then leads them to the First Warden, who in his turn verifies the work by passing his level over it, and says:
This work is defective.

The Deacon then causes them to make the circuit of the hall, which ended, he says to the Second Warden:
My Brother, the journey is ended.

The Second Warden repeats this announcement to the First, who in his turn transmits it to the Very Wise, who then says to the Candidate:
Qu.·. *What is the foundation of Masonry?*
Ans.·. *It is to love one's Brethren as one's self.*

The Very Wise then says to him:
Give the Venerable Second Warden the grip, the pass-word and sign of an Apprentice.

[9] When the Second Warden has received the grip, word and sign, he says in a low voice to the First Warden . . (See hereafter A:)
Venerable Brother, all is just and perfect.

Pass-word, ... (there is no Sacred Word in the Degree of Apprentice.)

     Grip . . . . . 1st phal . . . .
     Sign . . . . . (See the last on page 6.)

7 . . . (10)

The First Warden repeats the announcement aloud to the Very Wise, who then says:

Well, since it is so, Brother Second Deacon, cause the Candidates to make their second journey.

2nd Journey of the Candidates.

This journey is made in the same way as the first, (see, as to this, Accolade, page —.) When the announcement has been finished and the Very Wise is advised of it, he says to the Candidates:

Now, Brothers, why have you asked an increase of pay ?

One of the Candidates responds:

To acquire new light, and be enabled the better to relieve the needs of my Brethren.

The Very Wise says to them:

My Brethren, give the Venerable Second Warden the words, signs and grips of a Fellow.

When the Second Warden has received them, he says in a low voice to the First Warden:

Venerable Brother, all is just and perfect.

The First Warden, in his turn, says aloud to the Very Wise, that [10] all is just and perfect, and the latter orders as follows: ✢

Words:——— { Pass——— . C∴ H∴ . . . L∴ T∴
             { Sacred——— . . K∴ . . .

Grip:——— . . . . . . phal of 2d . . . . .

Sign:———See page 6.

V∴ ✢ W∴ Since it is so, Brother Second Deacon, cause the Candidates to make their third journey.

3rd Journey of the Candidates.

The third journey is proceeded with in the same manner as the first.—
When the announcement is finished, and the Very Wise advised, he says to the Candidates:

My Brethren, why were you deprived of everything metallic ?

One of the Candidates replies:

8 . . . (11)

Because at the time of the building of the Temple of Solomon, no noise caused by any working-tools was heard.

The Very Wise continues and says:

My Brethren, give the Venerable Bro. Second Warden the words, signs and grip of a Master.

When he has received them, as below, (B.) he says in a low voice to the First Warden:

Venerable Brother First Warden, all is just and perfect.

[11] The First Warden repeats this announcement in his turn, in a loud voice to the Very Wise, who says: ‡

[Words, { Pass:—. O∴ H∴ . . . O∴ N∴
          { Sacred:—. U∴ B∴ . . . K∴ . N.   (B)

Grip :———Cing points . . . . .
Sign :———See page   ]

V∴‡ W∴ Since all is just and perfect, Bro∴ Second Deacon, cause the Candidates to make their fourth journey.

Fourth Journey of the Candidates.

The fourth journey is proceeded upon in the same manner as the first.— When the announcement is completed, and the Very Wise advised, he says to the Candidates:

My Brethren, why are you barefooted?

One of the Candidates replies:

Because the place whereby we have passed is holy ground. For God said unto Moses, Take off thy shoes: the place where thou art is holy ground.

The Very Wise continues, and says to them:

My brethren, according to our custom, you should have made sixteen journeys; but, foreseeing that you would be wearied, I have reduced them to these four.

Here the Very Wise descends from his throne, goes to the rear of the altar, [12] which is set in the middle of the Temple; all the Brethren range themselves around it, and the Conductor of the Candidate brings him there, and causes him to kneel on his right knee at the foot of the altar, his left leg

9 . . . (12)

forming a square with the other; and he being in this position, the Very Wise, with his square, examines the work of the Candidates, and finding it bad, returns it to the Candidate, who, taking it with his two hands, the little fingers raised together, flings the stone over his left shoulder, and the Very Wise, addressing the Candidates, says to them:

My Brothers, give me, each of you, thirteen cents.

They reply:

I have no money.

The Very wise, addressing himself to the Bro∴ Second Sub-Deacon, says to him:

Bro∴ Sub-Deacon, search, yourself.

Then, turning to the Candidates, he says to them:

How, my Brethren!—Refuse so small a sum for the relief of suffering humanity? And yet the Grand Architect of the Universe will account to you for it.

At this moment, the Sub-Deacon tells one of the Candidates to demand their wages, and, taking him by the right hand, makes him stretch it out over the altar, as if to receive wages, open; at which instant the Second Warden, having a poniard in his hand, and who should be posted there, makes a show of endeavoring to cut off his wrist; and immediately the Very Wise, addressing the Candidates, says to them:

My Brethren, are you willing to take the obligation of the degree [13] *which you desire?*

They reply:

We are, Very Wise.

The Obligation, or Oath.

I, ... , do swear and promise, of my own free will, and in the presence of the Grand Architect of the Universe and of this august Assembly, to keep in my heart the secrets that are about to be unveiled to me. I swear also to maintain inviolate secresy as to all the decrees of the Sublime Lodges that shall be transmitted to me by their Grand Deputies and Inspectors. I swear also friendship and fraternity to all true and good Masons, and promise them assistance in their misfortunes, and to warn them against the snares that may be set for them by their enemies, if they come to my knowledge. I also promise not to have communication with any Mason who shall by perjury have broken his sacred engagements, and, in a word, been recreant to the duties which we reciprocally owe

10 . . . (14)

each other. And if I should ever myself become perjured, I consent to suffer the penalties invoked by me in my former obligations, and, moreover, to be excluded from all Lodges regularly constituted, over the surface of the two Hemispheres. Wherefrom, may God preserve me, and be my help accordingly. Amen! amen! amen!

Mode of Putting the Lodge at Refreshment.

[14] Qu.˙. Venerable First Warden, what is the hour?
Ans.˙. Very Wise, the Sun is at meridian.

Qu.˙. Venerable First Warden, announce to the respectable workshop that my intentions are to put the Lodge at refreshment.

———The two Wardens alternately repeat the announcement on their respective columns; and when the Very Wise has been advised in the ordinary manner that this has been done, he raps 8 with his mallet . . . . ; the two Wardens respond by four . . ˙. ., and the Second Warden by four others . . . . ., and at the last rap all the Brethren go to refresh themselves.

Mode of Resuming Labor.

The Very Wise raps 7 at equal distances . . . ., which are replied unto by the First Warden by 5 . . . . . ., and immediately after by the Second Warden by two . .

Upon these raps being given, all the Brethren re-enter the Lodge and retake their places, except the Candidates and the Bro.˙. Terrible, their Conductor, who remain in the ante-chamber.

Then the Very Wise, addressing himself to the First Warden, says to him:
Q.˙. Venerable Bro.˙. First Warden, what is the hour?
Ans.˙. Very Wise, the hour when the workmen ought to resume their labors.

FACSIMILE

11 . . . (15)

Q∴ Venerable Bro∴ Second Warden, announce to the respectable workshop that I am about to reinstate the works in activity.

Here the Bro∴ Tiler knocks with four equal raps . . . . on the [15] door of the Temple, but without opening it, to advise the Bro∴ Terrible to bring the Candidates to it. The latter responds by seven knocks at equal intervals . . . . , of which the Bro∴ Tiler informs the Second Warden in a low voice, who informs the First Warden, and he, in his turn, informs the Very Wise, aloud, *who then rders the Candidates to be permitted to enter* the Temple, which order is transmitted in the ordinary way to the Bro∴ Tiler, who immediately repairs to his post and opens the door.

The Bro∴ Terrible, preceding the Candidates, leads them directly to thg foot of the throne of the Very Wise, who then gives them the followine word, grip and sign:

Pass Word.

G∴ I∴ B∴ U∴ L∴ U∴ M∴

Sacred Word.

H∴ E∴ A∴ V∴ E∴——I∴ T∴——O∴ V∴ E∴ R∴

On pronouncing this word, the right hand is turned upside down, the ends of the two first fingers joined to the end of the thumb, as if one held a stone with them, saying, "What shall we do with this stone?"

1st Sign: of Order.

Index and middle finger of the right hand behind the ear.

2nd Sign: of Adhesion, or Assent.

Raising and stretching out horizontally the right hand.

3rd Sign: of Assistance.

The thumb and the two first fingers joined at their extremities, as if [16] one held a stone with them, and the other fingers closed.

12 . . . (16)

Grip.

Interlace the little fingers of the right hands, joining the two thumbs, raised perpendicularly, the other fingers closed.

Battery or Acclamation.

. . . . equal raps.

Explanation of the Medal.

We have in this degree, my dear Brethren, independently of these signs, a medal of gold, for a sign of recognition. On the first side are engraved in a circle, the baptismal and family name of the Bro.·. to whom it belongs, his Masonic quality of Mark Mason, and the Orient at which he received this degree; also the Mosaic pavement, on which is the altar of the Very Wise, and on the altar an open Bible; and on that a compass crossed above a square; and on the Mosaic pavement the plumb and mallet, and over all, and to the left, an eye surrounded with rays.

On the reverse side, and between two circles drawn on the upper part of [17] the medal, are the letters:

Hiram	Thir	wil	send	Jabulum	tou	King	Salomon
H.·.	T.·.	W.·.	S.·.	J.·.	T.·.	K.·.	S.·.
Hiram	Thir	veut	envoyer	Jabulum	au	Roi	Salomon

and in the centre an emblem appropriate to his profession, or any other that he may prefer, as *Force* represented by a *Lion*: or *Humanity*, by the *Pelican*, &c.

When a Mark Mason finds himself in need, he sends his Medal to a Bro.·. of the degree, asking of him the assistance which he needs. If such Bro.·., on sending him what he asks for, sends him back the Medal, it will show that what he sends him is a gift; but if he keeps the Medal, what he sends is a loan, to be repaid.

My Brethren, when you shall have adopted your device, you will see to it that it is recorded in the Book of Gold.

Go now, my Brethren, and make yourselves known to the First and Second Wardens.

FACSIMILE

13 . . . (18)

The Bro.·. Terrible leads the new Mark Masons, first to the First Warden and then to the Second, that they may give these the words, signs and grips, which received, the two Wardens say, each in his turn, to the Very Wise, that they are just and perfect. Which done, the Bro.·. Terrible leads the new Initiates to the East, and seats them there, on the left hand of the Very Wise, and the Bro.·. Orator reads to them the following discourse:

―――――·▶●◀·―――――

Discourse upon the Degree.

[18]

My Brother, among the great number of Workmen employed in building the Temple of the Grand A.·. of the Un.·. there were confusion and misunderstanding. Many imperfect pieces of work were found, which no one wished to own having made: wherefore it was decreed that every Workman should adopt a certain mark, which he could not afterwards change, and should be bound to have it registered. This was afterwards used to mark his work with. All alike used the eight initial letters of certain words, adding thereto the device which each had adopted, and the name of the Conductor of the Works. The Overseer who verified these directed the mode of payment, but sent away without pay those who work was not correct.

There was also in the office of the Treasury a wicket, through which each Workman had to receive his pay, and where were two Wardens, one of whom paid those who gave the true sign, and the other cut off the wrist of those who gave a false one. By this means all the bad Workmen were soon got rid of; which proves to you, my dear Brother, that, in this initiation, [19] we ought to rid ourselves, also, of the bad Workmen of our Workshop.

As to the thirteen cents, which were asked of you, it is to teach you that at that time the day's work of a Workman was thirteen cents; and that if you are asked for assistance, by a Workman, you cannot give him less than the value of a day's work in the country wherein you live.

If a Bro.·. of your degree, or higher, but not one of a lower degree, asks you to assist him in his needs, he may pledge his Medal for the loan; but he cannot pledge it a second time until he has redeemed it by paying the first loan. And in case a Bro.·. should find that no member of the Lodge can make him the loan which he needs, he will in this case apply to the Lodge itself, which cannot refuse him what he asks, he leaving his Medal there in pledge.

14 . . . (20)

You are also to know, my Bro.˙. that if, by any kind of misconduct, a Bro.˙. should lose the confidence of his Lodge, he would thereby, upon Masonic trial, inevitably lose all his titles, and the sentence against him be sent to all the regular Lodges of the two Hemispheres.

This degree is also known at Algiers; so that, my Brother, in case your business should lead you to that place, or you should by any chance find [20] yourself there, by means of your Medal, and first making yourself known, you will find there all the assistance that the case may require.

After this discourse or instruction, if the Orator has prepared another, and the Very Wise desires him to give it, the Lodge of Instruction will be opened (A.˙.); and he will pronounce it; immediately after which, the Catechism will be given.

Closing of the Labors.

Qu.˙. Venerable First Warden, what is the hour?
Ans.˙. Very Wise, the Sun has just disappeared.

Since this is so, Venerable Bro.˙. Second Warden, announce that my intentions are to dismiss the Workmen.

The First Warden makes this announcement, and then the Second; after which the same ceremony is followed as at opening (*See page 4.* ✣); which done, the Oath of Silence is taken, and all retire.

Catechism of the Mark=Mason.

Q.˙. Are you a Mark–Mason?
A.˙. I have made the sixteen Journeys, reduced to four.
[21] Q.˙. What do these sixteen Journeys signify?
A.˙. That every good Mason ought to work and travel without cessation, until he has attained the 16th Degree of Masonry, or that of *Master of Masonry.*

15 . . . (22)

Q∴ What does the reduction to *four* Journeys signify?

A∴ Its first signification is, that we ought to neglect nothing, in order to relieve the needs of our Brethren: the second, that we ought constantly to endeavor to instruct ourselves; the third, prevention of differences with one another; the fourth, relief of the widow and orphan.

Q∴ What was your condition on entering the Lodge?

A∴ My hair dishevelled, my shirt folded over like a girdle, a cord around my neck, my feet bare, deprived of all metallic substances, and my thumb and first two fingers of the right hand holding a stone.

Q∴ Why were you so prepared?

A∴ To teach me that every good Mason ought to be humble, and devoted to the will of his Brethren.

Q∴ Why did you carry the stone with two fingers and the thumb only?

A∴ Because that is the sign of assistance of the degree.

Q∴ What did your eyes first behold, on entering the Temple? [22]

A∴ An Altar set in the middle of the Lodge.

Q∴ What did you see upon that Altar?

A∴ A white marble Stone, which should serve as a model for all the Workmen, because it was perfect and without defects.

Q∴ Was there anything remarkable on it?

A∴ Yes: two circles, between which and around it were eight initial letters, of the words, Hiram, King of Tyre, resolved to send Jabulum to King Solomon.

Q∴ Where did you take your Obligation?

A∴ At the Altar which was in the centre of the Lodge, representing the wicket where the workmen who labored on the Temple received their wages.

Q∴ How did you ask for yours?

A∴ With my hand extended over the Altar, to cut which off a feint was made, to teach me symbolically that we ought not to ask for anything that we have not deserved.

Q∴ What was there demanded of you?

A∴ Thirteen cents.

Q∴ Did you give them?

A∴ I could not, having been deprived of everything metallic; but a Sub-Deacon paid them for me.

Q∴ What was afterwards said to you? [23]

A∴ That every good Mason ought always to find the means of assisting his Brethren.

16 . . . (23)

Q∴ Why, to resume labor, does the Very Wise raps *Seven* times with the Mallet, the First Warden *five*, and the Second Warden *three?*

A∴ The *Seven* call the *Masters* to labor; the *five*, the *Fellows*; and the *three*, the *Apprentices*.

CEREMONIAL OF THE SECOND APARTMENT.

Preliminary Observations.

As this pretended 5th Degree of Mark-Mason, according to the copies of Bro∴ Fourt∴ does not seem to me to be, according to other copies, and even to his own, anything more than the degree that immediately follows that of Master, I here consider it as such only; and with so much the more reason because it is said in it, (page 23, line 6), '*It is a Bro∴ who demands to be received in the degree of Mark Mason*': (page 27, line 15), *Is that a perfect work of a Master?*' '*Undoubtedly it is by mistake this Bro∴ has been received in this degree &c.*' Nevertheless, I make no change in his Ceremonial, except that I no where mention in it the pretended qualification of *Master marked*. Moreover, for the signs, words and grips, reference is made to those of the so-called 4th degree; that is to say, to the 1st part of the Cahier.

---

[24]   TITLES OF THE BRETHREN.

The Grand Master.   The Grand Secretary.
The First Grand Venerable Warden.   The Bro∴ Terrible.
The Second Gr∴ Ven∴ Warden.   The Master of Ceremonies.
                Conductor of the Candidate.

When all the Brethren have repaired to the Second Apartment, and the Ven∴ First Gr∴ Warden has made due report to the Gr∴ Master, the latter raps four equal raps . . . . and says:

With me, my Brethren!

FACSIMILE

17 . . . (24)

At the same time all the Brethren come to order, (*See page 15*); the Grand Master then descends from the East, and stands at the foot of the steps, his face towards the door of the Temple, the First Grand Warden at his right, and next him the Second Grand Warden; and by degrees the other Brethren form a circle, with them, so that the last of all is on the left of the Grand Master.

Then the Grand Master gives the First Warden the grip, and whispers in his ear the Pass-word (*See pages 15 & 16*) and the First Warden in reply gives him the Sacred Word. (*See page 15.*)

Then the First Warden turning, in his turn, to the Second Warden, they go through the same ceremonial, and it is so done all around the circle, until the Bro∴ on the left of the Gr∴ Master gives him the grip, and whispers in his ear the Pass-word, and the Gr∴ Master responds by giving him the Sacred Word.

The Gr∴ Master then takes his hat and says:

My Brethren, the Lodge of Perfection of Mark Mason is opened.

The Brethren then return to their places, and the Gr∴ Master or- [25] ders the reading of the last labors; which done, he announces what the labors of the day are, and the two Wardens transmit in the usual manner this announcement upon their respective columns.

If the work is to be the reception of a Candidate, the Grand Master will order the ballot to be passed around. If it is favorable to the Candidate, as there is reason to believe it will be, he will be informed of it, since he ought to be in the Antechamber, with the Master of Ceremonies, who immediately prepares him for his reception, taking from him all metallic substances of every kind that he may have about him; passing a rope four times around his neck, and causing him to hold a perfect piece of work in his right hand. (A).

Entry of Candidates into the Temple.

The Candidates being thus prepared, the Master of Ceremonies brings them to the door of the Temple, on which he gives four equal knocks . . . . upon which the First Warden repairs to the door, opens it, and asks:

Q∴ Who is there?

The Master of Ceremonies responds:

18 . . . (26)

A.·. Certain Past-Masters who ask advancement to the degree of Mark-Mason.
Q.·. Are they well prepared?
A.·. Yes.
Q.·. Have they the Pass-Word?
A.·. No: but I will give it for them.

[26] The First Warden then closes the door, re-enters, returns to his place, and standing, and at order, (see for mode of this, page 15), says to the Grand Master:

Grand Master, certain Masters ask their advancement to the degree of Mark-Mason.
Q.·. Are they prepared?
A.·. Yes, Gr.·. Master; they are.
Q.·. Have they the Pass-word?
A.·. No: but their Conductor will give it for them.
Q.·. What are their names?
A.·. (He gives the names.)
Q.·. Are the Brethren satisfied with them?

If all the Brethren are satisfied with the Candidates, they make it known by the Sign of Adhesion, which is to lift up and stretch out horizontally the right hand: and then the Gr.·. Master will say:

Let these Candidates enter.

Entrance of the Candidates into the Temple.

The Bro. Terrible goes and opens the door, and the Master of Ceremonies enters, preceding the Candidates; and when they are between the two columns, the Grand Master directs the Master of Ceremonies to cause the Candidates to make their 4 journeys, which consists in going four times, amid profound silence, around the hall.

When, at the end of the first journey, they pass in front of the East, the Gr.·. Master raps once with his mallet on the altar; at the second time, twice; at the third, three times; and at the fourth, four times. At the last of these raps, the Second Warden assumes a grave air. The Master [27] of Ceremonies, followed by the Candidates, strikes four blows upon his shoulder. The Second Warden rises, and turning towards them, asks the Master of Ceremonies:

19 . . . (27)

Q∴ *Whom do you bring there?*

A∴ Certain Past-Masters who ask to be received in the degree of Mark-Mason.

Q∴ Are they prepared?

A∴ Yes; Grand Venerable Warden; they are.

Q∴ Have they the Pass-word?

A∴ No: but I will give it for them.

Q∴ To become a Mark-Mason, one must present a perfect piece of work—where is it?

A∴ They bring it to you, Grand Venerable Warden; and it is here.

Q∴ But, my Brother, are these really perfect pieces of work of Past Masters? Undoubtedly it is by inadvertence they have been received in this degree. In my opinion, far from being advanced, we ought to put them back among the Apprentices. However, I cannot judge of these works; lead them, therefore, these Candidates, to the First Venerable Grand Warden.

The Master of Ceremonies conducts the Candidates to the First Warden, who, like the Second, affects to be serious and pre-occupied. He gives him 4 equal raps on the shoulder, at which he rises, and turning to the M∴ of Cer∴ says:

Q∴ *Whom bring you here?*

[The other questions and answers are the same as those embraced on the two preceding pages by the lines on the margin.]

[28] The First Warden having in his turn sent them to the Grand Master, they repair to the foot of the Throne, where the Master of Ceremonies claps 4 times at equal intervals, on the shoulder of the Gr∴ Master, whereat he rises and turning to them with the most serious air and tone possible, asks the M∴ of Ceremonies:

Q∴ *Whom bring you there?*

[See page 27: the rest of the questions and answers, to the foot of that page only, which through with, the Gr∴ Master will say to the Candidates:

Q∴ *Are these, to be sure, your perfect pieces of work. My eyes do not tell me so: but let us see!*

The Grand Master takes the Compasses from the altar, tries the circles with it, and then applies the Square, and after full examination says:

This work is not at all what it ought to be.

He puts it to one side, and says to the Lodge:

Q∴ *My Brethren, what is your desire with respect to these Candidates?*

20 . . . (28)

The Brethren all decide in favor of their admission, and consequently give the sign of Assent, by extending horizontally the right hand.

Then the Grand Master directs the M∴ of Cer∴ to bring the Candidates to the East, where he causes them to take the obligation:

Oath of a Candidate.

[29]

I, ..., do swear and promise, that I will never reveal to any Profane the Secrets that are about to be entrusted to to me, nor even to any Mason whatever who has not been received in this degree of Mark Mason, in a Lodge of this degree, regularly constituted; that I will never change the Mark which I am about to adopt, nor ever put it in pledge into the hands of two persons at the same time; that I will comply, as far as may be in my power, with the requests which my brethren may make of me, when sending me their Mark; and in case I can not by any means do so, I promise to return their Mark at once, with a piece of money in testimony of my inability. I furthermore promise and swear, never to assist at a reception in this degree, of more than four brethren at once; and this under the penalties of my former obligations; and moreover, under that of having my wrist cut off, wherefrom I pray God to preserve me, and to give me aid. Amen!

The Grand Master causes the Candidates to rise, and receives them in this degree by four blows of the mallet, and then explains to them the characters engraven on the three sides of the square stone of white marble, (see the beginning of this book;) which done, the M∴ of Cer∴ leads the new Initiates to the left of the Gr∴ Master and seats them there; and the Bro∴ Orator reads the following discourse:

Discourse.

[30]

The most skilful of the Masons, desiring to give proofs of their skill, agreed to mark their work in a certain manner approved by all the workmen, and also registered in the Book of Gold. Some of the workmen, on presenting themselves to receive the wages of the work from the paymaster, not having entirely concealed their marks by the two last fingers of their hand, the

21 . . . (30)

others supposed that those who thus had the hand half closed, received more wages than they, and resolved to imitate them; but the paymaster perceiving the cheat, cut off the wrists of all who so exposed themselves. Thence it came that the Mark-Masons swore to preserve their secret, and to fulfill their obligations, under the penalty of having the wrist cut off, in case of violation of their obligation; and the better to recognize each other, they also agreed that, besides their mark, they would use hieroglyphics, not only incomprehensible to the vulgar, but even to Masons of degrees below that of Mark-Mason; which mark consists in the characters engraven on the Cubic Stone.

Note:—This seems to have been intended as a second and concluding part of the degree.

Wherever the word '*Past-Master*' is used, the original MSS. had simply '*Maitre*' or '*Maitres*.' The alterations have been made by another hand, evidently to let in the Past Master's as the 4th degree.   [P.

ROYAL ARCH.
7th *Degree of the Ancient Rite.*

[32]

1st *Apartment.*

This Apartment is lighted by four lights. In it the Master of Ceremonies prepares the Candidate, taking from him everything of a metallic nature, his coat and vest, causing him to wear his shoes as slippers, and blindfolding him with his apron. In this Apartment the 3d Grand Master presides.

22 . . . (32)

2d Apartment.

This Apartment should be lighted by three lights, and hung with *blue*, as the door is also: by the side of which is *a burning bush;* a rod or stick, at the end of which is an inflammable match; and a table, on which are three candles and a Bible. In this Apartment the 2d Grand Master presides.

3d Apartment.

This Apartment is hung with *red;* and there is an altar, on which are a Bible, three candles, and two vases, in one of which is water, and in the other, red wine. In this Apartment the 1st Grand Master presides.

4th Apartment,
or
Sanctuary.

The ceiling and door of this apartment are painted *blue*, and the hangings are red. At the east end, and on the left of the High Priest, who presides there, is a stool for prayer; and on his right appears a large ring of iron, [33] attached to a trap in the floor, covering a vault underground, in which are three arches, each upheld by three columns, and one over the other. In the interior and at the bottom of the lowest arch is set A TRIANGULAR STONE, on which are three medals, on one of which is engraved the word of Merit, on the second the Pass-word, and on the third the Sacred-word; the two last by separated syllables.

Order of places in this Apartment.

The High Priest————————————occupies the Altar.
The 1st∴ Grand Master——————to the right of the High Priest.
The 2d∴ Gr∴ Master————————to the left of High Priest.
The 3d∴ Gr∴ Master————————to the right of the 1st∴ Gr∴ Master.
The Gr∴ Orator——————————to the left of the 2d∴ Gr∴ Master.

FACSIMILE

23 . . . (34)

The Gr∴ Secretary————————to the right of the 3d∴ Gr∴ Master.
The Gr∴ Treasurer————————to the left of the Gr∴ Orator.
The Royal Arch Captain—————sits in front of the High Priest, and facing him.

The other Brethren Companions are seated, part beyond the Gr∴ Secretary, and part beyond the Gr∴ Treasurer.

The High Priest wears on his head a tiara, on the front of which are the words HOLINESS TO THE LORD. On his chest is hung, to a black belt, an enamelled square plate, at the top of which are in large letters the two words DOCTRINE and TRUTH. This plate hangs at the end of a chain of gold, passing over the neck. He wears also two other plates behind the back.

The 1st∴ Grand Master is clothed in a *purple* robe, over which is a [34] *yellow* mantle. He wears his jewel at the end of a Cordon worn across the body, i. e., from the right shoulder to the left hip.

The 2d∴ Grand Master is clothed in a *white* robe, over which is a mantle of the colour of *gold*. He wears his hat; and his jewel is worn like that of the 1st∴ Grand Master.

The 3d∴ Grand Master is clothed in a *blue* robe, over which is a *yellow* mantle. He wears his hat; and his jewel is worn like those of the other Grand Masters.

All the other Brethren wear also the *flame-colored* Cordon, across the body, with the jewel, and have their hats on. With this jewel a key is also worn.

The jewel worn at the end of the Cordon is a delta of gold, a *whole* plate, without hollow.

The Royal Arch Captain has also a staff, about six feet in length, at the end of which is a halber.

————•▸•◂•————

Grand Cordon and Jewel.

This Grand Cordon is of purple colour, at the end of which hangs the Grand Medal of the Arch, of Gold. On the side of this medal is engraved an open trap, with its door near it, on which is a large ring in the centre: two men, standing face to face at the opening, on opposite sides, are drawing up with a rope, another man from the vaults. On the other side of the medal is a glory, in the middle of which is a delta (A).

There is also another jewel, on which are engraved three arches, of three pillars each, one above the other; on the frontispiece of which arches are the letters S∴ R∴ H∴ R∴ H∴ A∴ (B.)

24 . . . (35)

Opening of the Chapter.
[35]
The High Priest wearing his tiara, and all the Companions their Crowns, the High Priest says to the Royal Arch Captain:
My Companion, ascertain if we are well tiled here.
The Royal Arch Captain goes out, and on his return says:
High Priest, we are well tiled.
The High Priest then says:
Companions my Brethren, aid me to open the Chapter of Royal Arch.

Here the two first Grand Masters join the High Priest, who will have descended from his throne to below the last step of the Orient, and they and the others each way from them, three by three, form with their right feet a triangle, each brother pressing and seizing with his left hand the upper side of the upper part of the arm of the other, to represent the three arches, raising the arms afterwards, to represent the 1st∴ Arch. In this position they give to each other, by three times, and by syllables, separated, the Sacred Word, and in such manner that he who pronounced the second syllable, pronounces the first, the second time, and the third, the third time, &c. Before and after pronouncing this word, they say, alternately raising and lowering their arms; '*we three, by friendship and confidence united, agree to endeavour to find again the Sacred Word; and to that end we do declare the Chapter of Royal Arch opened.*'

This ceremonial finished, each group says to the High Priest:
[36] *All is correct and perfect.*
Then all resume their places, and the High Priest says:
Companions my Brethren, the Chapter of Royal Arch is opened.
The High Priest orders the reading of the works of the last Session, and has them approved in the usual manner.

Reception of a Candidate.

1ST∴ APARTMENT: *The 3d∴ Grand Master presiding.*

[*See in detail, page 32, and the condition in which the Candidate is, when prepared for his reception.*]

The M∴ of Ceremonies brings the Candidates to the door of this Apartment, and gives six equal knocks . . . . . . The 2d∴ Grand Master,

FACSIMILE

25 . . . (36)

who is at the door, opens it, and asks, *Who is there?* to which the M∴ of Cer∴ replies:

A∴ It is the Bro∴. . . . ., Super-excellent Mason and Royal Master, who, having governed a Lodge, seeks to be admitted into the Temple of the Grand Architect of the Universe, to work without wages or reward.

Q∴ Is he prepared to contract the obligations by which we are bound in the degree of Royal Arch?

A∴ Yes.

Q∴ By what means does he hope to obtain the favour that he asks?

A∴ By the Pass-word, and it is his Conductor who answers for him.

Q∴ Has he that Pass-word? (*See page* 45.)

A∴ No, but his Conductor will give it for him. [37]

The M∴ of Ceremonies hands a medal to the 2d∴ Grand Master, on which is the Pass word of this Apartment; and he permits them to enter.

The M∴ of Ceremonies conducts the Candidates directly to the altar, and causes them to kneel there on one knee, the right hand on the Bible which is opened at the 3d chapter of Exodus, and the 3d Grand Master causes him to take his obligation as follows:

Oath.

In the presence of the Grand Architect of the Universe, I renew all the obligations I have heretofore contracted, promising moreover never to shed the blood of a brother Royal Arch, nor in any wise to injure him in fortune or reputation; that I will never reveal his secret, unless it be for cause of high treason: to obey the regulations of perfections: never to assist at a reception of more than three Brethren in the degree of Royal Arch; and if I should perjurously violate this obligation, I consent to have my skull and brain laid open, my body reduced to ashes and afterwards flung to the winds: from which may the Grand Architect of the Universe preserve me: Amen!

All the Brethren now align themselves in two ranks, to form the Vault of

26 . . . (38)

Steel, in the middle of the Apartment. The M∴ of Ceremonies causes the [38] Candidate to rise, and make three journeys, in search of the Word of Merit, (*see it, at page 44*), in order that he may reach the Second Apartment, where the Candidate is soon to present himself. All the Brethren pass to the rear of the stool for prayer, before which the Brother Orator is seated, who reads the 3d chapter of Exodus, to the 16th verse; and at the moment when he reads, 'I AM THAT I AM,' a pistol shot is fired close to the Candidate's ear (he being all the time blindfolded with his apron). [*Note:* That he will have been made to put off his shoes, where this is directed by one of the said verses]. This ended, all the Brethren pass into the 2d Apartment, behind the door whereof the 1st∴ Grand Master will have posted himself, and where the 2d∴ Grand Master is about to preside.

2d∴ APARTMENT: *The 2d∴ Grand Master presiding.*
[*See description of it at page 32*].

The M∴ of Ceremonies conducts the Candidates to the door of this Apartment, and knocks as at that of the 1st∴, 6 equal raps . . . . . .
The 1st∴ Gr∴ Master, who is posted there, within, opens it, and asks, *Who is there?* The M∴ of Ceremonies responds as at the first door. [*See the questions and answers designated by the brace in the margin, at page 36*].

These questions and answers completed, the M∴ of Cer∴ hands to the 1st Grand Master the medal of the pass-word, which he found in the search made in the first apartment; who takes it, and permits the Candidate and his Conductor to enter; and he is conducted directly to the Altar, which is on the left of the door, and around which all the Brethren are arranged, and the Bro∴ Orator is seated, near the 2d∴ Grand Master. There the Orator reads the 4th chapter of Exodus, during which reading, which is [39] slowly done, to give time for the ceremony to proceed, the M∴ of Ceremonies for an instant raises the apron that covers the Candidate's eyes, that he may see the B∴ B∴ (3), causes him to give the Sign (see p. 45), and then causes him to light at the burning bush the match [cartouche], inserted in the staff, at the end. The Grand Master then gives a sign with his hand to commence the test (4), which finished, the M∴ of Ceremonies replaces the apron over the eyes of the Candidate and remains with him in this Apartment, while all the other Brethren pass into the third.

27 . . . (39)

3d∴ APARTMENT: *The 1st∴ Grand Master Presiding.*
[*See description of it at p.* 32.]

The Brethren, being in this Apartment arrange themselves around the altar, where the 1st∴ Grand Master is, who presides there, the 3d∴ Grand Master being behind the door.

All being so arranged, the M∴ of Ceremonies repairs with the Candidate to this door, and knocks as at the doors of the other Apartments, 6 equal raps . . . . . . and the 2d∴ Grand Master who is within, opens the door and asks, *Who is there?* to which the M∴ of Ceremonies responds as at the other doors, [*See the questions and answers, marked at page 36*].

These questions and answers finished, the Candidate hands to the 3d∴ Gr∴ Master a third medal of the Pass-word, which he takes, and he lets them enter. The M∴ of Cer∴ leads the Candidate immediately and directly before the altar of the 1st∴ Gr∴ Master, around which are arranged all the Brethren of the Chapter, 4th of Exodus, during the following ceremony. The M∴ of Ceremonies raises for an instant the apron which covers the Candidate's eyes, and causes him to give the Sign of the Water, [40] [*See page* 44], which ended, he covers his eyes anew, and remains with him in this Apartment, while the other Brethren pass into the 4th.

4TH APARTMENT: *The High Priest presiding:*
or
THE SANCTUARY.

The Brethren being in this Apartment, the Royal Arch Captain guards the door, and the Candidate has not his eyes bandaged as in the three others.

The Master of Ceremonies conducts the Candidate to the door, and knocks as at the others, six equal raps . . . . . . The Royal Arch Captain opens, and asks *Who is there?* The M∴ of Ceremonies replies as at the other Apartments. [*See the questions and answers designated at p.* 36.]

These questions and answers ended, the M∴ of Ceremonies hands the Royal Arch Captain a medal of the Pass-word, which he takes, and he lets them enter. The M∴ of Ceremonies places the Candidate in the West, facing the High Priest, who asks him the following questions:

Q∴ *What do you desire?*
A∴ *The favor of being admitted near you.*
Q∴ *Come hither, my brother.*

28 . . . (40)

The Master of Ceremonies and Royal Arch Captain accompany the Candidate to the altar of the Sanctuary, on which the Royal Arch Captain lays the 3d medal which he has just received at the door, and, addressing himself to the High Priest, says to him:

[41] *This Aspirant making an offering of the price of his labours, asks the favour of working in the Temple of the Supreme Being, without wages or rewards; but he begs you, O High Priest, to give him the word of Royal Arch.*

The High Priest, addressing the Candidate, says to him.

Seek, my Brother. Perhaps God will permit you to find it. As to me, I cannot give it.

The M∴ of Ceremonies then gives the Candidate a crow-bar, and having caused him to search carefully, leads him to where the trap is, and causes him to insert the crow-bar in the ring of the covering of the trap, and having caused him to raise it, passes a long rope under his armpits, by means of which he is lowered into the vault, after being instructed to pull upon the rope at each arch he may meet with, so that he may be drawn up three times. At the 3d time, he finds himself at the bottom of the vault, and there sees on a small table, triangular in shape, and through a transparency, the Sacred Word, above it the Pass-word, and below, the word of Merit. He pulls upon the rope, the two brethren (representing Joabert and Stolkin, when they drew Gibulum out of the vaults), draw up the Candidate from the Subterranean, and at the moment when they grasp him, to lift him out of the trap, they do it by the grip of Companion Royal Arch, saying *Gibulum is a good Mason.*

The Candidate goes immediately to the High Priest, tells him the result of his search, and gives him the Sacred Word, Word of Merit and Pass- [42] word; at seeing which, all the Brethren place themselves under the Sign of Admiration [*see p. 44*], and the High Priest, pointing to the words, says to all the Brethren:

Behold the Holy Name of the Eternal found again!

[*See the Sacred Word, page* 44].

The High Priest then descends from his throne, embraces the Candidate, and says to him:

My Brother, through your difficulties and disinterested labours, you have attained the centre of virtue. Reflect well, my dear Companion, on all the ceremonies of your reception, and you will see that they symbolize the only way that men can follow to attain perfection. Walk therein, then, constantly with us, my dear Brother; the satisfaction of the Soul is the only

29 . . . (42)

reward of the virtuous man. This awaits you, if you always perform your duties.

Go now and clothe yourself, my Brother, and then return to share our labours.

[*Note :* The right to speak is asked directly of the High Priest, giving at the same time the sign of the skull.

Re=entry of the Candidate into the Sanctuary.

The M∴ of Ceremonies knocks again at the door of the Sanctuary, but now with seven raps, of which six are equal, and one slow, ...
The Royal Arch Captain opens, the M∴ of Ceremonies conducts the new Companion Royal Arch to the East, and the High Priest says:

Companions, my Brethren, let us congratulate ourselves upon the acquisition by us of our dear Companion A . . . . F . . . . .

All the Brethren rise, and give, with the H∴ Priest the Sign of the [43] Skull, and afterwards the plaudit, ...

1st∴ Sign of the Skull or of Order :
Grand Sign of the Degree.

The Sign of the *Skull*, or of *Order*, consists, my Brother, in holding the right hand horizontally, as if to cut off the upper part of the skull.

2d∴ Sign, of the Staff (A.), or of the Pass.

The Second Sign, of the *Staff*, consists in letting fall the Staff (or rod) on the ground, by the large end, and taking it up immediately by the small end. It symbolizes the first miracle which God made Moses to perform, when he told him to take a serpent by the tail, and it became a rod in his hand.

30 . . . (43)

3d. Sign: of the Leprosy.

This third Sign consists in putting the right hand into the bosom (*l'estomac*), to take it out, and turn it and examine it on the back and palm with astonishment—(it is supposed to be covered with the leprosy)—to replace it in the bosom, draw it forth and examine it again—(the person is supposed now to see that the leprosy has disappeared)—and put it back in the bosom. This Sign symbolizes the second miracle, of the leprosy, which God caused Moses to perform.

4th∴ Sign of the Water, and of Recognition.

To make one's self known in this degree, one takes wine in a tumbler, and presenting it to a Bro∴, asks him *what it is*, to which he replies '*It is blood.*'

[44] (A) Upon this Sign being given, when one presents himself to obtain entrance into a Lodge, the Royal Arch Captain demands the Pass-word, which being given him, he opens the door and says, '*Pass!*'

This Sign symbolizes the third miracle which God caused Moses to perform, directing him to fill a shell with water from the river Jordan, which was immediately found to be turned into blood.

5th Sign of Admiration.

☋ This Sign, my Brother, consists in spreading out the arms, as a Priest does when he says *Dominus vobiscum!* then carry the right hand, palm upwards, to above the eyes, opening these wide, the left leg and body to the rear, thus making a genuflexion.

Grip.

☋ The *Grip* [Attouchement] or *Token*, consists in putting mutually the hands under the armpits, as if to raise one another, saying 'Gibulum is a

31 . . . (44)

good Mason;' and so give each other the Sacred Word, by spelling it, G∴ I∴ B∴ U∴ L∴ U∴ M∴

Sacred Word.

G∴ I∴ B∴ U∴ L∴ U∴ M∴   J∴ E∴ O∴ V∴ A∴

Each of these words is spelled by three Brethren, forming a triangle with their feet, and the arch with their arms.

Word of Merit.

S∴ A∴ I∴ N∴ T∴ E∴ T∴ E∴ A∴ U∴   S∴ E∴ I∴ G∴ N∴ E∴ U∴ R∴
[*Holiness to the Lord.*]

It is given in the same way as the preceding.

Pass-Word.

[45]
J∴ E∴ S∴ U∴ I∴ S∴ C∴ E∴ Q∴ U∴ E∴ J∴ E∴ S∴ U∴ I∴ S∴ S∴ E∴ M∴ C∴ H∴ A∴ M∴ E∴ T∴ J∴ A∴ P∴ H∴ E∴ T∴ responded to by A∴ D∴ O∴ N∴ A∴ I∴
[I∴ A∴ M∴ T∴ H∴ A∴ T∴ I∴ A∴ M∴]

The Bro∴ Orator then reads the following history of the degree.

32 . . . (45)

History of the Degree.

I am not now about to give you, my dear Brother, the amplified history of the Royal Arch, *which you will find in that of the Great Patriarch-Masons*, whom Solomon appointed to be the twelve chiefs of the Temple, and to each of whom he assigned the government of a Province or Tribe, to conduct and distribute the works; *giving to the Gr∴ Hiram the general inspection of all*. I shall limit myself to giving you a recital of the principal facts.

The Brothers Royal Arch were all sons and descendants of the race of Joshua, whose line was always distinguished in the wars waged by the children of Israel to conquer the land for *the twelve Tribes*, promised by the Supreme Architect to the descendants *of Abraham, Isaac and Jacob*.

Solomon, having prepared everything for the erection of the Temple to the honour and glory of the Supreme Architect, made an intimate alliance with Hiram, King of Tyre, with whom the Prophet King had also been closely connected, as his nearest neighbour, and a great lover of the Sciences, [46] which attained great excellence in his realm, in order to avail himself of the attainments of that celebrated Architect and expert in the knowledge of the metals, in building that edifice.

It is well here to instruct Masonic posterity in regard to an event which is so much the more interesting, because it has transmitted to us the mystery, most excellent of all, of the Royal Arch, the discovery whereof seems to have been due to chance, as is the case with the greatest things, by the pettiest causes. For the understanding of the matter, it is also necessary to say, that independently of the mysteries attached to each different degree of Ancient Masonry, and of which we ought never to lose sight, there was THE GREAT SECRET, which the wise Founder of the Art entrusted only to *Hiram* surnamed *Abif*, and to *Mahabon*, another Chief, also his favourite, for their talents and long standing in Royal Arch. Some historians pretend, however, that Solomon entrusted this great work to Hiram the King; but our history contains nothing in respect to that. Moreover, Hiram the King, not being of the Jewish religion, could not be initiated into the mysterious secrets of the Temple; but it is true that they were connected together by the closest friendship, like that which he had borne for the Prophet-King, father of Solomon.

The respectable Hiram Abif having been assassinated by the three wretches, who, to obtain that secret, had conspired, but in vain, against him, the Elus and the history of the Patriarchs will instruct you as to his [47] sad end.

33 . . . (47)

The Temple and its ornaments being finished, Solomon confided this Great Secret to Jachin and Boaz, requiring of them an oath not to reveal it, and this *under the penalty of the withering excommunication of the whole body of the Sages adepts.* But many other distinguished Masters entreated Solomon to grant them admission to this sublime degree; but that wise Prince, faithful to his oath, gave them the rewards due to their talents and labours, and said to them; "Go, my friends and work! Persevere, and some day the Sublime Architect will give it you;" and this promise was indeed fulfilled, as you will see hereafter.

Solomon and the Masters united with him, wishing to transmit this profound mystery to posterity, had themselves constructed in a deep and unknown place under ground a special Lodge or laboratory, where they worked in a manner worthy of the profound knowledge wherewith the Supreme Dispensor had endowed them, and herein they deposited it.

Although this place had no visible outlet or entrance, that could even be suspected to exist, nevertheless chance or a supernatural inspiration occasioned the discovery.

At their return from their captivity at Babylon, the great Zorobabel caused excavations to be made in the ruins of the Temple, and there discovered a primitive tabernacle, supported by three columns, immense sums in ingots of the purest gold, and the inextinguishable fire which enclosed the Sacred word.

The Temple destroyed, Zorobabel abandoned the excavation of this [48] work; and a certain time elapsed after the death of Jesus Christ, and in the reign of Titus, Son of the Emperor Vespasian, some zealous Masons assembled, and resolved, for reasons unknown, to dig in the rubbish of this famous Temple, then entirely destroyed. One of them, named Gibulum, of an old race of the first Masons, while digging there, found his pick caught in a large iron ring. He called his comrades, and having carefully examined the place, they saw that the ring was attached to a trap of the same metal, which they could not even move; but by the aid of levers they succeeded in raising it, and at first saw only a kind of funnel in a rock, and that very dark. Gibulum, full of ardour, offered nevertheless to descend into it, and for safety had himself girt with a rope, and fixed upon a signal whereby he could have himself immediately drawn up out of the place. He had hardly penetrated into the hole, when he perceived that it was made by mining, and that its vaults were upheld by great arcades, one above the other.— The darkness of the place, and the cold at first so lessened the ardour of Gibulum, that reaching the third arcade, he gave the signal agreed on, and

34 . . . (49)

was drawn up. When he had emerged from the shaft, his brethren questioned him, and he told them that he had seen a vault, terrible even to the [49] most intrepid persons; but that, nevertheless, if one of them would accompany him, he would descend again. But no one offering to do so, he persued his undertaking alone, and penetrated further than before into the subterranean, whose extreme depth caused him to tremble again; his senses were chilled, he shook the rope, and was drawn up; but he recovered his senses only to resume with greater ardour his undertaking, despite the obstacles and even the danger which he had seen there. He supplied himself with a blazing torch, a pencil and paper, invoked the Supreme Being, and prepared to encounter new perils, and the prophecy of Solomon was about to be accomplished. He was let down and reached the last arcade. He struck a blow with a hammer, on a place where a responsive echo showed him that the wall concealed another spacious apartment. — He redoubled his zeal, and worked there with so much ardour that he at last succeeded, but after inexpressible toil, in piercing the wall and by degrees making therein an aperture large enough to enable him to pass. The reflection of the flame of his torch falling upon something extremely brilliant, dazzled him at first, and he perceived that this brilliancy came from the reflection of his torch upon a magnificent Sun and an altar of gold, of triangular form, on the front whereof were the initial letters which informed him of an agreement between Solomon, Hiram the King, and Hiram Abif, [50] and which were S∴ R∴ H∴ R∴ H∴ A∴, and above these S∴ R∴ H∴ A∴ M∴ B∴, which signify Solomon the King, Hiram Abif and Moabon.

These three illustrious Architects had caused this place to be constructed, for the celebration of their most secret and Great Mysteries, which they had written in letters of gold on a tablet of white marble.

The first movement of Gibulum, at the sight of this luminous place, was to bend the knee, and hold the right hand, palm upwards, over his eyes: sign of dazzlement, awe and admiration.

Then he drew nigh to the altar, and attained a knowledge of the great Mysteries and the oath and conditions, prescribed under the greatest penalties, written by these three illustrious and ancient sages, depositories of the Sciences.

Gibulum, marvelling at his discovery, returned thanks for it to the Most High, and for the third time pulled upon the rope. He was forthwith drawn up, and coming to the surface, all the BB∴ surrounded him, seeing his eyes gleam with a perfect satisfaction, and gave him the fraternal embrace, say-

FACSIMILE

35 . . . (51)

ing, *"Vivat! Gibulum is a good Mason."* He then told all of them what he had seen, *but carefully concealed from them what he had learned.*

So that of this lineage came the Ecossais, those illustrious Masons who from that time forward distinguished themselves in the wars of the Crusades; but to whose arms it did not please the Supreme Being to give all the [51] success which they hoped for. But their fervent zeal was only increased, and their hopes augmented. They returned to Europe with the Knights of the West, where they won the greatest celebrity, as well by their lofty deeds as by their wealth and power. Thence descended the Ancient Templars, whose history ended with the death of De Molai, the Great.

———•◆•———

This lecture ended, the High Priest causes the Pouch of Propositions to pass along the columns, and after it the box of the Poor: and after this he proceeds to close the works as follows:

Closing the Works.

My Brethren Companions, assist me to close the Sovereign Chapter.

Here the two Grand Masters unite with the High Priest, & [See the Ceremonial to be followed, marked at page 35] marked ✠, at the end wherof the groups of three Brethren say:

We three, united by friendship and confidence, declare that it is our purpose to close the Sovereign Chapter of Royal Arch.

Each Brother then repairs to his place, and the High Priest causes each to take the oath of silence and discretion; and says;

Let us retire in peace, my dear Brethren and Companions. The Sovereign Chapter of Royal Arch is closed.

REPRINTS OF RITUALS OF OLD DEGREES

FACSIMILE

37 . . . ( )

PAST MASTER: VENERABLE OF THE LODGE.

4TH DECREE OF THE ANCIENT RITE.

―――――•▸•◂•―――――

Opening.

The Lodge is opened by five raps and the ordinary questions.

―――――•◂•―――――

Reception.

The Candidate has a rope around his neck making four turns, round the body at the known place, and the two arms. The jewels of the First and Second Warden. His shirt is rolled around his waist and the two sleeves let down, the knee naked.

The Conductor raps as a Master.

The Bro∴ Tiler replies from within, *Who is there?* and announces to the Venerable, A Master who desires to enter the Sublime Council.

He is asked *if he has worked his time? As Apprentice, Fellow and Master?*

(After these usual questions)

He is caused to enter and make four circuits around the Lodge, halting at the Second and First Warden, as is customary, and at the Ven∴ who asks him all the questions.

He is then conducted to the steps of the throne, where he is made to kneel, on the tracing-board, and takes his obligation on the Bible, after the Venerable has received from him the signs, words and grips of the three preceding degrees.

Obligation.

I, P . . . . . . C . . . . . . do swear and promise never to reveal the secrets of this part of Masonry, which you are about to confer on me; never to write it, trace it or engrave them; never to entrust them to

38 . . . ( )

any Mason of an inferior degree; to be faithful to my engagements; to aid and assist my Brethren, and to keep their secrets as my own, except in case of murder or treason; to warn my Brethren of dangers that threaten them, except in case of war; and never to seduce the wife, daughter or sister of my Brethren: the whole under the penalties contained in my former obligations, Amen! Amen! Amen!

Then he is made to rise, and the sign, word and grip are given him, and the word of a Past Master.

The Word of a Past Master.

M∴ A∴ h∴ O∴ B∴ m∴ O∴

Sacred Word.

G∴ I∴ U∴ M∴ B∴ V∴ L∴

The Venerable puts into his hands all the instruments of a Ven∴ and his jewel over his neck, saying to him. *"In the name of this Respectable Lodge I make you Past Master or Venerable of the Lodge."* Then he makes him sit in the arm chair of the Ven∴ and all the Brethren pass four times before him, saluting him by the sign of each degree in succession, to each of which he responds.

This done, all take their places, and the Ven∴ takes the place of the Ex. Ven∴ The works ended, the Candidate closes the Lodge in the usual form.

FINIS.

Index

A
Aaron 55, 61
aleph, beth, lamed 126
Alpha et Omega xxiv
Amasaphus 41
American Eagle Mark Lodge No. 1, Charleston, SC xi, xii
A-montra 70, 78
Arimathea 70
Astier, Hyacinthe ixn2
Auld, Isaac xiii

B
Bideaud, Antoine xvii
Boaz 233
Bold, Thomas Lonsdale xvi

C
Caiphas 70
Calvary 70
Capharsoleum 70
Carlile, Richard xxv, 109
Chibbelum (Past Master's word) 59. See also Giblum (Past Master's word)
Columbian Council No. 1, R&SM, New York City xxiii
Concorde, Lodge, Cuba 195

D
Dalcho, Frederick xii, xiii
 ritual collection xxxv
Degree of Mark Master, A. Mackey xi–xiv. See also Mark Master Mason Degree
de Lachelle, Achille Huet 192, 193, 194
 manuscript xxii
 Royal Master Degree xxiii
 ritual collection xvii, xxi
De La Motta, Emanuel xii
Duhulquod, Pierre Joseph
 Mark Master jewel *xviii*
 ritual manuscript xvii, xx, xxii
 Royal Master Degree xxiii
Dunckerley, Thomas x, xv, xvi

E
Early Grand Encampment
 Wigan ritual xiv–xvi, 129–148
 Christian armor 136
 emblems 140
 obligation 137–138
 openings 135–136
 signs 139
Ehihu or Elihu 70
Eleazer 55, 61
Eli, Eli, Lama Sabacthani 70
Emanuel 70

F
Fourtaud, Bro. 194
Fourteau, Bro. 194

G
Gabaon 177
Gethsemane 70
Giblim 98
Giblum (Past Master's word) 59, 66. See also Chibbelum (Past Master's word)
Gibulum xx, xxii, 211, 231, 234. See also Jabulum (Jabulon, Jahbuhlun)
G.I.U.M.B.V.L. 238
Golgotha 70, 137, 147

Grand Maitre Ecossais (Grand Master Ecosé)
Degree xxxv–xxxvi, 167–195. *See also* Scottish Elder Master and Knight of St. Andrew Degree
- closing 186–187
- compared to Sovereign Grand Inspector General xxxv
- form of the lodge and clothing 169–170
- knighting 181–182
- lecture 185–186
- obligation 175–176
- opening 171–172
- oration 182–184
- reception 172–178
- signs and words 177

Grand Overseer xiii

H

Harby, Solomon xii
"Heave it over." 211
Hiram Abif 232
Holiness to the Lord 55, 61
Holland Mark Lodge, New York City xx

I

"I am that I am." 55, 61, 70, 231
I. H. S. (Jesus Hominum Salvator) 139
In hoc signo vinces 78, 137

J

Jabulum 212
Jabulum (Jabulon, Jahbuhlun) xix, xx, xxi
  transition to Gibulum *xxi*
Jachin 233
Jao-bul-on 49, 70
Jehova 177
Jeova 231
Jerusalem 70
Je suis ce que je suis 231
Joabert xx
Joppa 98

K

Knight of St. Andrew Degree. *See* Grand Maitre Ecossais (Grand Master Ecosé) Degree
Knights Templar Degree xxv–xxxiv, 69–84
- charge 79–81
- closing an encampment 73–74
- English ritual 151–166
  - closing the encampment 155–156
  - installation 156–166
  - libations 163–164
  - obligation 159–160
  - opening the encampment 153–155
- installation ceremony 74–76
- lecture 81–84
- obligation xxix–xxx, 76–79
- opening an encampment 71–73
- passwords 70
- qualifications for the admission of a Candidate xxvii
- signs of the order 69–70

L

Lodge Réunion des Coeurs, Haiti 194
Lodge Réunion Désirée, Haiti 195
Louisiana, Grand Lodge of xvii, 191
Lowndes, Thomas xxiii

M

Mackey, Albert G. xi–xiv
Mahabon 232
Maher-shalal-hash-baz 70
Mahershalalhashbaz 78
M.A.h.O.B.m.O. 238
Manual of Freemasonry, R. Carlile (1836, 1845) x, 109
Mark Man Degree 39–43
  catechism 39–43
Mark Mason Degree xvii–xviii, xix–xxi, 191, 194, 201–221
  arrangement of the lodge 201–202

INDEX

candidate, preparation of 201
catechism 214–216
closing 214
discourse 220–221
grip 212
lecture 213–214
medal 212
oath of a candidate 220
obligation 209–210
opening 202–203
reception of a candidate 204–206
signs 203–204, 211
Mark Master Degree
catechism 43–46
jewel xix
Mark Master Mason Degree x–xiv. *See also* Degree of Mark Master, A. Mackey
Master Mark Mason Degree 87–106
 charge 98–99
 closing 106
 form of the lodge 89–90
 history 99–102
 lecture 102–106
 obligation 97–98
 opening 91–92
 reception of a candidate 93–97
Melita 70
Mitchell, John xiii
Moabon 234
Mohabon xxii
Morin, Stephen xx
Moses 55, 61

N

Noah xxiv

O

Oliver, Dr. George xi

P

Passed Master Degree xvii–xviii

Past Master Degree xxii, 191, 237–238
 jewel *xxii*
 obligation 237–238
 opening and reception 237
 tracing board *xxii*
 words 238
Perseverance, Lodge, Cuba 195
Phile, Frederick xix

R

Ramsay, Rite of xxxvi
 degrees. *See* Scottish Elder Master and Knight of St. Andrew Degree
Rancliffe, Thomas Baron xiv, xv
Regime Reforme on Rectifie of Dresden 167, 190.
 See also Scottish Elder Master and Knight of St. Andrew Degree
Réunion des Coeur Lodge, Saint Domingue xvii
Rite Ancien Maçonnerie d'York xvii–xviii
Royal Arch Degree xvii, xvii–xviii, xxii, 47–68, 107–128, 191, 221–235
 apartments 221–223
 charge 49–50
 closing 51, 128, 235
 cordon and jewel *xxiii*
 exaltation 52–53
 grand cordon and jewel 223
 grip 230–231
 history of the degree 232–235
 lecture 59–69
 oath 225
 obligation 53–54, 115–119
 open a chapter 47–49
 opening 224
 original signs 67–68
 Passing the Veils 54–55
 reception 224–225
 re-entry of the Candidate 56–59
 signs 123–126, 229–230
 words 231

Royal Master Degree xvii, xxiii–xxiv

S

Saintete au Seigneur 231
Scottish Elder Master and Knight of St. Andrew
    Degree 167–195. *See also* Grand Maitre
    Ecossais (Grand Master Ecosé) Degree
Scottish Master and Knight of St. Andrew of the
    Thistle Degree xxxvi
Sem Chamet Japhet 231
Spirit of Masonry, The, W. Hutchinson (1775)
    xiv
Stodan 41
Stolkin xx
Super-excellent Mason xvii

T

Templum Hierosolyma 67
triple Tau 125

W

Waite, Arthur Edward xxxvi
Webb, Thomas Smith xiii, xviii

Z

Zabulon. *See* Jabulum (Jabulon, Jahbuhlun)
Zorobabel 233

Arturo de Hoyos, 33°, Grand Cross, is Grand Archivist and Grand Historian of the Supreme Council, 33°, Southern Jurisdiction, Washington, DC, and a member of the executive staff at the House of the Temple.

His Previous Books Include:
The Cloud of Prejudice: A Study in Anti-Masonry (1992)
Rituals of the Masonic Grand Lodge of the Sun, Bayreuth, Germany (1992)
Liturgy of Germania Lodge No. 46 F&AM (1993)
The Book of the Words—Sephir H'Debarim: With an Introduction by Art de Hoyos (1999)
Albert Pike's Esoterika: The Symbolism of the Blue Degrees of Freemasonry (2005)
The Rituals of the Swedish System of Freemasonry: The German Große Landesloge (2005)
The Scottish Rite Ritual Monitor and Guide (2007)
Light on Masonry: The History and Rituals of America's Most Important Masonic Exposé (2008)
Masonic Formulas and Rituals Transcribed by Albert Pike (2010)
Freemasonry's Royal Secret (2014)

In Collaboration with S. Brent Morris:
Is It True What They Say About Freemasonry? The Methods of Anti-Masons (1994)
Freemasonry in Context: History, Ritual, Controversy (2004)
Committed to the Flames: The History and Rituals of a Secret Masonic Rite (2008)
The Most Secret Mysteries of the High Degrees of Masonry Unveiled (2011)
Allegorical Conversations Arranged by Wisdom (2012)

As Editor and/or Author of Introduction/Preface:
(ed.) *Collectanea* (Grand College of Rites, 1994–2015)
(ed.) *Miscellanea* (Grand Council, Allied Masonic Degrees, 2001)
(ed.) C.F. Kleinknecht, *Forms and Traditions of the Scottish Rite* (2001)
(ed.) L.P. Watkins, *Albert Pike's String of Pearls* (2008)
(ed.) L.P. Watkins, *International Masonic Collection, 1723–2011* (2012)
(intro.) S. Dafoe, *Morgan: The Scandal the Shook Freemasonry* (2009)
(intro.) A. Bernheim, *Un certaine idée de la franc-maçonnerie* (2009)
(ed./intro.) R.L. Hutchens, *A Bridge to Light: A Study in Masonic Ritual & Philosophy* (2010)
(preface) A. de Keghel, *Le défi Maçonnique Américain* (2015)

REPRINTS OF RITUALS OF OLD DEGREES

Book layout and design by Steven L. Adams 32°
Composed in InDesign CC using Minion Pro, American Scribe,
Berthold Akzidenz Grotesk BE, Hoefler Text Ornaments, and Adobe Woodtype
Ornaments.

Related Titles from Westphalia Press

Ancient Mysteries and Modern Masonry: The Collected Writings of Jewel P. Lightfoot, Edited by Billy J. Hamilton Jr.

Jewel P. Lightfoot. Former Attorney General of the State of Texas. Past Grand Master of the Masonic Grand Lodge of Texas. From humble beginnings in rural Arkansas, he worked to become an educated man who excelled in law and Freemasonry. He was a gentleman of his time, well-known as a scholar, public speaker, and Masonic philosopher.

Essay on The Mysteries and the True Object of The Brotherhood of Freemasons
by Jason Williams

This isn't a reprint of a classic. It's a new rendition with new life breathed into it, to be enjoyed both by the layperson trying to understand the Craft and Masonic scholars taking a deeper dive into the fraternity's golden years—when the concepts of liberty and equality were still fresh.

Female Emancipation and Masonic Membership:
An Essential Collection
By Guillermo De Los Reyes Heredia

Female Emancipation and Masonic Membership: An Essential Combination is a collection of essays on Freemasonry and gender that promotes a transatlantic discussion of the study of the history of women and Freemasonry and their contribution in different countries.

Freemasonry, Heir to the Enlightenment
by Cécile Révauger

Modern Freemasonry may have mythical roots in Solomon's time but is really the heir to the Enlightenment. Ever since the early eighteenth century freemasons have endeavored to convey the values of the Enlightenment in the cultural, political and religious fields, in Europe, the American colonies and the emerging United States.

Freemasonry: A French View
by Roger Dachez and Alain Bauer

Perhaps one should speak not of Freemasonry but of Freemasonries in the plural. In each country Masonic historiography has developed uniqueness. Two of the best known French Masonic scholars present their own view of the worldwide evolution and challenging mysteries of the fraternity over the centuries.

Worlds of Print: The Moral Imagination of an Informed Citizenry, 1734 to 1839
by John Slifko

John Slifko argues that freemasonry was representative and played an important role in a larger cultural transformation of literacy and helped articulate the moral imagination of an informed democratic citizenry via fast emerging worlds of print.

Why Thirty-Three?: Searching for Masonic Origins
by S. Brent Morris, PhD

What "high degrees" were in the United States before 1830? What were the activities of the Order of the Royal Secret, the precursor of the Scottish Rite? A complex organization with a lengthy pedigree like Freemasonry has many basic foundational questions waiting to be answered, and that's what this book does: answers questions.

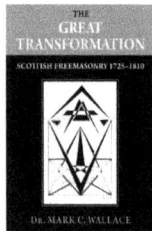
The Great Transformation: Scottish Freemasonry 1725-1810
by Dr. Mark C. Wallace

This book examines Scottish Freemasonry in its wider British and European contexts between the years 1725 and 1810. The Enlightenment effectively crafted the modern mason and propelled Freemasonry into a new era marked by growing membership and the creation of the Grand Lodge of Scotland.

Getting the Third Degree: Fraternalism, Freemasonry and History
Edited by Guillermo De Los Reyes and Paul Rich

As this engaging collection demonstrates, the doors being opened on the subject range from art history to political science to anthropology, as well as gender studies, sociology and more. The organizations discussed may insist on secrecy, but the research into them belies that.

The Great Transformation: Scottish Freemasonry 1725-1810
by Dr. Mark C. Wallace

This book examines Scottish Freemasonry in its wider British and European contexts between the years 1725 and 1810. The Enlightenment effectively crafted the modern mason and propelled Freemasonry into a new era marked by growing membership and the creation of the Grand Lodge of Scotland.

Getting the Third Degree: Fraternalism, Freemasonry and History
Edited by Guillermo De Los Reyes and Paul Rich

As this engaging collection demonstrates, the doors being opened on the subject range from art history to political science to anthropology, as well as gender studies, sociology and more. The organizations discussed may insist on secrecy, but the research into them belies that.

Freemasonry: A French View
by Roger Dachez and Alain Bauer

Perhaps one should speak not of Freemasonry but of Freemasonries in the plural. In each country Masonic historiography has developed uniqueness. Two of the best known French Masonic scholars present their own view of the worldwide evolution and challenging mysteries of the fraternity over the centuries.

Worlds of Print: The Moral Imagination of an Informed Citizenry, 1734 to 1839
by John Slifko

John Slifko argues that freemasonry was representative and played an important role in a larger cultural transformation of literacy and helped articulate the moral imagination of an informed democratic citizenry via fast emerging worlds of print.

Why Thirty-Three?: Searching for Masonic Origins
by S. Brent Morris, PhD

What "high degrees" were in the United States before 1830? What were the activities of the Order of the Royal Secret, the precursor of the Scottish Rite? A complex organization with a lengthy pedigree like Freemasonry has many basic foundational questions waiting to be answered, and that's what this book does: answers questions.

A Place in the Lodge: Dr. Rob Morris, Freemasonry and the Order of the Eastern Star
by Nancy Stearns Theiss, PhD

Ridiculed as "petticoat masonry," critics of the Order of the Eastern Star did not deter Rob Morris' goal to establish a Masonic organization that included women as members. Morris carried the ideals of Freemasonry through a despairing time of American history.

Brought to Light: The Mysterious George Washington Masonic Cave
by Jason Williams MD

The George Washington Masonic Cave near Charles Town, West Virginia, contains a signature carving of George Washington dated 1748. This book painstakingly pieces together the chronicled events and real estate archives related to the cavern in order to sort out fact from fiction.

Dudley Wright: Writer, Truthseeker & Freemason
by John Belton

Dudley Wright (1868-1950) was an Englishman and professional journalist who took a universalist approach to the various great Truths of Life. He travelled though many religions in his life and wrote about them all, but was probably most at home with Islam.

History of the Grand Orient of Italy
Emanuela Locci, Editor

No book in Masonic literature upon the history of Italian Freemasonry has been edited in English up to now. This work consists of eight studies, covering a span from the Eighteenth Century to the end of the WWII, tracing through the story, the events and pursuits related to the Grand Orient of Italy.

westphaliapress.org

www.ingramcontent.com/pod-product-compliance
Lightning Source LLC
Chambersburg PA
CBHW051537020426
42333CB00016B/1969